Communism in Western Europe

Communism in
Western Europe

>>>>>>>>>>>>>>><<<<<<<<<<<<<<

MARIO EINAUDI

JEAN-MARIE DOMENACH

ALDO GAROSCI

ARCHON BOOKS

1971

© 1951 by Cornell University.
Reprinted 1971 by Archon Books, Hamden,
Connecticut 06514, with permission and
without alteration or abridgement from
the 1953 printing.

International Standard Book Number 0-208-00411-4
Library of Congress catalog card number 77-143880

Printed in the United States of America

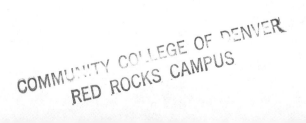

>>>>>>>>>>>>>>>>>>>> * <<<<<<<<<<<<<<<<<<<<

Foreword

THIS volume is the first of a series devoted to the political, economic, and constitutional problems of postwar France and Italy. It is the initial result of a "French-Italian Inquiry" started at Cornell University in 1949 in the belief that the changes brought about by fascism, revolution, and war in these two key countries of Western Europe were sufficiently significant to warrant their study.

First of all, some of the more far-reaching political ideologies of today, such as Communism and Christian Democracy, have developed there in an especially characteristic way, at the same time that new constitutional experiments and wide structural economic reforms have been undertaken.

Secondly, the parallel lines of many of the ideological and political developments of France and Italy offer an interesting opportunity, from a methodological point of view, to follow ideas and problems across national lines.

Finally, the one hundred million inhabitants of the two countries occupy a decisive position in determining the relationship of Europe to the United States and to the Soviet Union. A clarification of the nature of their domestic problems is useful both in formulating American policies and in understanding the essence of the struggle against the Soviet conquest of the continent.

This first volume deals with the phenomenon which is at the root of the difficulties of our times, communism. And among all the nations of free Europe, communism has developed as a dominant movement only in France and in Italy.

In the first part, the general nature of Western European communism is analyzed and some conclusions are offered on the conditions, both of renovation and of integration of French and Italian societies, which will make the defeat of communism possible.

In the second part, Jean-Marie Domenach, political essayist, member of the French Resistance, author of a biography of one of the founders of the M.R.P. *(Gilbert Dru, celui qui croyait au ciel,* Paris, 1947), editor-in-chief of *Esprit,* the influential and controversial organ of certain currents of French Catholic thought, writes a thoughtful study of the French Communist party.

In the third part, Aldo Garosci, author of books on Bodin and on France under the Third Republic, one of the leading members of the "Justice and Freedom" movement, draws a vivid picture of Italian communism against a broad historical background, showing its dual relationship to national problems and to Soviet communism.

It should be clear that each author bears responsibility only for his own essay. But the three parts integrate and confirm each other, each telling a different side of the same story, which is the Communist attempt to overthrow the established civilization of the West.

The Inquiry has been made possible by a grant from the Rockefeller Foundation to Cornell University. John Roche, Roy and Winnifred Pierce, and Eleanor Tananbaum have given me invaluable assistance during the various stages of preparation of this volume.

Mario Einaudi

Cornell University
September 1951

Contents

Part I by Mario Einaudi

COMMUNISM IN WESTERN EUROPE

I

The Areas of Communist Power

In any study of modern communism, three areas occupy a position of paramount significance. In two of them, the Soviet Union with its immediate satellites and China, communism has been successful in achieving what is its goal — a monopoly of totalitarian power; in the third, Western Europe, defined for our purposes as France and Italy, communism has developed into a dominant political and economic force.

Elsewhere, too, communism offers a fruitful field of study. But outside these three areas the scope of Communist power and its ability to influence in a decisive way the course of political life are far more restricted. Largely as an intellectual phenomenon, United States communism offers highly interesting possibilities of inquiry into the behavior of fringe groups and isolated individuals. The receding of the Communist tide in the United States has exposed the confused nature of the intellectual sympathies and emotions which caused its modest advance in the thirties and forties and deserves to be noted as an indication of the degree of spontaneous defense against communism that can be put up by a socially fluid, economically vital, constitutionally stable community. In the United States even the most underprivileged groups look coldly upon the messianic promises of communism because of the fairly substantial promise of the world in which they live.

In Great Britain, as in the Low Countries and Scandinavia, the successful reorientation or the harmonious development of the economic systems, the gradual and visible overcoming of the early maladjustments of capitalism, the absence of any disruptive quarrel between church and state, the long experience in the processes of constitutional democracy, all have kept communism within exceedingly narrow boundaries. Africa and Latin America have not received the imprint of communism, even though considerable uncertainty must prevail as to their future.

When one turns to the Soviet Union, China, and Western Europe, the different nature of the Communist problem in those countries becomes apparent, as well as the peculiar characteristics which color communism in each of them.

In the Soviet Union, communism has been in power since 1917, as a result not of a popular revolution but of a *coup d'état*. The November revolution was dominated by the thought and action of a few men who exploited the elements of Marxist doctrine stressing the leading role of the Communist élite and the decisive and far-reaching nature of the dictatorship of the proletariat. What mattered was not the prior support of the masses but the possession of ideas and plans and of tools of power that would make mass support unimportant. Soviet communism has interpreted Marxism in the light of Lenin's own understanding of it and on that basis has developed the practice of government by a Communist élite entrusted with the monopolistic task of carrying out its millennial role in Russia first, throughout the world later.

The Soviet revolution occurred in a country that was, in spite of the existence of a few large factories, industrially underdeveloped, and in which the simple process of eliminating a relatively small number of large landowners could for a time be described as the key to agricultural democracy. It occurred in a country that had not entered the main stream of western political and social change of the last two hundred years. Underdevelopment, immobility, and isolation were all justified or barely opposed by a governmental system which, as the end of World War I approached, had been seriously weakened. Exploiting conditions ideally suited to the creation of a revolutionary atmosphere, the Bolsheviks were successful in carrying off their conquest of power, and now, a third of a century later, they are well along in the fulfillment of their task of remolding the lives and thoughts and aspirations of the Russian people to fit the pattern of Marxian-Leninist theory and practice of communism.

In China, too, communism is in power. It got there, however, at the end of a process rather different from the Soviet one. With a relatively short series of revolutionary actions, the Bolsheviks secured their triumph essentially according to the romantic nineteenth-century notion of revolution (there is a striking resemblance between the paintings immortalizing the street fighting in Paris in 1848 and the attack by the Kronstadt sailors against the Winter Palace in St. Petersburg in 1917). On the other hand, the Chinese Communists achieved success after a long and complicated struggle (which sometimes even included a "popular front" type of agreement with the Kuomintang) in the course of which they acquired the larger popular support that the Bolsheviks lacked for many years. This enabled the Chinese Communists, shortly after the end of World War II, to be generally recognized as the core of the government of China.

Chinese Communists accept the typical elements of twentieth-century communism. Mao proudly relies on Marxian orthodoxy, as filtered through the Leninist-Stalinist interpretations. This common Sino-Soviet doctrinal ground is, of course, of the essence and explains the early development of characteristics that are everywhere an integral part of the exercise of Communist power. These are the use of force and the disregard of "formal procedures," which are considered irrelevant to the solutions of the "substantive problems" with which a real Communist statesman must deal. The fact remains that Chinese communism distinguishes itself from Soviet communism because of the larger popular support it enjoyed *ab initio*. The drowning of "élitist" communism in the vast ocean of "popular" communism is without significance insofar as the ultimate assertion and operation of a totalitarian dictatorship is concerned, but it creates important temporary problems of interpretation, as the Chinese Communist drive to power is measured and evaluated in terms of the interests of other nations. This explains the flourishing of the myth of "agrarian reformers," the inability of many governments to resist the claim to recognition put forth by the Chinese government, and the discomfiture and lack of prestige of non-Communist forces in China.

On the other hand, the same conditions of underdevelopment, immobility, and government failure that were present in Russia were present in modern China. This had come about in the midst of one of the oldest and most refined of civilizations and in spite of the so-called "modernizing" efforts of western capitalism. Rigidity of relations and overpopulation had continued to characterize Chinese agriculture, while the setting up of wholly separate and isolated areas of political authority favored the disintegration of governmental processes.

The Chinese Communists have successfully exploited the demands of a people ready for change but unable to get it. Having gained power not in the name of Marx or Lenin but in the name of the interests of the community and of the defense of its integrity, Chinese Communists are now forced by the logic of their ideology to develop a very different balance between the satisfaction of the commitments which their ideology demands and the satisfaction of the promises which they have made to the people. As always in the history of dictatorships, a way out of the dilemma of power or the people's welfare is being sought by resort to coercion and to appeals to nationalism and war. In spite of this, no one is likely to underestimate the reality of the power of the Communists within China itself and the revolutionary attraction which they exercise over all the peoples of Asia living in conditions similar to those of China.

The issue of the validity of Lenin's interpretation of Marx will probably continue to be debated for a long time in spite of the evidence that Lenin's gloss was well founded and that he crystallized the key elements of the Marxian revolutionary doctrine. What cannot be debated is that Western European Communist parties have today accepted the Leninist evaluation of Marxism and the Soviet revolution as the symbol and pattern of all proletarian revolutions. Their acknowledgment of the tie that binds them to the Soviet Union has been open and uninterrupted since that winter of 1921–1922 when both the French and Italian Communist parties were founded. Upon these roots European communism has grafted a great variety of native elements appealing strongly to different social groups. It is the combination of ideological self-sufficiency and certainty, of encouragement derived from the presence of a powerful and successful Soviet government, and of strength based upon the appeal of complex national themes that explains the notable advances of communism in postwar Europe, making of France and Italy one of the focal points of Communist influence.

But unlike communism in the Soviet Union and China, communism in Western Europe is not in power, even though (1) it has developed in countries where, according to Marx, some of the necessary preliminary phases of bourgeois rule and of capitalistic transformation have taken place, and (2) it has now a larger popular support than Soviet communism was ever able to achieve during the first half of its existence or than Mao has today. Thus we are confronted with the unique issue of mass communism within societies that are fighting back politically and institutionally. What lends particular importance to the conflict is that it is waged inside two countries that have for long been at the center of the culture communism is trying to supersede and in the heart of a continent occupying a key position between the United States and the Soviet Union.

II

The Sources of Communist Strength in Western Europe

SINCE 1947 Western European communism has been deprived of all participation in national governments and has been exposed as the agent of the aggressive aims of the Soviet Union. But communism, drawing upon notable sources of strength, has either held its ground or has made further advances. This successful maintenance of Communist positions has occurred in the midst of societies that are still essentially free and where the processes of democratic discussion and persuasion are still functioning.

IN THE PAST

French and Italian communism exploits the tradition of the revolution of 1789. The appeal to the eighteenth century is ever present in Communist writings. Togliatti introduces Voltaire to his followers as a writer embodying the idea of a revolution whose consequences Italy has never fully felt and as a Communist *avant lettre* because of his faith in the power of man and of his efforts to open the path to the renovation of society. Roger Garaudy, the intellectual historian of French communism, praises eighteenth-century materialist philosophers. These men, he states, struck at the divine sources of authority, since its true source was to be found in experience and utility. They painted in brilliant colors the progress of technology, of science and of reason.

Materialism, rationalism and optimism are the signs of the youth and strength of this philosophy, which is revolutionary also because, against the myth of the eternal immobility of divine perfection..., it has discovered the law of movement.... Our materialists have mobilized matter, man, and society. Movement has entered the world and will not leave it again.

To a large extent, communism has identified itself as the carrier of the traditions of revolutionary change. This is useful, for there is evidence on all sides that France and Italy have not yet completed the cycle that in the United Kingdom and the United States has brought about the modernization of economic and political life and the use of power in the public interest.

The social structure of the two countries has maintained rigidities and cleavages favoring the class warfare approach of the Communists. The following are some notable examples: (1) the excessively rigid defense of the private property system; (2) the lack of pliancy shown by a codified legal system; (3) the attitude of certain classes which, having lost the power to influence national life, have not given up their claims to special recognition as bearers of past values; (4) the habits of secrecy and manipulation ingrained in many entrepreneurial groups and accompanied by possessive claims with regard to the distribution of public bounties; (5) the fear of the unknown and novel which has retarded technological advance; (6) the inadequacy of an educational system which, however noble and attractive in its stressing of classical and humanistic values, does not come close to the majority of the people, except on the barest levels of elementary and technical instruction; and (7) in the south of Italy, the arrogance of certain landowning groups which, themselves bankrupt morally and economically, have in the past fought against emigration because it would tend to decrease the available pool of cheap man power, and today fail to co-operate in the working out of measures aiming at the increase of the common welfare.

Important changes have, of course, been under way, chiefly as a result of two World Wars, but to the independent observer the striking thing is not the beginning of change but the persistence of the defense of old attitudes, in spite of the evidence that communism will make headway in societies which remain closed and static.

France and Italy have thus offered partial justification to one of the basic contentions of Marxism, that in a bourgeois capitalistic society workers and peasants would be deprived of the advantages that all have a right to expect from the community in which they live. According to the foremost French Communist theoretician, Henri Lefebvre, *"la vie privée"* of individualistic society has become *"une vie privée"* of all reality, of all ties with the world — a life deprived of all that is human. As far as the working classes were concerned, the processes of integration and acceptance which had been visible for a long time elsewhere were slow to appear and reluctant to develop in France and Italy. Thus, a serious economic issue superimposed itself upon a social issue. As it nourished the fires of rebellion among large strata of the working classes, it provided the basis of Communist power.

The strength of the rebellion derived from the worker's resentment at being a merely passive and exploited witness in the life of the nation, which unaccountably proceeded on its way without sufficient regard to his rights and interests. The specific grievances were many, and even though not all of them could be properly inscribed to the debit of the ruling classes, they all contributed to the building up of an antagonism which communism could later nourish. For French and Italian capitalism exhibited well into the twentieth century some of the characteristics typical of early nineteenth-century capitalism. The state was either the enemy to be fought or the keeper of a public treasury to be mulcted. The workers, on the other hand, were to be exploited to the greatest possible extent without regard to the social consequences of such a policy. In this respect, the French *patronat,* or industrial class, has been notoriously bad. When its hand was forced a few years before World War II, it set in motion reactions which contributed to the easy triumph of fascism in 1940. By 1950 French industrial wages had not yet recovered their prewar level. The sense of intolerable injustice which such policies create is strong and cannot be underestimated.

Italy has faced additional difficulties deriving from the presence of a population larger than the French in a country half as large as France and not as productive. The strength of communism in many agricultural areas has come chiefly from the unsatisfactory nature of the relationships binding the peasants to the land and from the feeling that some extraordinary effort was necessary to relieve population pressure on a land which could not possibly sustain more than half of the people living on it. The fact that the Italian land problem was not one of redistribution of property but one primarily of heavy capital investment and of directed resettlement of populations did not undermine the Communist position if the peasants felt that governments were not interested in undertaking any of the necessary steps, or that the situation was so hopeless that revolution was the only way out.

Over all has floated the sense of insecurity caused by the weakening economic positions of France and Italy. While Germany and the United States after World War I, and even England after World War II, were capable of large-scale industrial and economic progress, France and Italy were standing still or losing ground. Some of their major industrial enterprises no longer were, or never were, viable. French mines were getting to be very expensive to exploit, and their coal seams were running out. The silk industry was undermined by a technological revolution which France and Italy could not stop. Many of Italy's heavy industries had no sound economic basis on which to operate. Awareness of economic doom favored defense of government policies such as only a totalitarian government might enact. Communism found many supporters for its theory that economic salvation would come not from free operation of the market, which was impossible to achieve, but from an economic system which, regardless of costs, would seek at least to maintain the *status quo*.

In the years following the adoption of the Marshall Plan, the conviction spread that, in the name of efficiency, competition, and international integration, the United States stood for a policy of suppression of high-cost industrial enterprises. In an irrational attempt at self-defense and to protect their immediate visible interests, many workers chose to cling for the time being to the Communist solution, which promised them national autarchy and insulation from the risks of a competitive world in which weak economic units would be eliminated. Thus static capitalism, confronted at long last by the exigencies of modernization, was itself a cause of the strengthening of static communism.

Next to the social and economic issues stands the religious issue, which on the continent of Europe is kept alive by the memories of 1789, by the persistence of traditional slogans, which even changed circumstances have not obliterated, and by recent evidence of a renewed direct interest of the church in political matters.

The Established Church has for a long time appeared in England as the capstone of a constitutional-religious edifice which in no way seeks to exercise repressive and harsh powers over the political and moral life of men. The strong traditions of nonconformism have, on the other hand, nourished a current of liberalism and of autonomy with respect to Anglicanism, and have in later years been the spring of a large part of British socialism. Mr. Attlee's well-known statement, "We are all Christian democrats," is taken as a simple yet basic statement which even a Socialist society finds no difficulty in admitting. A similar lack of antagonism between religious and civil spheres has existed in modern times in the United States, owing to the exceedingly complex fragmentation of religious life. Under these conditions, the principle of separation in a broad sense has been accepted, the religious issue has been lifted, at least until recently, out of the sphere of political debate, while the political class has maintained that sense of reverence toward religion which underscores the absence of conflict.

In France and Italy neither separation nor co-ordination has allowed political life to proceed without regard to religion. Modern Europe has developed under the influence of Cartesian philosophy and of the battle waged against a pre-Reformation ecclesiastical structure which either claimed or exercised domination over the lay world. Laicism represents the defense against clericalism. These two words, unknown to the Anglo-Saxon world, are fighting words in Europe today as they were in the eighteenth century. It is true that by the end of World War I the conflict between church and state seemed to fade away. On the one hand, the lay state had become aware of certain spiritual and moral values which in the name of science, positivism, and rationalism it had relentlessly rejected until then. On the other hand, many influential groups within the church had recognized the role of the independent political community and the importance of the educational and economic functions that the state was bound to exercise, apart from the church. Thus a reconciliation might have been possible with good will, peace, and the absence of abnormal threats to the survival of the existing political and religious systems.

But World War II brought to the surface opposite trends. Just as it caused a great strengthening of Christian democracy, conceived both as a softening of the asperities of bourgeois morality and as a defense against Communist atheism, it resurrected those elements within Christian democracy that had been longing for a revival of the historical alliance between civil and religious authorities for the triumph of Christian civilization. One of the logical and most profitable areas of past co-operation had been the educational field, and the efforts to reinstate the church in some of its lost positions in the schools have been particularly noticeable in Italy, where Christian democracy has had a near monopoly of power since 1948. Similarly the school issue has flared up anew in France, where the efforts made on behalf of private (and therefore most often religious) schools have been in part objectively justified by the inability of the state to carry out adequately its educational responsibilities in the postwar period.

But, regardless of the particular circumstances, the Communists have paraded as the defenders of a school system free from ecclesiastical interferences. The priest as the enemy of liberty and as the proponent of every dark and magic formula that the modern world has rejected is still a potent symbol in the hands of those who say they are defending the freedom of man to act politically regardless of metaphysical commands. Today European communism appears as the strongest supporter of a materialistic approach which vindicates for the community rights which the church is charged with trying to take away. In the particular case of Italy, the failure of the Christian-Democratic party to clarify its positions, as well as its half-admitted and half-visible moves tending to confuse the lines of lay and ecclesiastical jurisdictions, has without question strengthened the hand of communism, which relies on the traditional antireligious attitudes of the majority of the working class.

Thus the needed restatement of moral values in political life has led too often to the reinstatement of merely ecclesiastical values. In societies rent by class antagonisms and poverty, this trend has sustained the belief that what is required is a revolution and not a return to relationships tending to perpetuate, as they in the past created, a way of life that no modern community can adopt. Exploiting the reaction against the claims of a metaphysical dogmatism, communism has succeeded in making some people forget the reality of its own temporal totalitarianism.

Finally, the French and the Italian crisis has political roots. Neither country has succeeded in developing a political class conscious of its responsibilities and an administrative machinery fully able to perform the tasks of a modern state. There is no desire here to speak too harshly of systems of government which at times have made possible significant advances, or of parties which, as in France in 1951, have shown extraordinary cleverness in defending themselves against the extremism of right and left; nor of political leaders who have often stressed values cherished as an essential part of the tradition of the West, a tradition which the legendary visitor from Persia at the beginning of the eighteenth century found impossible to define except by saying that it was felt in the air. The literary abilities of the statesmen of the Third Republic have undoubtedly been greater than those of any other group in a similar position anywhere in the world. Their training and

outlook on life made them, as well as their Italian fellow-states-
men, ill at ease in dealing with the complex problems of the
modern state. Too often technical incompetence was accompanied
by surrender to special interests, thus giving added appearance
of substance to the Marxist-nourished mass belief that the state
was nothing but the instrument of greedy capitalistic interests
and that it was the duty of all those who loved freedom and progress to oppose such a state, conquer and destroy it, and replace
it with something better. France and Italy today are suffering from
their failure to moderate the sense of hostility and contempt
towards the state which remains the dominant feeling of large
groups of the population: hostility, because of the gulf which is
believed to exist between the actions of the state and the interests
of the community; contempt, because of the obvious obsolescence
of the tools of government. Both countries are still far removed
from the developments which in England have, within the last
century, brought to a position of command a political class substantially independent of private interests and in the United States
have led to the New Deal, that is, to the rebirth of the concept of
the common welfare.

IN REVOLUTION AND WAR

Fascism has been the touchstone of European politics between
the two World Wars. In dealing with it communism has demonstrated an uncanny ability to lead different lives simultaneously
or in succession without apparent harm to itself.

Fascism, as it developed in Italy and in France, was both a rebellion against the failure of parliamentary government and of the
party system and an attempt *in extremis* of certain property-
owning groups to safeguard positions which they felt were threatened. The inadequacy of the pre-Fascist ruling class and its inability to adapt political life and constitutional techniques to
the post-World War I era cannot be denied. In spite of this, the
monster of fascism that grew out of the crisis was certainly not all
its doing. But the historical fact remains that the French and the
Italian bourgeoisie were given the main responsibility for the

havoc of fascism. When fascism led to a totalitarian aggressive state, as in Italy, or to a police state at the service of a foreign totalitarianism, as in France, the direct or indirect supporters of fascism were forever branded as the enemies of democracy and freedom and progress. In a postwar world dedicated to the task of restoring democracy, freedom, and progress, those who could say that they were the champions by definition of antifascism stood to gain considerable advantages.

As one considers the Communist parties of Western Europe in terms of their ruling élites, one cannot doubt their opportunistic attitude *vis-à-vis* fascism. Their thoughts and actions were from the beginning controlled by the requirements of Soviet policy. Thus, before the Popular Front days of 1936, Communist leadership refused to make any distinction between Fascist and non-Communist anti-Fascist forces. They were all mere variants of anticommunism and, as such, to be all lumped together as "social fascists." The threat posed by Hitler to Soviet Russia's safety pushed the Communist leaders, under Moscow's orders, into a hitherto-despised alliance with other democratic groups in a common anti-Fascist front. The further reversal in Communist policy that occurred with the signing of the Nazi-Soviet pact of 1939 had no consequences in Italy, where communism was still outlawed, while whatever shock was produced in France by the Communist betrayal of the anti-Fascist cause and of the national interest was soon overcome as the Communists took the leadership in the resistance to nazism from 1941 to 1945.

The crucial point here is this: the somersaults and about-faces have concerned, in effect, the top Communist leadership alone, made up of revolutionists who consider such matters as normal developments within the long-range Communist pattern. As far as the millions that make up the Communist rank and file are concerned, there has never been any change, for their history is the history of the last ten years. Without deviation, they have been led under banners inscribed with the slogans of antifascism, battle for democracy and peace. To an amazing extent the Communist leadership has been able to create in their minds the image of the

Communist party as the party which, by definition, is the anti-Fascist party and, therefore, the party of freedom and peace.[1]

Communism has also been able to exploit all the derivative elements of the struggle against fascism. As Domenach vividly describes, the Resistance created sympathies which the Communists have successfully turned to their advantage. The Communists had no monopoly of the Resistance, as some very effective non-Communist Resistance groups were organized, not by the older and discredited political parties, but by new movements (such as Italy's "Justice and Freedom") which for a time hoped to be able to develop into meaningful competitors of communism in the postwar world. But the long tradition of secrecy, of centrally directed organization, and of toughness of training, the unrelenting pressure from above, and the feeling that the historical occasion was at hand that would permit a Communist revolution to triumph throughout the world made Communist resistance so effective as to implant firmly in people's minds the conviction that its role was decisive. This was not a small asset among the many who felt that the postwar world was to be illuminated by the elements of courage, unselfishness, devotion to duty and to ideals as against the corrupted and selfish past that had to be obliterated entirely.

After the war, Europe felt as never before the emergence of the Soviet Union as a dominant power. Czarist Russia had never shed the position of inferiority to which its regime had condemned it in the eyes of the liberal societies of the western world. Later, resentment had accumulated against a revolutionary government which had caused painful losses to many French purchasers of the bonds of imperial Russia. Still later, the Soviet regime had seemed re-

[1]This particular issue shows how misleading it would be to think of European communism in terms that are appropriate for American communism. In the United States the contradictions and untenable positions into which the party has been forced by Soviet directives have been more strongly felt and have exposed the party to public, and damaging, ridicule and contempt, because American communism has been a static movement, its membership made up of intellectuals with scant working-class representation, its theater of operations far removed from the wars and revolutions that have marked Europe.

mote and primitive and uninteresting. On the eve of the war the Soviet opposition to Munich had created an uncomfortable reaction among those Europeans who were convinced of the virtues of peace bought at any price. But after 1945 Russia's impressive military might and the importance of the role which she was clearly going to play in Europe led to a fresh appraisal of her position at a time when the illusion of co-operation between the democratic world and the Soviet Union was not yet dissipated. Communism was therefore able to attract both those who were "realistically" impressed by the presence of Soviet armies so close to the Rhine and those who thought that support of the Soviet Union meant support of new methods of democracy adapted to the exigencies of the postwar world. Not all the ground thus gained was lost after 1947, when the Soviet world began to appear in all its crudeness, for by then the Soviet theme had been reproposed in terms of the defense of peace.

Lastly, communism filled the political vacuum left by fascism and war. The crisis was such that it created support for those who proclaimed a knowledge of infallible means to be used in its elimination. In an atmosphere compounded of pessimism and great expectations, and amid an awareness of the radical changes of structure that had to be introduced, communism offered a program of action, an avowed confidence in the future if only men were willing to surrender their freedom of decision into hands capable of guiding them. The myths of the plan and the planners, of the equality and plenty of tomorrow, were used to rally the dispossessed, who by the end of the war included many members of the middle classes. They attracted those who had nowhere else to go, those who felt that socialism was only a pale and ineffective replica of communism and that all other parties were either clerical or tendentially Fascist, those who were unable to replace with anything else the steadying hand of Fascist dictatorship, and, finally, those who, in peace, had not shed the exhilarating habits of wartime violence.

The appeal of communism was based upon a clever manipulation and combination of the symbols and slogans of the democratic world and of the instruments of mass control. It gave rise to a belief that the "neutralization" of the working class would be ended and that the worker would get his share of power in a truly democratic system, together with the purposive and controlled direction of his life and activities which a merely formal parliamentary system would never give him. In this way the two simultaneous cravings of freedom and status were to be satisfied. The bourgeois state had given everybody a loose and uncertain freedom, and status to only a few. Fascism had denied freedom to all but had experimented with an integrated corporative system. Communism would give to all social freedom as well as an assigned role within a sheltered society.

IN THE PRESENT

With the end of the arrangements based upon an alliance among Christian-Democratic, Socialist, and Communist parties which dictated the formation of French and Italian postwar governments until the spring of 1947, communism reverted to its traditional role of outsider. But its greatly augmented size and the sharply defined terms of the crisis made it possible for communism to become also the main opposition party. In Italy this is still true, while in France the rise of de Gaulle has added the Rassemblement du Peuple Français to the ranks of the opposition. But even in France the Communist party has been largely alone in the field of parliamentary opposition up to 1951.

Communism has therefore been able to gather the fruits that a strong opposition party will gain by virtue of the wear and tear and the popular dissatisfaction that always accompany the exercise of power by the majority parties. While British dissatisfaction with the Labor party redounds to the advantage of the Conservatives, French and Italian dissatisfaction with the Third Force and Christian-Democratic governments has redounded to a great extent to the advantage of the Communists, if only by permitting them to retain positions that might otherwise have been seriously threatened. Thus, in the 1951 Italian elections a vote for the Communists has often been a protest vote against the government in office. That this should be so is not surprising when one remembers the loss of popularity between 1945 and 1950 of as stable, skillful, and democratically minded a government as the British Labor government.

Furthermore, the very seriousness of the Communist threat has forced anti-Communist parties to modify in some instances their attitudes. The totalitarianism of communism tends to breed a total defense of the *status quo.* The extremity of the danger brings about an extremity of reaction which, by the logic peculiar to the political game, can only be to the extreme right. Thus, neofascism and Gaullism appear as attractive alternatives, while even within democratic parties the shift is from the left to the right in contrast to the historic nineteenth-century shift from the right to the left. The Radical Socialists in France are more conservative today than ever before. Within Socialist ranks there appear such personalities as Jules Moch, who thirty years ago would have been considered as a conservative bourgeois. Christian Democracy is torn to pieces. In France some leaders and many voters gravitate to de Gaulle, while in Italy the party is almost paralyzed by the defensive attitude of those members who interpret the appeals of Christian Democracy to moral values and individualism as meaning a defense of clericalism and of property rights.

The polarization toward the extremes is, of course, nothing new in the recent history of Europe, except for today's reduction of everything to desperate alternatives. The sliding of anticommunism toward the right has of necessity brought about an increase of sympathy for communism. This is especially true for those who identify the extreme right with the known and personally felt atrocities of fascism and of nazism but who insist in keeping alive a much more attractive picture of what a Communist state might be in Western Europe.

>>>>>>>>>>>>>>>>>>>>> * <<<<<<<<<<<<<<<<<<<<<<<<<

III

From Thorez to Boulier

Wɪᴛʜ nearly three million members and from twelve to fifteen million voters, the French and Italian Communist parties are complex political machines. The case studies that form Parts II and III of this volume discuss the matter in some detail and contain a good deal of novel information. What will be attempted here is a general analysis of the composition and attitudes of the main groups, both within and without the two parties, upon which the total power of communism is based.

The most striking initial fact is the continuity of the top Communist ruling class. In Italy, Togliatti and his "Piedmontese" group have been in command since 1921. In France, the political bureau elected at the twelfth party congress in the spring of 1950 included the names of Thorez, Duclos, Marty, and Cachin, with whom the entire history of French communism is associated. The conclusion is well founded that, with relatively minor exceptions, Western European communism for the past thirty years has been led by the same group of men who have throughout managed to retain the confidence of Moscow.

This general statement has to be clarified in one important respect. The continuity of leadership does not, of course, mean that no serious clash has ever arisen with the Kremlin. Almost certainly, for instance, a serious crisis developed in the course of 1950, and both Thorez and Togliatti felt the discipline of the iron hand of the Soviet Union.[1] But what matters is that the readjustments

[1]See below, pp. 31–33.

and corrections of policy imposed by the Kremlin have been made
without any drastic change in the top party leadership. There
has never been any open deposition *à la* Browder. The agonies and
humiliations of the chief leaders have been suffered in the secrecy
of French and Italian politburo meetings or, when publicity was
required, admitted in such terms as not to affect their standing.
As far as the overwhelming mass of party followers is concerned,
the Communist movement has brought to maturity and to positions of command trusted native leaders with deep roots in the
national soil, who are believed to be no mere puppets of an outside power but are seen as the authentic defenders of the aspirations of the French and Italian working classes.

This development, so favorable to the strengthening of western
Communist mythology, has, of course, been due to the fact that
communism has so far been unable to seize power in Western
Europe. The Soviet Union recognizes that, as opposition parties,
French and Italian Communist parties must be permitted to have
leaders who will not be subjected to the truculent and ruthless
control that is reserved for Communist party leaders in office.
The rapid wear and tear of the Communist élite begins once the
Communist parties have achieved power and have come under
the control of the Soviet government. The same wholesale and repeated replacements of Communist leadership that have been
witnessed during the last three years throughout eastern Europe
would take place in France and Italy under similar circumstances.
Both Thorez and Togliatti, and with them a host of other old
leaders, would be purged as guilty of a great variety of capital
crimes according to the Soviet Communist code. For the moment
they are far too useful to the Soviet Union. The repressions are
hidden and in public they are allowed to continue to play the
roles that properly belong to independent and national leaders of
the working classes.

Thanks to the many vicissitudes and changes in party line that
they have survived and the keen perception that they have acquired of the substance of Soviet power and of the nature of the
revolutionary struggle in which they are engaged, the top leaders

have developed over a period of thirty years a tough cynical realism, an ability to dominate the party machine, and a steadfast
dedication to the party's fortunes that are quite useful both to
the designs of the Soviet Union and to the effectiveness of party
operations. There is no possibility of disenchantment amid this
group, which is, without question, one of the ablest and most
dangerous products of twentieth-century communism.

The younger leaders who have emerged in the course of the last
decade add greatly to the national influence of their parties. One
finds here literary and professional people, many of them of
bourgeois origin in sharp contrast to the preponderantly working-
class derivation of the old leaders, intellectuals who in the
crucial years of the war and the Resistance have found in communism the only possible appeasement for their troubled minds.
These younger leaders have so far seldom obtained any position
of effective power. They are the shock troops of communism in its
dealings with the rest of the population and in its efforts to persuade the nonbelievers that communism is a truly national phenomenon embracing the democratic and politically conscious elements to be found in all classes. A good many of them are far removed from the world in which the top leaders live and bring to
their efforts a ring of sincerity and of faith in a millennial future
of which the Communist party is to be the herald. Some of them
have been attracted to communism by promises of freedom and of
recognition of the value of individual contributions, which could
not be fulfilled in the machine-ridden party structure. They were
soon forced to accept Laurent Casanova's rule for Communist
intellectuals that discussion can be free only if it is started by the
party and is not directed against it.

But apart from a small number of personal crises, the ranks
have held, for the party pressure has been heavy and many are
too weak even to contemplate the difficulties that a rebellion would
entail. A vague hope persists that somehow Soviet totalitarianism will not reach into the West and that a humanistic communism will be able to avoid the grimness of the *univers concentration-
naire* which was and is the foundation of the Marxist and Soviet

systems. As decoys, the intellectuals were highly valuable for the first few years after the war, but the rush to join the Communist party that was then so much in evidence has stopped now and no important additions to their numbers have been counted since 1949. The ranks of the second-string leaders are becoming frozen. One must look at the mass for any fresh evidence of fluidity.

If the rank and file is defined to include both party members and Communist voters who are not party members, three groups may be identified: the militants, the ordinary party members, and the voters.

The militants are the party organizers, the cell leaders, the trade union bosses, and the factory foremen, that is, the trained and active Communists who are performing, or who at least are told to perform, specific jobs which are important in determining the effectiveness of Communist party action. Their numbers have been kept at a high level. Taking France and Italy together, there may be about 400,000 of them, a figure equal to 15 per cent of the total party membership. There is no evidence that their strength has decreased in recent months but, rather, evidence that new militants are being trained and that most of them can still be counted upon to provide the party with its workers' army should one be needed in the open field of battle.

If the militants have gained in numbers and effectiveness, the number of ordinary party members has probably declined to some extent. This decline in membership, of no more than 10 or 20 per cent in any case, gave origin, early in 1951, to optimistic reports about the waning strength of communism in Western Europe. What was not realized was that as long as the hard core of militants and the electoral strength of the party remained intact, the power of communism would hardly be affected, and that the possibility still existed of Communist expansion.

In the Italian spring elections of 1951, which, although municipal in name, were in effect fought on a national basis, the Communist vote in certain regions increased substantially over that of 1948. In the Sicilian provinces of Catania and Palermo it went up from 125,000 to 210,000. It is important to note, therefore, that as late as 1951 no fixed boundary line existed everywhere in Italy (as apparently it did in France) between Communist and anti-Communist forces, but that a war of movement of large proportions was still being waged, with the decision at times going to the Communists. This underlines, on the one hand, the effectiveness of Communist propaganda and, on the other, the importance of immediate economic fears that may drive great masses of voters to the Communist side in spite of the contrary pull of well-reasoned long-range arguments. In politics, even when communism is at issue, the match between short-range and long-range interests is an uneven one.

But to list the top leaders and the subleaders and the three layers of the rank and file does not mean to list all the elements that compose the sum total of strength of European communism. There still remains the Abbé Boulier who writes of Communist man as having "that touch of sweetness, tolerance, goodness and human tenderness, that certitude on the glory of truth which, as a perfume, reveals the Christian soul."[2] There still remain the various progressive fringes that surround communism, lending it whatever support they can without ever committing themselves fully to a support of the party itself. There one finds those who accept Communist politics while rejecting Communist theses, as Julien Benda does,[3] those who accept generic Communist goals but

[2] See his preface to Pierre Debray, *Un Catholique retour de l'U.R.S.S.* (Paris, 1950).

[3] "For the last fifty years, Communists have been the only ones, as a party and without qualifications, to defend those values of justice to which I, as a spokesman of many intellectuals, remain attached. They have defended them, no matter what their motivations, at the time of the Dreyfus affair and of the Ethiopian, Spanish, and Czech affairs. They defend them today in their positions on epuration, on Franco, and in their determination to see the working class represented in the government. It is not my fault if I must join my hands with those of a party whose theses I mostly reject, since the bourgeoisie to which I belong by birth, education, and taste has for the past fifty years betrayed in the most cynical fashion the values it should defend" (*Ordre*, Sept. 4, 1947; quoted in *Nouveau Dictionnaire des girouettes* by Orion [Paris, 1948].)

reject Soviet practices,[4] representatives of the traditions of the

[4]The acceptance of Communist goals along with the rejection of Soviet practices appeared in a 1947 manifesto of a group of Resistance leaders (*L'Heure du choix,* by Claude Aveline, Jean Cassou, André Chamson, Georges Friedmann, Louis Martin-Chauffier, and Vercors [Paris, 1947]): "We remain firmly attached to a program of rational reconstruction of institutions founded on social justice and human dignity, in a word, to socialism. . . . The U.S.S.R., whose immense effort has long since attracted our active sympathy, remains an example, but for the western world it cannot be taken as a model."

To Martin-Chauffier, whose tragic experiences in a Nazi concentration camp have been movingly recounted in his *L'Homme et la bête,* capitalism means liberty without justice, but the Soviet Union means justice without liberty. Europe must seek liberty and justice: "This is the task of Europe. Europe remains the one community in the world to keep alive the notion of man which has been slowly elaborated in centuries of dialogue between Christian humanism and agnostic humanism. It is the one part of the world where socialism can best be realized with the least violence and alteration of principles which are not new for Europe. A socialism which will incorporate, with all its humanity and with all its strength, the ideals of communism, whose main weakness is its rigidity and whose main virtue is its rigor. Clever in manipulating ideals, in clarifying them rather than in obfuscating them . . ., on familiar terms with revolutions whose sweep will leave behind not ruins but a pure and clear perspective, Europe has acquired enough wisdom and practice . . . to be able to bless and render fruitful the legitimate union of freedom and social justice."

And if Europe cannot nourish this hope, Vercors believes it better for her to be destroyed by an atom bomb. Together with Jean Cassou in 1949 he denounced Soviet communism as not keeping faith with the people. But even then he summed up his position in this way: "I love humanity above all and France because it has been the symbol of its destiny for the last 150 years, and the Communist party because it is the only one which wants and can . . . fulfill this destiny and promise man his liberation. As long as the Communist party will not abandon these admirable goals, I will never be counted amongst its enemies. . . . If one day the party should be attacked, I will be found fighting in its ranks. But, if in its name a mistake or a crime is committed, or simply a lie is told, it will be my love for humanity and my respect for the party . . . which will lead me to denounce such acts without reserve" (Jean Cassou and Vercors, "Il ne faut pas tromper le peuple," *Esprit,* December 1949).

In their latest common statement (*La Voie libre,* Paris, 1951), Aveline, Cassou, Martin-Chauffier, and Vercors take a much firmer stand against communism. They refuse in the name of reason and truth to accept the Communist party position that "no analysis or views of the political situation, no appeal to the conscience of men, can take place outside of the strict control of the party." They are appalled at the Communist technique of "retroactive

French revolution such as Pierre Cot,[5] and Christian progressives. They generally disclaim outright support of communism but find it impossible to work against it and altogether feasible to co-operate with it. They find comfort in the fact that in the 1951 national elections, the French Communist party ran everywhere as the "Republican Resistant and Anti-Fascist Union for National Independence, Bread, Freedom, and Peace."

They write movingly of the moral "rigor" of communism and establish as their task the softening of what are described merely as the "rigidities" of communism. They feel that as long as the Communist party is the party of the working class, it is impossible to be against it as the working class is the class that needs redemption and liberation from the injustices that are committed against it, and what the world needs above all is justice. Their contribution is not a substantial one in terms of votes but it is a significant one in terms of prestige, in terms of the paths it keeps open to Communist infiltration and persuasion. It is an important one in keeping alive an almost incredible confusion concerning basic issues of freedom and rights and the meaning of justice, which should have been settled a long time ago in the light of the clear meaning of Communist doctrine, of Soviet practices, and of the emerging reality even in such western countries as Czechoslovakia, where the so-called "western variant" of communism should by now have come to life. In times of deepening crisis, the voice of the progressive fringe is one to which many people will listen as the awful moment of decision approaches and men begin to look desperately for an avenue of escape.

---

defamation." But, perched uneasily on the fence, they seem convinced that capitalism needs war to survive, that the Atlantic Pact is a "Munich upside down and an international slaughterhouse project," and that no new form of civilization can do without the economic and social contribution of Marxism.

[5]Author of the rejected first Constitution of the Fourth Republic, Pierre Cot crossed the final bridge facing all "progressives" and stood for re-election on the Communist list in the 1951 elections for the French National Assembly.

IV

The French and Italian Communist Parties in Their Thirtieth Anniversary Year

THE year from the spring of 1950 to the spring of 1951 was a busy one for the French and Italian Communist parties.[1] Acting in unison, both parties held national congresses after an interval of three years. Both parties celebrated the thirtieth anniversary of their founding. Both parties devoted a good deal of attention to their programs. Both faced the handicap of the serious illnesses of their chiefs, Thorez and Togliatti. Both parties had to suffer Cominform criticism and to admit that their Central Committees were not quite up to the standards required of a Communist party Central Committee. Both had to meet a developing threat of Titoism within their ranks. Both, finally, had to test their strength in local or national elections in May and June 1951.

In their reports to the national party congresses, Thorez and Togliatti followed what has now become a standard pattern of argument. They both highlighted the sharp contrast between the

---

[1]The important dates and occasions to remember for this period are: (1) the twelfth national congress of the French Communist party in April 1950; (2) the meetings in September and October 1950 of the Central Committee of the French Communist party; (3) the meetings in October 1950 of the Central Committee of the Italian Communist party; (4) the seventh national congress of the Italian Communist party in April 1951; and (5) the meetings in April 1951 of the Central Committee of the French Communist party.

warlike intentions of the United States and the peaceful activities of the Soviet Union, underlined the disastrous economic policies of the French and Italian governments, enslaved by American capitalism, and described communism as the defender of true national aspirations and honor. Thorez said that only the Communists carry "the memory of our intellectual traditions, of our qualities of taste, of measure, of elegance and probity, all the qualities that have made the greatness of our country." Togliatti was full of patriotic praise for the valor of the Italian army and referred with nostalgic affection to the liberal symbol among the builders of modern Italy, Giolitti. Thorez restated once more his policy of the outstretched hand, telling Catholics that "rather than quarrel to find out whether there is a paradise in heaven, let us unite so that this world shall no longer be like hell." Togliatti, on the other hand, felt obliged to say that there were no true progressive elements among Christian Democrats and that all parties and all non-Communist organized groups were hopelessly anti-Communist. Communism alone was the party of all-embracing democracy and peace and of defense of constitutional and republican freedoms. But both leaders felt impelled to criticize the vice of Communist sectarianism, defined as a sense of superiority which prevents the Communist militant from working effectively with non-Communist workers and intellectuals.

Reports such as those of Thorez and Togliatti reveal the current leading propaganda themes and cannot be dismissed as meaningless generalities since they influence a good many people. But it is clear that one must look elsewhere for clues to the substantive nature of the Communist program. Needless to say, there is no hope of finding any advance written confirmation of the establishment of a state in which all personal political freedoms are lost. But, interestingly enough, there is an important body of information dealing with economic policies which offers a self-incriminating picture of a quite primitive type of economic thinking. While the identification of communism with political tyranny is generally conceded outside the circle of the faithful, there are still at large all kinds of legends concerning the identification of communism with economic progress. For this reason anything contributed by Communist sources themselves to obliterate such identification deserves particularly careful attention. Two instances may be examined, the agrarian policy of the French Communist party and the industrial policy of the Italian Communist party.

Self-sufficiency and high costs appear as standard Communist policy, as economic isolation follows the isolation of Communist political thinking. It is, therefore, not surprising to see the Communists advocate first of all the elimination of all foreign competition through a customs barrier high enough to keep foreign foodstuffs out. Expropriation without indemnity of all lands belonging to big capitalists and with indemnity of the smaller properties largely belonging to the professional bourgeoisie is to follow. Expropriated lands will be distributed to peasant owners or to landless peasants, who will receive an "absolute consecration of [their] rights to the continuous and hereditary enjoyment of the lands they cultivate."[2] This "absolute consecration of rights" does not mean a guarantee of the property rights of the French peasant in keeping with the individualistic traditions of France and the plain meaning of words. In keeping, rather, with the paradoxes of Marxian dialectics, it means the establishment of a future collectivistic paradise preceded by an immediate hell of peasant serfdom. For the party has been at pains to repeat that the long-range "theses on the agrarian question of the French Communist party" adopted in November 1921 have never been repudiated. They read:

The revolutionary task is that of preparing the peasants to face the new problems...and of substituting the notion of a common interest for that of individual interest. The use of heavy machinery ..., the participation in production and exchange co-operatives will tear the peasant away from his present isolation and will lead him to understand that his interest lies not in conflict with his fellow peasants or in merely living next to them, but in living with them in an ever-closer collaboration.... Defeated by the new tech-

[2]On the Communist agrarian program, cf. *Cahiers du communisme*, May 1950.

nology, by the propaganda of speech, press, and school, egoism will disappear. The peasants will form production associations in increasing numbers, waiting for the dawn of the day when of their own free will they will destroy the boundary lines which have kept them divided for centuries.[3]

This collectivistic paradise in the party's own estimate is not a near one. One may remember the objections of principle advanced by Lenin against attempting to forecast the length of the dictatorship of the proletariat, that is, of the period intervening between the revolution and the advent of the perfect Communist society. The "disappearance of egoism" envisaged by the French Communists belongs to the category of long-range and painful changes which Lenin said must be effected before the revolution has achieved its true goal. It is downright unscientific, owing to the lack of precedents, to try to predict how long it will take a workers' state to get there. Mere human beings are, therefore, justified in their anxiety to know what is to happen in the long interval between the Communist seizure of power and the final fading of egoism.

It is clear that the French Communist party is not going to wait a long time for the "dawn of the day" in which the boundary lines will be erased. For what is to develop at once is a condition of serfdom, with a conspicuous lack of interest in property rights and in spontaneous individual mobility. At its twelfth national congress, the French Communist party again adopted as the fifth point in its agrarian policy the "interdiction of all purchases and sales of land, in order to keep the land for those who work it and in order to prevent any renewed transfer of land to capitalists and speculators." Thus is achieved the double purpose of destroying all property titles of the small owners which a moment earlier the Communist party seemed eager to protect, at least in interim fashion, and of transforming the proud peasant owners of France into slaves permanently fixed to their bit of land.

The attachment of the Communists to feudalism, inefficiency,

[3]*Le Parti communiste et la question paysanne,* preface by Waldeck Rochet (Paris: Editions Sociales, 1949).

and obsolete economic policies is indeed chronic. Speaking before the Central Committee of the Italian Communist party in October 1950, one of the two "tough" vice-secretaries, Luigi Longo, in effect lamented as tragic the increasing productivity which is beginning to show up as an encouraging factor in Italian industry. While in 1948 fourteen minutes of work were required to produce one pound of rayon, in 1949 nine minutes were enough. The biggest motor car factory increased its labor force between January and September 1949 by 14 per cent, but increased its production by 46 per cent. And while the cotton industry increased its labor force in 1949 over 1948 by 0.6 per cent, it increased its production 20 per cent. Further, by lumping together the rates of production of a tank arsenal and of a typewriter factory, of cotton cloth and of a Fascist-invented fiber, Longo sought to create the impression of wastage of basic industrial assets. In effect, in most instances normal peacetime industries have not only been using their full prewar capacity but have greatly expanded it, while the tank, gun, and warship arsenals are, of course, idle and other industries which cannot readily adapt themselves to a freer world market are meeting with serious difficulties. What Longo is defending is, again, the isolation of Italy's industrial system from the rest of the world and the continued exploitation, no matter what the economic cost, of obsolete and unnecessary Fascist plants which should be scrapped to make room for other activities of a more modern and profitable type. Again, what the Communists are proposing in the West is not a rational utilization of natural resources but the freezing of an industrial system which, instead, needs revision if it is to meet the needs of the democratic community of nations.

Programmatic issues were not the only ones to occupy the parties' attention in their thirtieth year. No less important was the organization of a machine that had to be prepared for the contingency of war between the Soviet Union and the western world, when the role of Communist parties would be that of military agents of the Soviet Union. The pressure exercised by Moscow in favor of a tightening up of the party apparatus has been considerable ever since the outbreak of the Korean war. It explains, on the one hand, the internal party tensions that became visible at the meetings in October 1950 of the Central Committees of the French and Italian Communist parties and, on the other hand, the beginnings of a Titoist movement in northern France and in northern Italy.

At the meetings of the two Central Committees, Pietro Secchia and Auguste Lecoeur uttered criticisms which can only be interpreted as an indirect attack on the two top leaders, Togliattti and Thorez, who were both at about that time to become so critically ill as to necessitate a long period of cure in the Soviet Union. Secchia complained that party leadership reacted with great slowness to the outbreak of the Korean war. Local Communist federations did not arrange for mass meetings and failed to mobilize public opinion. These criticisms apply, Secchia continued, to the members of the Central Committee of the party, who must learn to act more rapidly and with greater initiative, for under present conditions it is necessary not only to know how to do things but above all to do them. A similar accusation of incompetence and laziness was leveled in even stronger terms by Lecoeur at the members of the French Central Committee meeting ten days later and in the absence of Thorez. The Central Committee, which included such veterans as Duclos and Marty, was forced to admit that its ideological foundations were weak, that its practical work was of poor quality, and that its organizational efforts were inadequate. It approved unanimously the following resolution presented by Lecoeur:

The members of the Central Committee of the French Communist party..., conscious of their responsibilities, engage themselves: (1) to strengthen their ideological education by devoting regularly the necessary amount of time to the study of Marxist-Leninist classics as well as of all essential party documents and documents of the Cominform and other mass organizations, and to prepare carefully the meetings of their study group; (2) to improve the quality of their work and to organize each meeting of the Central Committee in such a way as to bring the most constructive elements to the discussion and formulation of the political line; (3) to double their efforts to clarify political problems and to control carefully and rigorously the total execution by those concerned of the decisions reached, since the political line must not simply be proclaimed but must be executed.[4]

The warnings delivered by the "tough" party leaders against the softening of the party under the quasi-bourgeois rule of Thorez and Togliatti were followed by a long series of criticisms of the French and Italian Communist press and organization appearing in the Cominform bulletin, *For a Lasting Peace, for a People's Democracy!*[5] On December 8, 1950, the Italian Communist party daily, *Unità,* was found wanting because

it does not adequately reflect the activities of local peace committees or the work of the mass democratic organizations fighting for peace.... Frequently it shows an insufficiently critical approach in using information and reports circulated by bourgeois news agencies on questions of international life. There are instances when, dealing with questions of culture and art, the newspaper does not adhere to a consistent Marxist-Leninist viewpoint; it does not devote sufficient attention to ideological work among the progressive intelligentsia and, as yet, makes insufficient use of correspondents drawn from its readers, particularly workers and peasants.

On January 12, 1951, it was the turn of the *Cahiers du communisme,* the official organ of the central committee of the French party:

It strikes the eye, for example, that too little space is devoted to questions of Marxist philosophy, sociology and political economy. ...It should also be pointed out that although the journal did publish Comrade Stalin's work on Marxism in linguistics, it did not, however, print any articles illustrating the full significance of these works by Comrade Stalin for the further development of Marxist-Leninist theory.[6]... The struggle against the ideology of

---

[4]For Secchia's address, see *Verso il VII congresso del partito comunista Italiano, Per la discussione precongressuale* (Rome, 1950); for Lecoeur's, *Cahiers du communisme,* December 1950.

[5]The following quotations are from the English language edition of the Cominform weekly published in Bucharest.

[6]This glaring omission was happily remedied in the June 1951 issue of the

social-democratism is weak. . . . There is a tendency to regard the consequences of the war economy as something that is unavoidable, something ordained by fate, as if the working class and its allies — the middle strata in town and countryside — cannot wage an effective struggle against the government policy of war and poverty.

And on March 23, 1951, both the French and Italian Communist parties (along with a few other small western Communist parties) were warned to eliminate present shortcomings and to develop criticism and self-criticism "as a means of purging the party of enemy filth and scum." Party meetings should be carefully prepared and constant control should be exercised over the carrying out of party decisions. This open invitation to drastic discipline and purging of party ranks is in keeping with the general trend of Soviet policy since 1947 of maintaining as far as possible the mass appeal of western communism, but of reinforcing at the same time the military discipline of its inner revolutionary core against the day when either war or the gradual redemption of European society will force communism to retreat upon its line of last defense.

The scattered outbreaks of Titoism in France and Italy are certainly a reaction against the increasing Moscow domination so completely accepted by the present Communist leaders. National communism in the West is only a generic and distant threat, but it has the quality of a nightmare for the official party organization. Tito has joined the enemies of the Stalinist world, and his influence is feared in the West since communism there does not have at its disposal the full governmental apparatus of repression which in Communist states permits the elimination of dissent. In an atmosphere of freedom, even Communist dissent might flourish.

It should be noted, however, that the Titoist movement in Italy started in the Bologna area, where within the last fifty years extreme manifestations of syndicalism, fascism, and communism

---

Cahiers, in which Georges Cogniot published an article on "Les positions de Parti dans le domaine idéologique à la lumière des travaux de Staline sur la linguistique."

have found a natural environment, due in part to the seriousness of the agrarian issue. It is described by its authors as due to the development within the party of a mechanical atmosphere and to the supine acceptance of decisions imposed by a dictatorial apparatus. The lack of freedom of discussion inside the party has apparently prevented the flowering of that democratic grass-roots communism which was fleetingly glimpsed in the mythological world of *Ordine nuovo*.[7] But the two Titoist leaders, Deputies Cucchi and Magnani, proclaim themselves revolutionary Marxists, enemies of the United States, of the Marshall Plan and the North Atlantic Treaty, of the Italian bourgeoisie, and of the present Italian government. It seems probable, therefore, that the contribution of Titoism to western democratic parties will remain small and that a strong Titoist movement will be unable to develop in France and Italy so long as French and Italian Communist parties remain opposition parties. As such, relieved of the responsibilities of government, they will not be required to carry out policies dictated solely by the interests of the Soviet Union. As long as they cannot set up a slave state under Russian control, they will parade as the champions of freedom and national independence. The greatest direct stimulus to Titoism will thus be missing.

The spring elections of 1951 provide the latest accurate record of the popular strength of communism in France and Italy. An over-all evaluation of the results might proceed as follows:

In the five years between 1946 and 1951 France has seen a good measure of economic recovery. Furthermore, France has been the source of some of the more original and hopeful ideas for the future integration of Europe, and in France some of the best of European postwar political leaders have asserted themselves. Statesmen like Schuman have impressed not only the French people with the breadth and originality of their ideas. The election returns of June 17, 1951, seem to be based upon a recognition of these factors and to show a modest measure of hopefulness for the future. The Communist vote has therefore declined by 7 per

[7]See below, p. 157.

cent, or from 28 to 26 per cent of the total votes cast. Nor is this decline altogether nullified by the vote for de Gaulle.

In the industrialized areas of northern Italy no benefits similar to those reaped by France have as yet been realized. But a beginning has been made toward the modernization of industrial plants and the general improvement of economic conditions. The Communist vote in the municipal elections of May and June 1951 is a little below that of 1948.

Central and southern Italy is an agrarian region still contemplating a future that over large areas holds out very little hope indeed. The start of agrarian reform has been recent and on a small scale, and population pressure has not been relieved. Voters are still swayed by immediate personal considerations and fears and move amid an almost complete lack of the kind of intelligible information that might make the issue between communism and anticommunism understandable. Profiting from these conditions and from the strengthening of a party structure which three years ago was still weak, the Communist vote increased everywhere, with the maximum increase in Sicily.

With the support of 26 per cent of the voters in France and of 37 per cent in Italy (the Italian percentage includes a substantial "captive" Socialist vote which makes up more than one-third of the total), communism in 1951 was still the strongest and most effective single political force in Western Europe. But the tide had started to recede where the initial foundations of new conditions of life and of new ideas had been laid down.

V

Communism and Europe's
Position in the World

W ESTERN European communism is a major factor in determining the nature of the key triangular relationship of power in our times, that of the United States, Europe, and the Soviet Union.

Since 1947 it has been the policy of the United States, and one from which there has been no deviation in spite of Asiatic complications, to devote a main part of its foreign effort to the task of making Western Europe a strong and independent unit of the free world and, therefore, an ally of the United States. Motives ranging from a generous determination to maintain the integrity and increase the welfare of a community that has played a vital role in the growth of American society, to an awareness of the requirements of American military security, have contributed to the steady and large-scale application of a policy of assistance to Europe. Following the outbreak of the Korean war in 1950, military exigencies have tended to overshadow everything else at a time when, of all European countries, only England had precariously achieved a balanced and rather uniformly prosperous level of national life. Within England, therefore, the country's responsibilities as military ally of the United States were not too seriously questioned; in France and Italy the proponents of a full military effort on the side of the United States were faced by a far more serious challenge.

Furthermore, the challenge did not, as in England, come from men such as Bevan who are part of a common democratic system, but from revolutionary leaders who have in effect placed themselves outside the societies in which they live and are yet capable of exercising a tremendous influence on those societies. This is not to say that, even on the continent of Europe, the majority has not already chosen between the United States and the Soviet Union, since people in the position of making a free choice have realized that a choice in favor of the United States is only an initial choice, which does not bar the way in the future to a great variety of other choices, as those other choices gradually become possible in a world that has managed to stay free. But the minority is highly organized, powerful, and capable of using the techniques of propaganda which mass totalitarianism has perfected, and has not been reduced to the acceptance at any point of the other side's position. The Communist minority can also appeal on the question of the choice between the United States and the Soviet Union to a non-Communist neutralist element, which, because of the complexity and gravity of the issues, hopes to be able to avoid making any choice at all. It, therefore, matters a good deal to understand what are the unsolved difficulties, what the psychological factors and the legends, which communism is using in an attempt to control Europe's mind.

A summary of the views of those Europeans who still judge the United States on the basis of a mythical interpretation of its economic system and of a negative view of its political life, and who believe that American policy can lead only to the most catastrophic outcome, follows:

The American economic and political system is inapplicable to European conditions. No good, therefore, can be expected from any firm association with a country whose institutions are irrelevant and foreign to European experience and needs. They are not only inapplicable but inherently bad. American capitalism, which dominates the economic life of the United States, is exploitive and monopolistic and extolls a money conception of life flouting the humane and social values which the modern world should stress. No explanation to the contrary has so far persuaded these groups that the United States is anything but a civilization of robber barons, extreme concentration of economic power, and artificial and materialistic values which the rest of the' world has decisively rejected. Politically, the institutions of the country are described as obsolete and inflexible, making possible the worst kind of group discrimination and lending the dignity and majesty of judicial bodies to racial crimes and persecutions against which Europe fought the anti-Nazi battle. It is this combination of economic greed and of belief in the superiority of the American people that leads to imperialism and war. Americans are the natural allies of Franco and of the surviving Nazis whom they are trying to spare from the gallows. In their fear of the Soviet Union, which is in effect a subconscious fear of political and social change, Americans are ready to risk war and to use the atom bomb, that supreme affront to the civilized mind. They promise political freedom, but what is that freedom worth if it is to follow the total destruction of the world as a result of war?[1]

American policies in Europe since the inception of the Marshall Plan and, more particularly, since the beginning of the Korean war have often been interpreted in the light of these misconceptions. The visible and all-pervasive presence of the United States government on the European continent since 1948 has placed America at the center of controversy. The precipitate disappearance of American military might after the end of the war has been followed by the return of great numbers of American government and economic experts, by the signature of agreements between the United States and European governments concerning the European recovery program, and by the establishment of the complicated administrative procedures necessary for its management. The tying of the policies and fortunes of European governments to the United States, as a result of the Marshall Plan, is one of the outstanding phenomena in postwar Europe. The frictions and misunderstandings which have inevitably resulted must be judged by any impartial observer as relatively minor ones, given the novel-

---

[1]See for an attempt to deal with this obsessive image, Mario Einaudi, "Controverse sur l'Amérique: Lettre à *Esprit*," *Esprit*, June 1951.

ty, the scale, and the ultimate significance of the issues involved. But they have appeared as major issues to the ill-disposed, and the Communists have cleverly magnified them into proof of a deliberate American intention to bring about the submission of Europe to its interests. Normal relationships of the French and Italian governments with Washington have been translated into evidence of subservience and slavish renunciation of national independence.

The deepening of the crisis since the Korean war has imparted to American policy a new sense of urgency and of the importance of military considerations. The United States is in such a position of responsibility as to be forced to favor unpopular policies and to issue from the midst of plenty and incredible wealth orders that require the hardest kind of sacrifice from communities living on the edge of poverty. It is forced to exact painful efforts and dedication to duty from a continent still not recovered from the shock of war. American pressure for economic reform has been replaced by pressure for rearmament, for a life of even grimmer austerity, and for a postponement of economic plans deemed vital by the peoples of Europe. As the 1951 report of the Organization for European Economic Cooperation points out, "This means that in all cases a smaller proportion of the total output will be available for civilian purposes." This dislocation of a barely normal way of life has alarmed many people, and the Communists have not been slow to exploit the advantage. Intelligent and critical minds were convinced in good faith that the increase in prices due to the stock-piling and war production policies of the United States since the outbreak of the Korean war had, by the spring of 1951, already caused France greater damage than all the benefits derived from the Marshall Plan.

The requirements of the North Atlantic Treaty have led to the re-establishment of a number of military bases throughout Europe in which United States participation is preponderant as is its contribution to the total defense effort. The hardships and tribulations which inevitably follow the entry of the military into a hitherto peaceful landscape are for the Communist proof of the ruthlessness with which Americans, as the Nazis ten years ago, are dealing with France:

The happiness of May is bursting open upon a land softened by the rising lymphs of spring. They love our sweet France, the Americans do, as the Germans loved it. They too are here, in the heart of France, in this Bourbonnais of mountains and groves where, under a fleecy sky, fat silken cows pasture in meadows covered with lucent grass. On the left, a quarry of red sand cuts sharply across a green hill. Here the Nazis shot forty-two patriots. To the right, the Americans have the insolence to install one of their military depots for the coming war.[2]

All this must be realized in weighing the handicaps which the United States has to surmount in order to help those Europeans who are determined that communism shall not decide the position of Europe in the world.

But what must also be taken into account is the image of the Soviet Union that communism is placing before the West. Just as the United States is everywhere visibly present in the West, so is the Soviet Union visibly absent. For it can use agencies not available to the United States to carry its message. And that message is not a stern reminder of the conditions of survival but an invitation to contemplate rivers flowing with honey and milk. The propaganda machine of French and Italian communism daily describes how in Russia atomic energy is used to move mountains and rivers and to water deserts, and how the energies of the Soviet government and people are concentrated on peaceful endeavors. New material is continuously fed to the campaign of local Communist parties through Soviet interventions before international bodies which admirably serve Soviet purposes. Speaking in Geneva in comparative terms carefully calculated to achieve maximum effect, the Soviet delegate to the United Nations Economic Commission for Europe happily announced in June 1951 that a gigantic new power station now under construction on the Volga will produce more power than all of Italy or all of France, and twice as

[2]Simone Téry, "La grande enquête de *l'Humanité* sur l'occupation américaine en France: Ils installent la mort américaine au coeur de la France," *Humanité*, May 8, 1951.

much as the Grand Coulee dam. As the *New York Times* pointed out:

This picture of a peaceful and booming Russia, contrasted to a struggling, inflation-ridden, west may sound pretty funny to some Americans. In the opinion of United States officials involved in the struggle to keep the western world from falling apart at the seams, it does not sound so funny and may sound pretty good to far too may Europeans. There can be no doubt whatever after this ECE session that it is the story the Communists are relying on to win the intellectual battle in Western Europe.[3]

European communism identifies the United States as its enemy because the Soviet Union recognizes that it is the power of the United States that offers the main obstacle to its plans of expansion. But European communism opposes the United States not only as the enemy of the Soviet Union but as its own particular enemy, because the United States is striking at the roots of Communist strength through its support of the modernization and integration of the structure of Europe. While the aims of the Marshall and Schuman Plans are primarily economic at this stage, they are bound to bring about far-reaching social and political changes that will create the conditions under which communism will not be able to survive.

Therefore, the problem of the defense of the United States and of its system of alliances against the Soviet Union, and of the defense of the exposed areas of the democratic world against the disintegrating influences of domestic Communist parties, must be met by the parallel policies of increase in the striking power of the United States and of support of the measures capable of ensuring the necessary reorientation of Europe's economic life. The rearmament of the United States can be undertaken, as it has in effect been undertaken, at once. But the support of basic economic plans must be continued also. For the effective rearmament of Europe is something that will follow and not precede the establishment of a substantial belief among Europeans in the reality of the new Europe which the Marshall and Schuman Plans ultimately envisage.

[3]Dispatch from Geneva, June 12, 1951.

VI

Communism and the Marshall and Schuman Plans

COMMUNISM opposes the two key reconstruction measures of post-war Europe because it realizes that the Marshall and Schuman plans aim to recover Europe's independence and strength *vis-à-vis* the Soviet Union and at the same time to reconstruct Europe's economic system in such a way as to eliminate some of the conditions which have led to communism.

The Marshall Plan has been in operation since the spring of 1948, and up to December 31, 1950, it had provided 2.2 billion dollars for France and 1.2 billion dollars for Italy. When in the elections of May-June 1951 the Communist vote increased in Italy and decreased only slightly in France, doubts were raised in the United States concerning the effectiveness and validity of huge foreign expenditures.

The fact of the matter is that up to the end of 1950, roughly 75 per cent of Economic Cooperation Administration expenditures in France and Italy had been used to prevent a further deterioration of the conditions which existed in 1948, while only 25 per cent had gone into the building of the plant upon which a modernized industrial Europe depends. Without the 75 per cent France and Italy would today be in a condition of far graver political instability. But it is from the 25 per cent that any substantial effect upon the 1948 strength of communism must be expected. This will not happen for some years to come, not before approximately 1955–1960.

The use of Marshall funds for emergency or short-range purposes, though necessary, could not lead to changes of permanent significance. Gratitude is not part of the normal human baggage; memories are short-lived; and if basic conditions remain the same, the strength of communism remains the same. But once the two billion dollars' worth of iron and steel, oil, automotive, chemical, power, and other industrial plants built or to be built with ECA assistance in France and Italy has come into full and efficient operation and has in due course led to expanded and more efficient activities of subsidiary industrial operations, there will then be in sight the framework of a modern industrial society within which communism cannot live. The 1951 strength of French and Italian communism still reflects the consumer type of ECA expenditure and not yet the capital type of ECA investment. This is merely another way of saying that the issue of Communism in Western Europe is not to be solved in a few years, after which the long-promised return to normalcy will take place, but that it will stay alive until many of the long-range problems of European society are solved.

The affinity between communism and bankruptcy and the incompatibility between communism and expansion and economic progress can be shown with the help of some figures revealed at the 1951 national party congress by one of the top Italian Communist leaders, Luigi Longo. In his report Longo produced data permitting the construction of what might be called the "bankruptcy index" of Communist party strength. In the great Ansaldo works, largely a collection of obsolete war plants and shipyards, without any possibility of use either in peacetime or in wartime and therefore facing complete bankruptcy and ultimate elimination, 85 per cent of the workers and technicians are enrolled party members. In the Ilva steel works, where a modest beginning has been made toward modernization of the mills, 77 per cent of the workers are Communist. In the Fiat motor works, in which as in any automotive plant retooling is a faster process than is modernization in a steel plant, 70 per cent of the workers are party members. In the Olivetti typewriter and office equipment factories, where renovation is far along, 66 per cent of the workers are Communist. In the Rossi textile mills, which because of a boom in textile exports have been able to provide both an efficient plant and steady and expanding employment, 58 per cent of the workers are Communist. It is true that in the last instance the presence of many women among the workers may account for the lower percentage. It is true also that all the figures of Communist strength are still fearfully high. But the trend seems clear, and the expectation is that it will develop with accelerated speed once modernization becomes a more general pattern. It is certain that there exists a correlation between economic soundness and confidence in the future and the worker's freedom of political choice, on the one hand, and, on the other, a similar correlation between economic distress and the attachment of workers to communism because of its shelter and defense values. The long-range effect of the Marshall Plan should be the elimination of obsolete economic units and their replacement by more productive plants better suited to the natural and man-power resources of such countries as Italy. When that day dawns, the strength of communism will begin to wane. It is against the dawning of that day that the Communist leaders are fighting.

Just as the Communists oppose the Marshall Plan because it stands for the modernization of Europe, so are they opposed to the Schuman Plan because it stands for the ideal of an open society. The combination of an invigorated economic system and a faster circulation of goods and men denies the basic premises of communism, which are those of the inflexible allocation of men to the performance of fixed tasks in a society from which the experimental approach and the free trade of ideas have been banned.

The preamble of the Schuman Treaty states the purpose of the European Community of Coal and Steel to be created for the management of these key industrial sectors by saying that peace may be safeguarded only by efforts measuring up to the dangers which menace it; that the contribution which an organized and vital Europe can make is indispensable to the maintenance of peace; that Europe can be built only by concrete actions creating effective solidarity and establishing common bases of economic development; that the expansion of production is necessary to raise the standard of living; and that the creation of an economic community will provide the foundation of a broad and independent association among peoples long divided and will lay the bases of institutions capable of giving direction to their future common destiny.

The Coal and Steel Community will have the mission of contributing, according to Article 2, "to economic expansion, the development of employment and the improvement of the standard of living in the participating countries through the institution, in harmony with the general economy of the member states, of a single market." The Community shall, according to Article 3,

a) see that the single market is regularly supplied, taking account of the needs of third countries;

b) assure to all consumers in comparable positions within the single market equal access to the sources of production;

c) seek the establishment of the lowest prices. . .;

d) see that conditions are maintained which will encourage enterprises to expand and improve their ability to produce. . .;

e) promote the improvement of the living and working conditions of the labor force in each of the industries under its jurisdiction so as to make possible the equalization of such conditions in an upward direction;

f) further the development of international trade. . .;

g) promote the regular expansion and the modernization of production as well as the improvement of its quality. . . .

The treaty recognizes as practices and policies which are incompatible with the single market for coal and steel and which are, therefore, abolished and prohibited within the Community the following:

a) import and export duties. . .and quantitative restrictions on movements of coal and steel;

b) measures or practices discriminating among producers, among buyers or among consumers, specifically as concerns prices, delivery terms and transportation rates as well as measures or practices which hamper the buyer in the free choice of his supplier;

c) subsidies or state assistance...;

d) restrictive practices tending toward the division of markets or the exploitation of the consumer....

The High Authority, established under the treaty and under conditions which should guarantee an effective international approach on its part to the tasks confronting the Community, has the means, sometimes in conjunction with the special Council of Ministers and under the over-all review of the Common Assembly but more often alone, to carry out the purposes of the treaty, which are purposes of integration, of the liberation of productive forces, and of the creation of all the benefits that will flow from the establishment of a common market where cheap goods produced in the greatest quantity will circulate freely.

This is a new and daring plan, above all for the spirit that moves it and for the supranational approach it uses. Substantial power is given to instrumentalities endowed with an independence of decision and action that lifts them from the narrow boundaries of national states. There is, of course, no assurance on paper that the Community will be a success. But if the goals of the Community are kept in mind and if the supreme direction is entrusted to statesmen of courage and imagination such as Jean Monnet, then Europe will gradually move toward a common market for the most basic raw materials of modern industrial societies — a common market from which the inefficient and high-cost producers will gradually be driven out, and in which increasing quantities (by 1953 a minimum of thirty-eight million tons a year) of cheap steel will be made available on equal terms to anybody within the market who wants to buy it — a common market which above all will help to create the sense of common destiny to which the treaty preamble refers.

With the Schuman Treaty, the bases are laid for an economic revolution which will ultimately affect, as it must, the infinite variety of economic activities depending on cheap steel. This is the most farsighted effort of Europe to face the fundamental problem of the inadequacy of the small traditional national units and of the impossibility of their continuing in a world in which the satisfaction, on an increasing scale, of the needs of the people has become a primary condition of life.[1]

If the creation of a common market for the cheapest possible steel is the central goal, then one can say that John Strachey's view of the Schuman Plan as a scheme of restrictive-minded capitalists is wrong. Nor are other critics closer to reality when they feel, with the disarming simplicity typical of a certain approach to the study of world problems, that this is just another move in the Vatican drive for a Christian Europe.

The Schuman Plan is not a clerical conspiracy and, if it lives up to its promise, is not a cartel. For it is not restrictive nor is it interested in the maintenance of high prices or in the untroubled security and high profits of the coal producers and the steel masters under its control. Indeed, many European industrialists are fighting the Coal and Steel Community because they realize that, by coming under its jurisdiction, they will lose their freedom of movement and decision and will have to subordinate their policies to the achievement of a wider European concept of welfare.

It is remarkable indeed to see, in addition to the Communists, vested industrial interests and the more dogmatic Socialists fighting side by side against the ideals of the Community. All are victims of rigid modes of thought which prevent them from getting at the changing reality. Some industrialists believe that the days of the private association typified by the French Comité des Forges can somehow be brought back. The more dogmatic Socialists are unable to go beyond their old obsessive conclusion that no plan

---

[1] The United Nations Economic Commission for Europe, in its study of the economic bases of the Schuman Plan, has provided both a justification of the Plan and a hopeful appraisal of its ultimate beneficial results. The Commission expresses the hope that the High Authority, fearing the shock that will accompany the introduction of a really free and common market, will not support measures likely to obscure the final objectives and hinder their realization. Cf. "The coal and steel industries of Western Europe," *Economic Bulletin for Europe*, October 1950.

which does not include nationalization of industry is any good. So far, the Schuman Treaty is a triumphant demonstration of the fact that the main virtue of the statesman is to push aside ruthlessly the worn-out clichés, the egoistic points of view of interested groups, and to fathom the essence of the future. The problem was rightly judged by men like Monnet, who have been working in France ever since the end of World War II with both nationalized and non-nationalized industries, not as that of a mere legal transfer of property titles from private hands to governments, but as that of the use of all available resources under the best possible conditions and for the benefit of the whole European community.

The rumblings that have accompanied the Schuman Treaty negotiations have been the best proof that Europe was on the right track and that for once statesmen seemed to be on the winning side and in full control against technicians, special pleaders, and men weighed down by all the prejudices of those who cling to closed systems of thought.

The link binding the Marshall to the Schuman Plan should be made clear at this point. For one of the more significant, if as yet still hidden, consequences of the Marshall Plan is the renovation of the European steel industry which it permits. As a result of investments made with Marshall funds, the Schuman Treaty countries in a few years will be producing steel under roughly comparable conditions with regard to costs. The difficulties of an agreement would have been much greater had national differences as to production costs continued to be as great as they had been in the past. By making it possible for European countries to renovate their steel plants, the United States has made a contribution of the first order to the success of the Coal and Steel Community; for it has tended to remove from the conference table the specter of too drastic and painful national readjustments.

But the opposition of communism to the Schuman Treaty is irrevocable. It is against it because that "traitor of the working class," Léon Blum, supported its principles at a conference of Western European Socialist parties on April 28, 1948, when he said, "It is of the highest importance for the future of the United

States of Europe that the industries of the Ruhr and of the Rhine-
land be integrated into a vast combine together with the coal, iron
and steel, and chemical industries of Belgium, the Saar, Lorraine
and northern France." It is against it because the left-wing leader
of German Christian democracy, Karl Arnold, said on December
30, 1948, "Germany's neighbors must form an economic union
with the Ruhr." It is against it because, on January 1, 1950, the
ECA published a declaration of Robert Schuman in which the
outlines of the plan were envisaged: "We intend to place our iron
and steel industry at the disposal of a united Europe."

But communism is against the Schuman Plan not only because
the intellectual leaders of anticommunism are for it, but because
the Schuman Plan threatens the survival of communism's economic theories. The official organ of the Central Committee of
the French Communist party laments the fact that the Schuman
Plan will force the closing of inefficient coal mines as well as the
closing of some older iron and steel plants at Saint-Etienne, Caen,
and Saint-Nazaire. It is true that, as against these future con-
tingencies, the full development of the promising new coal fields
of Lorraine will be accelerated. It is also true that France has,
thanks to Marshall Plan aid, built the greatest continuous rolling
mill plant in Europe, which, with another similar plant, will produce 1,800,000 tons of rolled steel products per year, or twice as
much as the highest peacetime French consumption of these products up to now. But the Communists do not view this as a substantial contribution to the raising of the standard of living of the
French people but merely as an obvious preparation for war forced
upon France by American imperialism.[2]

With such logic, the French Communist party has waged relent-
less war against the Schuman Plan. The campaign started with the
formal declaration of the French politburo on May 11, 1950, that
"the Schuman Plan will undoubtedly have as a result the entry of
Germany into the aggressive bloc of the Atlantic Pact, will prepare, therefore, its rearmament and will aggravate the conditions

[2] Cf. Pierre Froment, "Le combinat franco-allemand pour le charbon et
l'acier," *Cahiers du communisme*, June 1950.

of life of the laboring masses of France." It was continued up to the eve of the 1951 national elections when, on May 17, Jacques Duclos delivered a speech at a mass meeting in Paris in which the "nefarious" Schuman Plan was attacked along with the reconstitution of the Wehrmacht and the imperialistic adventure against the Korean people.

Communism is on the defensive when confronted by such novel ideas as the Schuman Plan, and it must attack them as it must equally fight any effort to introduce a breath of fresh air, any lowering of the barriers that separate peoples into air-tight compartments —anything, in brief, that may destroy the rigidities and primitivism on which, apart from the military might of the Soviet Union, is based its revolutionary appeal.

VII

What Must Be Done

To DEFEAT the Communist conspiracy for the conquest of the world, the unyielding resistance and the military might of the United States, developed in conjunction with that of its allies, are of the essence. Most Europeans understand that military defense is the vital premise and that a so-called "neutralist" position for Western Europe, interpreting neutralism as a refusal to make a choice now between the United States and the Soviet Union, is untenable.[1]

But the fact remains that the elimination of communism as a fifth column in Western Europe does not eliminate the political and social problem posed by communism. Communism as a military threat may be counterbalanced by military strength, and its constitutional significance may be half eliminated, as it was in France as a result of the 1951 electoral law. But the social, economic, and political issues remain, and with them the impressive scope of Communist power to act as a distintegrating and corrupting element within our society.

Thus, Western European communism cannot be considered wholly as a police problem, even though the police aspects of Communist activity have not escaped the attention of governments. It remains also a long-range political issue, to be met steadily through the successful affirmation of policies capable of creating a modern

[1]In the few electoral districts in which neutralist lists were presented in the 1951 French national elections, only a few thousand voters supported them. The Communist vote is not, of course, a neutralist vote because the Communists have chosen sides.

and open society where, by definition, communism cannot gain the upper hand.

It is by now clear that there is nothing inevitably leading modern democracies to communism, nothing to force the acceptance of the belief that communism is the coming form of political organization, nothing to compel man to embrace as final the prophecies of Marxism and to deny his ability to create the world he wants in the name of the future and not of the past. But it is also clear that one cannot, by standing still, claim immunity.

In considering France and Italy, one may assume that what is required is the acceleration of all processes tending to build more modern institutions, more substantial integration, and fully open societies. Some comments will be offered, by way of conclusion, on a number of specific problems.

The ideas of constitutionalism implied in the new French and Italian constitutions should be permitted to assert themselves fully, in order to give dignity and power to the state acting in the interest of the common good. First of all, the excessive claims of parties over constitutional life must be abandoned. From 1945 to 1951 parties have acted as if the sum total of wisdom were entrusted to their hands and as if they alone could speak for the national interest. The fact is that the more the demands of parties increased, the smaller became their hold on the people. The combined membership of the French Socialist and M.R.P. (Mouvement Républicain Populaire) parties fell from 535,000 in 1945 to 250,000 in 1950, or about one per cent of the French electorate. What appears necessary is a good deal of humility, a readiness to conceive of government as something higher and more flexible than the rigid application of party platforms, and a willingness to push party directorates far into the background and to allow parliament to function as an independent body acting for the benefit of the whole and in the light of the total information available to it. Unless this is done, parties will hardly be able to maintain their vital roles in political life as the vehicles and regulators of discussion, and will be subjected to the attacks of such authoritarian and antiparty movements as the de Gaullist and neo-Fascist movements. Unless satisfactory boundaries are established between the jurisdiction of parties and the jurisdiction of constitutional organs, crisis and paralysis will rule.

Second, the persistent suspicion of executive power must be abandoned. So little of the negative lessons of the French and Italian past and of the encouraging and applicable British experience has been learned. What is needed is a simplification of constitutional practices in this field, as well as an acceptance of the legislative, planning, and budgetary leadership of the cabinet, since such leadership cannot be found elsewhere.

Third, the moderation of party egoism and the improvement of the constitutional balance must be followed by a true acceptance of the spirit of the constitution. This is particularly required in Italy, where the Christian-Democratic party, in power since 1948, has failed to implement the constitution with the necessary laws, notably in the case of the constitutional court, which had been heralded in 1947 as the keystone of constitutionalism.

If this is accomplished, then the missing sense of national purpose and solidarity will begin to be restored, and in the common proprietorship of the visible instruments and symbols of government, there will come to life a sense of community typical of the countries where the development of democracy and constitutionalism have been parallel ones.

But France and Italy also need a higher degree of expert capacity in those fulfilling public administrative tasks and more adequate methods in the recruitment of future public servants. This would lead not only to a different outlook by the people upon their government, but also to the breaking down of the barriers which breed injustice and an excessive amount of social rigidity. The administrative machinery of France and Italy is inefficient and antiquated. It is certainly less efficient than the American, English, or German systems or than those of many smaller democratic countries in Europe. This is due to varied historical circumstances such as the traditional individualistic stubbornness of the inhabitants of France and Italy and the relative decline in the economic and political importance of the two countries. But administrative inefficiency and laxity cannot be continued for long with impunity. The vicious circle of stagnation, hopelessness, and obsolescence must be broken. An invigorated civil service does not mean an expanded one, but one using modern instruments of administration tolerably well and imbued with a stern sense of public duty.

What many people in both France and Italy have also resented, and these are some of the people who add to Communist strength, has been the separation between government and governed and the too easy control of governments by privileged groups. Government by the élite is a necessity even in democratic countries. But the governing élite must be one that cannot be purchased by any other. The arts of diplomacy and financial management, of public administration and arbitration, undoubtedly have to be placed in the hands of expert diplomats and financiers, administrators and arbitrators chosen with great care after a long process of selection and training. But no democratic society can last long if the diplomats are chosen on the basis of qualifications unrelated to the performance of their tasks, and if the financial inspectors and administrators are, in effect, co-opted by their predecessors and chosen from among an exceedingly narrow group of people. Thus, both the legend and the reality of the alien and remote state are created, against which any hostile action is justified and in which any flouting of social duties and any violation of civic responsibility are excusable.

The problems of government merge into the no less serious ones of social and economic life. The two World Wars have speeded up both social change and the reaction against the inadequacy of change. The transfer of property on a large scale from the bourgeoisie to the peasants, or from the less skilled producers to more adventurous ones; the rise from lower social strata of groups capable of seizing and exploiting, for the benefit of the entire community, the economic opportunities that wars and their aftermath create; the entrance into the channels of higher education of many who until ten years ago would never have been able to do so — all of these phenomena have contributed to a healthy circulation of groups and individuals.

But what has happened has not satisfied the demands of a restless age. Too many believe that *Christ Stopped at Eboli*, leaving multitudes of men in the uplands of southern Italy in a state of contemplative immobility and poverty. And the statistics of the French census of 1946 have been interpreted as showing obvious traces of a "hardening of the arteries," with too many people engaged in barely remunerative occupations, or in agriculture.

Also, the mental traits that favor social rigidities and class distinctions have not disappeared. Few things are more striking to the observer than the visibly held conviction that the "alienation" of the worker of which Marx spoke is still a contemporary reality. It is true that the "rejection" of the working class from the body politic, as noted earlier in this essay, was one of the historical causes that determined the break between Communist and non-Communist. In spite of the progress toward integration, much remains to be done to assure a basis of equal social dignity to the working class and the full realization by the dominant economic groups of the legitimate claims of the working man. It is true that wars and inflation have demolished to a large extent some of the traditional positions of the old capitalistic class and of the upper bourgeoisie, but their impoverishment has not always been accompanied by a decline in their arrogance, and often the benefits of the inflationary phase have gone to profiteers, whom neither the French nor Italian governments have been successful in reducing to their deserved state of nakedness.

The responsibilities of governments are immense in the economic field. Aside from the question of the changes that may have to be introduced in the management of private enterprise, public corporations own a very large quota of the total economic assets, industrial and financial, of France and Italy. Far more than with the Tennessee Valley Authority, it is in their power to set "yardsticks" of efficiency, standards for meeting the welfare of the public and the worker and for training managerial leaders interested in experimentation and progress. So far the public corporations of France and Italy have hardly set an inspiring example of imaginative and competent administration. Precisely because theirs are the areas of greatest Communist pressures, they will have to act in the future as examples of public policy serving the two essential goals of modernization of techniques and of reconciliation of conflicting groups.

The most encouraging sign for the future is that, in spite of their timidity and their yielding to the prejudices of the past and the vested interests of the present, the responsible leaders of France and Italy have shown their belief in that integration of the West which alone can create the conditions of permanent political and economic advance. For no effort to modernize the administrative system or to speed up social mobility will, in the end, achieve lasting results if it is not accompanied by the widest possible integration of the economic life of Europe. Discussing the need for the United States of Europe, the future President of the Italian republic wrote in exile in 1943:

We shall rise again from the present disaster only if we manage to go beyond the past and to establish a full solidarity among the peoples [of Europe]. . . . Only by giving up what we think we have as sovereign states — and this in truth is nothing and is of value only to small groups of plutocratic exploiters of the great majority of the citizens — shall we be able to secure a lasting prosperity.

While Europe is still unprepared for the political union that appears so simple to the dreamers of federalism, the continent is getting ready to test a functional approach that seeks to create at key points the conditions for subsequent political unity. The Coal and Steel Community is the prime example of the type of agreement that may spell the difference between a dying continent and one in a position at last to exploit fully its many skills and resources.

The statesmen of the West realize that this process of integration is the only way to strengthen Europe as a whole, to transform it into an equal and co-operative but not dependent member of the community of nations, and to put an end to the sense of inferiority which haunts so many Europeans today. European resentment against so-called American domination is misplaced, because Europe at this point needs the steadying and protecting hand of the United States. But both the United States and Europe will be benefited tomorrow by the rebirth of a much stronger continent capable of contributing fully to the continuous exchange of ideas and men and goods, in which lies the strength of free societies.

Under the multiple impact of constitutionalism, the modernization of governmental and economic institutions, the breaking down of social divisions, and an effective integration of economic and political areas of authority, communism in Western Europe is certain to show a high degree of vulnerability. The causes that attracted millions of men to communism will tend to lose their significance. As an expanding and strengthened community of nations, Western Europe should reap the full benefits of a prosperous and exciting free market of ideas. The sterility, repetitiousness, dogmatism, and irrelevancy of Communist slogans and programs should become increasingly clear. What many now consider the advantages of communism over democracy will become disadvantages. The rigid nature of Communist positions, which Communists today often succeed in labeling as a refusal to compromise with sin and the devil, will appear tomorrow as a refusal to accept reason and hope. The isolation of large numbers of individuals will not survive for long in communities which decisively mold their national and international life in ways that are opposed to isolation and discrimination. Inevitably the Communist parties of France and Italy will show the debilitating effects of protracted and vain opposition to an order of things that is showing evidence of vitality and change. The younger Communist generation, upon which the party has so heavily relied, since 1941, for its penetration into the fabric of society will gradually lose its *élan* with old age and will fail to attract the new recruits it needs to keep up the legend of the identity between communism and youth.

These political, constitutional, and economic changes are of the greatest complexity and difficulty. But the promise they hold is great, and their role is essential in the rebirth of a Europe united, free, and at peace with itself.

Part II by Jean-Marie Domenach
→→→→→→→→→→→→→→←←←←←←←←←←←←←←

THE FRENCH COMMUNIST PARTY

Introduction

THE French Communist party (P.C.F.) occupies an outstanding position in French political life. It has nearly 800,000 members, a very large number when compared with the membership of France's other large parties: the Socialist party, whose membership has fallen to about 150,000, and the Popular Republican Movement (M.R.P.), which does not have more than 100,000 members. Of these 800,000 members, many are militants who, unlike members of other parties, are not content merely to wear a pin or carry a card but consider themselves to be soldiers permanently mobilized in the service of their party. The present membership strength of the party reveals the extent of the decline that set in after a period of rapid growth. The figure of 1,000,000 members triumphantly announced at the Strasbourg Congress in 1947 had decreased to 900,000 in 1949 and, according to Communist data, to 787,000 in 1951. This decline certainly has its roots in specific Communist difficulties which will be discussed later, but it loses some of its importance when placed in the context of the general dislike with which many Frenchmen have recently viewed politics. The Communist party has lost relatively fewer members than the Socialists, the M.R.P., or even General de Gaulle's Rally of the French People (R.P.F.).

The French Communist party is equally strong on the electoral level. At the general elections for the first National Assembly in November 1946 it obtained 5,489,000 votes, or 28.4 per cent of the votes cast, while the M.R.P. received 4,989,000 and the Socialists 3,434,000 votes. At the June 1951 general elections the Communists still obtained 5,039,000 votes, or 26.5 per cent, while the M.R.P. votes declined sharply to 2,353,000 and the Socialists to 2,764,000 votes. Even General de Gaulle's party polled about 900,-000 fewer votes than the Communist party.

Therefore the Communists can still justifiably boast of being the "first party of France," in terms of popular support, if not any longer in terms of parliamentary representation. In addition, the Communists dominate the strongest trade union organization, the General Confederation of Labor (C.G.T.); and, through the vigor of its militants and the vastness of its propaganda campaigns, the party directs or uses for its purposes large groups of veterans, youth, women, and intellectuals. If the party is too isolated to be able to assume power through legal means, it is strong enongh to hold its own, by various means, against the policies of the government, and sometimes it even appears powerful enough to be considered on a par with the government itself. Governments have no respite from the party's propaganda and activities; each government must consider before anything else the difficulties the Communist party can create for it. It is the very existence and power of the Communist party which determine the composition of the government and which constantly influence the latter's policies. For it is essentially against the Communist party that the government governs, trying to deprive it of its means of action and of its eager audience, in order to force the Communists, in turn, to take the defensive. The government parties, divided on every issue, advocates of radically opposed economic solutions, find in anticommunism the justification — or rather the necessity — for their union.

While recent elections in Belgium, Norway, and Germany reflect a considerable decline in Western European communism, the French Communists have held their own, and are following a line of action that, in both the positive and the negative sense, is the determining factor of French political life. This is even more remarkable since it would appear that in many respects the Communists are obliged to collide head on with French tradition and mentality. How can one explain that in a country notorious for its vigorous and suspicious nationalism more than one-fourth of the electorate still gives its support to a party that openly adheres to instructions from abroad? How can almost a million Frenchmen of independent, critical, and frequently undisciplined bent blindly accept the discipline of the Communist party and devote themselves body and soul to the victory of sovietism? How can this people, this free people which fought the Great Revolution and which always succeeded in shaking off the chains of tyranny, give so large a proportion of its votes and its hopes to the supporters of a foreign totalitarianism? And how, so few years after the struggle against the Nazi occupation, can the French people cultivate at home the germs of a new dictatorship and, perhaps, of a new barbarism? Finally, how can it be explained why communism is widely and solidly rooted in a country that, in spite of the existence of a strong proletariat, has retained a rural structure, a foundation of peasantry, and where all classes have a common aspiration for the material security and comfortable existence which are the enticing privileges of the bourgeoisie?

Foreign communism among a chauvinistic people, totalitarian communism among a free and unsubmissive people, proletarian communism in a rural and middle-class France — these are the paradoxes for which we seek explanation. We will not succeed in our search unless, after having described the unique position of the French Communist party, we analyze it in the context of French political and social history of the last hundred years. French communism is indeed a foreign structure; it is a party whose organization and doctrine obviously contrast with a great many components of the French scene and character. Yet, it is also a French reality which responds to authentic needs and aspirations. The history of Tito demonstrates that it would be an error to regard every firmly established European Communist party as merely the agent of a foreign imperialism and to overlook that party's national roots.

VIII

The Communist Party's
Principles of Doctrine and Action

COMMUNISTS love to repeat with pride the words of Maurice Thorez: "Our party is not a party like the others." The Communist party is indeed radically different from the other French parties. The other parties are groups of men who have decided to work together in the political field. Brought together by common habits, common temperaments, common ideas, they agree to work for the victory of a common political formula, which is defined in terms of a program. The Communist party adheres to a doctrine — Marxism as revised and developed by Lenin and Stalin — and this doctrine is not only an armory of philosophical principles and political activity: it is also put forth as a complete system of historical interpretation and a complete faith, which is indivisible and from which it is impossible to eliminate one single article without causing the collapse of the entire structure. It is a philosophy; it is claimed to be a global and incontestable dogma. In the words of the official history of the Russian Communist party, "The Party possesses an infallible compass: the Marxist-Leninist theory." Other parties define themselves in terms of a program, which is certainly inspired by a latent philosophy but around which men of diverse religions and beliefs can rally. The Communist party, on the other hand, defines itself in terms of a philosophy, and its "programs" are never more than superficial and changing expressions of its political requirements. The significance of Communist political "programs" is secondary, and they should be interpreted only in terms of the immediate situation.[1]

This doctrine is not a body of principles to which one conforms one's actions by a series of compromises and readjustments. It is tied to action; it was born in action and it cannot exist without action. It is presented as a science, and by that token it profits from all the prestige attached to a system of rational interpretation; but it is also action, a transformation of the world — and it is at the same time a faith in the intimate connection between this science and this action which nourish each other and which lead to the same goal. Marxist-Leninist theory is, according to the Russian party history, "the science of the development of society, the science of the working-class movement, the science of the construction of the Communist society. . . . Marxist-Leninist theory is not a dogma, but a guide to action."

It is the proletariat that achieves the union, discovered by Marx, of theory and practice, of philosophy and action. Plunged into an inhuman situation, that class becomes aware simultaneously of its misery and of its mission. Communism is essentially class consciousness combined with the proletariat's own efforts for its liberation. In Marx's words, "Communism is the conscience of the proletariat."

The Communist party is the political expression of class consciousness, aroused and organized for action. It is necessary to stress this relationship between political action and class consciousness because it is essential to the Communist party; it is the core of its preoccupations and difficulties. Class consciousness is, certainly, the basis of political consciousness, but it is not quite

[1] I have thought it necessary to discuss briefly the basic principles of Marxist Leninism, on which the Communists base their thought and action. These tenets clearly apply to all Communist parties, as well as to the French Communist party, since all Communists base their actions on them — or think they do. Thus the best way to understand Communist activity is first to relate it to this ideological framework. But, confronting this ideological interpretation, there is the human factor, the individual equation, which is more personal, more complex, and necessarily more intangible. It is these human factors, which more often than not are irrational, that distinguish the French Communist party from all other Communist parties.

political consciousness. First it must be aroused, sharpened, systematized. The reason for this is — and this is the fundamental contribution of Lenin, who presided over the formation of Communist parties — that class consciousness left to itself becomes engulfed in the "economic struggle," narrows down to purely trade union activity, and does not attain political consciousness. As Lenin put it in *What Is to Be Done?*:

The workers can acquire class political consciousness *only from without,* that is, only outside the economic struggle, outside the sphere of relations between workers and employers. The sphere from which alone it is possible to obtain this knowledge is the sphere of relationships between *all* classes and the state and the government — the sphere of the interrelations among *all* classes.

The mission of awakening class consciousness and molding it in the course of political struggles falls to an élite of professional revolutionaries, who constitute the conscious vanguard of the proletariat. The Communist party is thus the instrument for connecting the élite and the masses, the vanguard and the class. Lenin replaced the Social-democratic concept of the mass party, as it had been organized in Germany and the Scandinavian countries, with the dialectical concept of a group of agitators who stimulate and direct the masses. When examining the policies of the Communist party, one must never forget that it has achieved this dynamic relationship formulated by Lenin: it purports to be the expression of the masses which it undertakes, at the same time, to direct. Thus the party's function is twofold: to create the state of mind upon which its slogans and propaganda will be based, and to start a movement of the masses in front of which the Communist party marches "one step ahead, but not further" (Lenin) — always agitating and interpreting at the same time.

Therefore, unlike the other parties, the Communist party is based on a class mission; but, the mission of this class being universal in scope, the Communist party does not restrict itself to the proletariat and claims to represent all the strata of the population with the exception of a minority of oppressors. The Communist spirit is indeed firmer and more vigorous among the proletariat, but other classes can also develop it by — to use Marx's phrase — "understanding the situation of the proletariat." Thus the second function of the Communist party is to extend the economic, political, and humanitarian demands of the proletariat to all social classes, and consequently to endeavor to convince the middle classes that their fate is identified with that of the proletariat.

Another difference between the Communist party and other parties arises from the fact that the former has a complete interpretation of society directed toward society's radical transformation and is incapable of limiting itself to "political" action in the sense that the bourgeois democracies understand the term. Utilizing effectively all the parliamentary and political liberties which the democracies extend to it, the party looks upon "political" action as never more than a temporary aspect of a struggle that must be maintained simultaneously on all fronts. As Lenin put it: "The revolutionary class, in order to attain its end, must know how to use all forms, without exception, of social activity. It must always be prepared unexpectedly and without delay to replace one type with another." If one wishes to gain an exact appreciation of the organization and power of a Communist party, he must never forget this polymorphous characteristic.

The originality of communism arises from its being, so to speak, a social reality of many dimensions, operating on diverse levels: mass organization *and* secret society, untiringly agitated electoral army *and* guerrilla organization for social warfare, parliamentary party *and* underworld gang. . . . When it is one, it does not cease being the other.[2]

All these factors must be taken into account in analyzing the Communist party: it has its militants, but it also has its theorists; its members of parliament, but also its working-class leaders; its political leaders, but also its military tacticians — it has its legal organization, but it can be turned overnight into a secret organization, for which permanent bases exist. It cannot be assessed only as a "party" organized for the political struggle, nor solely as a

[2]Jules Monnerot, *Sociologie du communisme* (Paris, 1949), p. 133.

"conspiracy" organized for the seizure of power; it is an immense machine, as complex as the state which it everywhere attacks. It is a discipline opposing a discipline, a university opposing a university, a police opposing a police, an organization of workers, women, children, old men, cripples, tenants, tradesmen, housewives, sportsmen, motion picture stars. It is a complete society which, in embryonic form, already exists inside the society it aims to replace.

IX

History of the
French Communist Party

Fʀᴏᴍ the complex history of the French Communist party under the Third Republic,[1] we shall select major trends which can aid us in gaining a better understanding of the party's present characteristics.

FROM 1921 TO 1934

First of all it is important to note that the Communist party in France did not spring from the void. Although its history begins in 1921, the tradition which it has utilized is much older: in France, Leninism was grafted upon a workers' movement which was certainly the most class-conscious and tumultuous in Europe. The insurrection of June 1848 and the Commune of 1871 were the most notable stages of a bitter and bloody struggle, which, as is well known, greatly aided Karl Marx in the development of his doctrine. The French proletariat, in a country which had its revolution in 1789, has nevertheless always been embued with a democratic consciousness: it will not for long separate its cause from that of the Republic, the "social republic," especially as it feels itself to be part of a nation which must once again show the world the road to freedom. This combination of democratic and nationalistic sentiments is in itself a barrier to Marxism; in addi-

---

[1]The best discussion is given in the objective study of Gérard **Walter,** *Histoire du parti communiste français* (Paris, 1948). The Communist party may be preparing a history of its own.

tion, it was France that had nurtured a large number of those utopian and reformist Socialist theoreticians whom Marx considered to be his chief enemies.

The Unified Socialist Party (S.F.I.O., or French Section of the Workers' International) had succeeded in combining sugar-coated Marxism with this democratic and Fabian tradition: Jaurès was the great architect of "socialist humanism." But the victory of the Bolshevik revolution in Russia forced all the Socialist parties to come to grips with the problem they had temporarily managed to avoid while building their great mass organizations: how could they eliminate the capitalist regime and do so quickly? The Social Democrats had capitulated before the strength of capitalism: they occasionally participated in a government and had committed themselves to a slow, progressive evolutionary process. In short, they had become infused with the bourgeois spirit. But the war of 1914 had demonstrated the failure of their internationalism and their pacifism, while in Russia, Lenin and his companions had just proved that it was possible, by a well-directed revolt, to effect the brutal transition from a structure still in a precapitalistic stage of development to a collectivistic structure through the medium of the dictatorship of the proletariat.

This revolutionary refutation of Social-Democratic opportunism, disrupted European Socialist parties. The congress of the French Socialist party met in Tours at Christmas of 1920. After hearing the report of its emissaries who had just returned from Moscow, the congress, by a vote of 3,208 to 1,033, decided to join the new Communist International. The Communist party, the French section of the Communist International, was born, while the minority reformed the old Socialist party.

One should not be deceived by the 1920 vote. Although initially in the majority, it was not long before the Communists lost a great many of those who had rallied to the party during the inital enthusiasm. Many idealists, attracted by the success of the Russian revolution, were unable to stand an atmosphere and conditions unlike those known to any previous French political party. At first, it is true, arguments went on at the party congresses where, in accordance with immemorial French custom, left, center, and right groups were formed. But soon peremptory orders, above debate, came from the Comintern. Those who did not want to obey them resigned or were expelled. The party was "bolshevized"; it lost the classic characteristics of a French political party to become a hard, disciplined party which endured no splits or factions. Its preoccupation became absolute conformity to the political "line" determined by the executive bureau of the Comintern, where the French Communists were represented.

The same characteristic appeared in the policy followed by the French Communist party with regard to other political organizations; it broke with the traditions of alliance and compromise, which were the substance of French political life. The Communists declared themselves intransigent and isolated — as hostile to the parties of the right as to the parties of the left, which, under the cover of verbal demagogy, were accused of prolonging the capitalist hoax. The same attitude persisted on the trade union level, where a Communist General Confederation of United Labor (C.G.T.U.) was formed apart from the Social-Democratic General Confederation of Labor (C.G.T.).

This attitude offended the mentality of the French left, which was accustomed to rising above differences in order to form coalitions against the "menace of reaction." Nevertheless, it was maintained in spite of disastrous results: the membership of the Communist party declined, its vote dropped also, and above all it lost deputies since they were unable to profit from the coalitions formed for the run-off vote when no candidate received a majority on the first ballot. In 1928 the Communist party received 1,064,000 votes and won thirteen seats in the Chamber of Deputies; in 1932, 800,000 votes and ten deputies. But during this same period the Communist party, having overcome its internal divisions, became a strong organization and it trained militants whose fidelity was constantly put to the test by this policy of isolation and by police repression. Thus it appeared that the Communist party had temporarily sacrificed growth of membership and electoral success to the formation of a structure capable of withstanding any ordeal. Here we again discover a basic law of operation of Communist parties: in order to direct the movement of the masses a party must first create the strong skeleton of a body which will take on flesh according to circumstances. When circumstances become critical, the body may be reduced to the skeleton, but the skeleton will not disintegrate.

The Communist party has known a period of prosperity (1934–1937) followed by a reduction to the skeleton (1939–1941), but the skeleton having been maintained, growth (1941–1947) became possible again. (See Figure 1.)

FROM 1934 TO 1939

At the end of 1932 the Communist party did not have more than 25,000 members; at the end of 1934, it had 50,000; at the end of 1935, 70,000; at the end of 1936, 329,000; at the end of 1938, 350,000.[2] This growth reflected the change in policy which occurred in 1934. In that year fascism, already established in Italy, attained full power in Germany and began to extend toward other countries. The U.S.S.R. and the Communist parties felt themselves to be threatened and everywhere adopted a policy of a "united front" against the common enemy. Maurice Thorez, secretary-general of the party since 1932, made a public profession of patriotism; for the first time, the French Communist party voted credits for national defense; to meet the menace of French fascism, symbolized by the riot of February 6, 1934, it urged the formation of a Popular Front in collaboration with the Socialists and the Radical Socialists. The election of 1936 was a victory for the Communist party, which won 1,488,000 votes and 72 seats. But above all, the Communist party appeared for the first time not as a party of agitators under foreign direction but as a French party, participating in the national defense and sharing in the heritage of patriotism and of the French revolution, as a party in the parliamentary sense and almost as a government party. But Communist distrust of the Socialists was too great to allow partic-

²Figures given by André Ferrat, a former Communist, in "Le parti communiste," *Esprit*, 1939, no. 80.

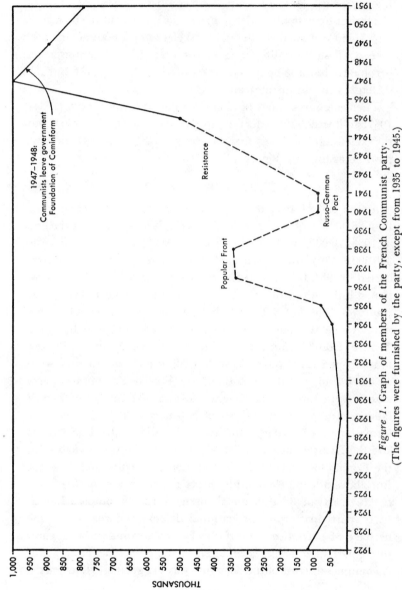

Figure 1. Graph of members of the French Communist party.
(The figures were furnished by the party, except from 1935 to 1945.)

ipation in a government where it would not have the majority; it preferred to remain in contact with the working class, which, by a wave of major strikes, was indicating that it expected structural changes which the new government was incapable of effecting.

The Popular Front coalition soon broke up. The Communists, who had supported a government in which they did not participate, moved again into the opposition, amid the worsening atmosphere of the Munich pact. The Communist party alone voted against the "capitulation at Munich." But this unyielding attitude cost it a great number of the members gained between 1934 and 1938; the defeat of the general strike of November 1938 marked this new decline.

FROM 1939 TO 1941

The Communist party began its journey toward a "tough" period in which it could no longer rely on any but proven party workers. When the Nazi-Soviet pact was signed and, in spite of its efforts, the Communist party seemed once again excluded from the national community, and when in September 1939 the Daladier government dissolved the party and arrested its chiefs, it could not count on more than 100,000 members, but they were devoted and ready to follow it to the very end.

The Nazi-Soviet pact and the entry of Soviet troops into Poland provoked the gravest crisis that the Communist party had ever known. In a few days it completely altered its slogans: the war that had been described in the days immediately following its outbreak as a just defense against the Fascist aggressor became a war between imperialisms which, through the intervention of the U.S.S.R. and the European proletariat, would be transformed into civil war. The tactic of the united front against fascism was succeeded by the purest Leninist slogans of revolutionary defeatism. Confronted with this sudden reversal, some deputies resigned and many militants were troubled.[3] The cadres as a whole, how-

[3]There is evidence of this perplexity in the first volume of Louis Aragon's latest novel, *Les Communistes* (Paris, 1949).

ever, quickly adapted themselves to the new policy, and one can say that the organization so patiently perfected between 1924 and 1934 held fast and permitted the Communist party to survive a crisis that would have overcome any other party. This was decisive proof of the discipline of the militants and of their faith in Soviet infallibility.

The party went underground. Several of its leaders were arrested, but the most important, such as André Marty, Jacques Duclos, and Maurice Thorez,[4] escaped. The policy of the French Communist party between September 1940 and June 1941 is extremely difficult to trace, first of all because it was carried on in secrecy and secondly because it was ambiguous. Rossi has used numerous party tracts and newspapers to show that after the defeat of France the party favored the creation of a "workers' and peasants' government" which would utilize Soviet friendship to sign a peace treaty with Germany.[5] This attitude, which is the principal object of complaint by the anti-Communists, did not prevent the party from following at the same time another line of action, inspired by popular patriotism and the struggle against the invader.

If it seems undeniable that certain members of the party thought of getting in touch with the German occupation authorities in order to get permission to carry on their propaganda publicly again, it is no less undeniable that several of its members, including some of the leaders, as early as June 1940 embarked on a campaign of resistance against the Germans.[6]

Rossi admits that the formation of the National Front of Struggle for the Independence of France, a broad Resistance organization

[4]Thorez, after having rejoined his regiment, deserted and disappeared. He did not turn up in public until the end of 1943 in Moscow. The date of his trip to the U.S.S.R. is still a mystery; his enemies put it in 1940, his friends, in 1943.

[5]*Physiologie du parti communiste français* (Paris, 1949). For the Communist version of policy at this period, see Florimond Bonte, *Le Chemin de l'honneur* (Paris, 1949).

[6]François Goguel, *La Vie politique de la société française contemporaine*, vol. III; a course taught at the Institut d'Etudes Politiques, University of Paris, 1948–1949 (Paris, n.d.).

created by the Communist party, dates from May 27, 1941, three weeks before the invasion of Russia.

But beyond doubt it was June 22, 1941, the date of the invasion of Russia, that marked the complete and unequivocal entry of the Communists into the Resistance and the beginning of a new period in which the Communist party, because of its patriotic policy, again rallied to its banners large masses of followers.

FROM 1941 TO 1947

The Resistance played an essential role in the formation of the present French Communist party; indeed, it marked its rebirth. During the Resistance the party was able to give dramatic evidence of patriotism in a nation which for many years had measured the fidelity of its citizens in terms of the blood spilt for it. Defiance of death and torture characterized almost all Communists from 1941 to 1944. Many other Frenchmen showed the same courage, but no other organization showed it so completely, and to the point of its becoming more a collective trait than an individual one. In spite of the suppression which began in September 1939 and did not end until September 1944, the French Communist party was the only prewar political party which appeared during the occupation as an organized Resistance force.

No history of the French Resistance yet exists. It is estimated, however, that the Communist party and the men under its control furnished about half of the military resistants and a third[7] of the civilian resistants. From 1941 on, the party's isolation was ended. It once again was in contact with other organizations, and once again it could utilize its old tactic of the "united front from below." It extended its influence over large sectors of opinion through the medium of the National Front (which was joined by priests and Catholic intellectuals like François Mauriac). On the military level, it enrolled its members and sympathizers in Franc-Tireurs and Partisans of France, which, in the spring of 1943,

[7]Here we refer to active participants, not to the mass of those who were, in one way or another, involved in the activities of the Resistance.

amalgamated with the non-Communist Secret Army to form the French Forces of the Interior (F.F.I.).

The importance of the party's position made possible the admission of Communist representatives into the new governmental organizations: the National Council of the Resistance and the provisional government of Algiers. For the first time the party entered the government; it appeared to have become a "party like the others."

This attitude was confirmed in the days after the liberation: the Communist party did not use its armed forces and its prestige for an insurrection. The party itself gave the signal for the dissolution of the Patriotic Militia and agreed that the French Forces of the Interior should be incorporated into the regular army. Evidently the prosecution of a war in common with the U.S.S.R. justified such a policy. As soon as the war ended, the French Communist party — *le parti des fusillés* — became the "party of the French renaissance."

The benefits of this attitude were considerable: the Communist party dominated strong Resistance organizations (National Front, Union of French Women, National Union of Intellectuals, refugee organizations, and others), which little by little were transformed into quasi-political organizations. It had men on all the Committees of Liberation; it seized in each department a daily paper, which often doubled as an organ of the National Front. By March of 1945 the number of its members had soared to 545,900;[8] the number of its voters reached 5,000,000.[9] This was a repetition, on a larger scale, of the rapid rise of 1934–1936, with the difference that this time the Communist party accepted governmental responsibilities. There was another difference also: the dissolution of the Comintern in 1943 eliminated an overt allegiance which had caused a great deal of embarrassment to Communist propaganda.

[8]Figure supplied by the report of the eleventh national congress of the party.

[9]In comparing this figure with that obtained by the party in the 1936 election it must be remembered that women voted for the first time after the liberation.

The French Communist party, having won an accolade for patriotism during the Resistance and having accepted government responsibilities, while no longer taking its bearings from an International directed from abroad, appeared in the eyes of an ever-increasing number of people to be an authentic French party — the largest, the most dynamic "government party."[10] To them it appeared to be the "party of the French renaissance" — the best qualified to carry out successfully a "policy of French grandeur"; the best qualified to lead the working class, reunited in a single confederation whose most active elements were under Communist control, in the urgent task of reconstruction.[11]

SINCE 1947

But a new reversal was in the making. The colonial policy of the government and the problem of wages and prices created a gap, which widened daily, between the government and the Communist party.

Since the liberation, the Communist party followed a tactic, both subtle and dangerous, which consisted in masquerading as a government party while retaining a monopoly of revolutionary hope and action. This led to the double game which it never ceased to play and to the "hostile support" that it gave to the governments in which it participated. As a revolutionary party, it denounced colonialism, the war in Indo-China, [and] clerical reaction...and supported the demands of the workers. As a government party, it preached the gospel of work and the reconstruction effort, eliminated antimilitarist propaganda, endeavored to gain cadres by raising the salary scale, and obtained followers, who were attracted by the promise of jobs and advantages. Until the spring

[10]"We are a government party, a party that has placed two of its members in the government of the Republic. Communists have been called to high positions in the state administration. Others serve in the army; others in production. Our militants run thousands of communes, including the largest ones. Or else they have been placed by the confidence of the masses at the head of great organizations.... We must be conscious everywhere of the gravity of our responsibilities before the party and before the nation" (Maurice Thorez, *Rapport au Xe Congrès du PCF* [Paris, 1945]).

[11]In many speeches, notably at Waziers before the miners, Thorez invited the workers to wield their tools with the same patriotic ardor with which they had wielded their guns.

of 1947 the party had taken no step toward renouncing this unstable compromise between its tradition and the requirements of the moment. But the strike wave, either begun spontaneously or by anti-Communist unions, brought home to the party the immediacy of a danger that it will never underestimate — the risk of being outflanked on its left.[12]

The renewal of the strikes was, without doubt, the occasion for the departure of the Communists from the government, but other causes played a part. Since 1946 tension had been growing between the United States and the Soviet Union, and in March 1947 the break occurred at Moscow. Paralleling this, anticommunism was regaining its strength among the Socialists, the Radicals, and the Popular Republicans. The departure of the Communists from the government in May 1947 reflects an evolutionary parallel in the international situation and in the political situation within France. It reopened a phase which still continues, in which the French Communist party, after a governmental interlude, has returned to a "tough" position of solitary opposition.

Moreover, this attitude was only a preface to the complete intransigence which the Communists started to show in September 1947. In September a conference of nine European Communist parties took place in Poland. This meeting decided, after hearing Zhdanov, the delegate from the Communist party of the Soviet Union, to accentuate everywhere the struggle of the working masses against American "imperialism" and to found a Bureau of Information (Cominform) for the purpose of co-ordinating this struggle in the different countries. Thorez, who, like Togliatti, was accused of laxity and opportunism by the Communist party of Yugoslavia, confessed that the French Communist party had delayed too long in recognizing the threats hanging over national independence and in organizing the struggle against the Marshall Plan and what it concealed — "an attempt by warmongering American capitalists to enslave Europe." Beginning with this self-criticism,[13] the French Communist party emphasized its class posi-

---

[12]Raymond Aron, *Le Grand Schisme* (Paris, 1948), p. 190.

[13]This speech by Thorez was delivered at the meeting of the Central Committee of Oct. 30, 1947.

tion, combined in the same condemnation the Socialists and the de Gaullists as "agreed on the same policy," and urged the mass of patriots to the defense of "national independence and peace." Having decided not to "underestimate the power of the working class," a sin of which it had been accused in Poland, the French Communist party wholeheartedly supported the strikes which began in November as a result of the wide disparity between wages and prices. These strikes, directed by a central strike committee dominated by the Communists, soon assumed the aspect of a test of political power and at certain moments seemed like the preliminaries to a revolt. But one section of the workers, upset by the political implications of the strike, or perhaps coerced by poverty, returned to work. This one-month strike miscarried and resulted in the splitting of the General Confederation of Labor, which had been re-established after the liberation. Force Ouvrière, a trade union confederation hostile to the Communists, was created alongside the General Confederation of Labor. Thus on the trade union level also the situation tended to resemble that prevailing before 1934. In 1934, however, it was the C.G.T. which was non-Communist and the General Confederation of United Labor which was Communist.

The succession of "tough" and "mild" attitudes is, as we have seen, a constant factor in the history of the French Communist party and corresponds to an accompanying cycle of shrinking and swelling in the party's ranks. But the French Communist party, having returned to a position of revolutionary intransigence, once again dependent upon an International even though a more limited one, the Cominform, does not seem as yet to have suffered the collapse that its history would lead one to anticipate. Is this collapse only retarded, and if so, why? Or are there new factors that will permit the French Communist party to maintain the strength which it acquired in the exceptional climate of the Resistance? This is what we will now try to discover, by studying its structure, its men, its influence, its tactics, and its propaganda themes.

X

The French Communist Party:
Its Organization and Militants

As was emphasized earlier, the Communist party bases its action on a philosophy. One must go to this philosophy to find the principles of an organization which makes the Communist party a party "unlike the others."

THE PRINCIPLES OF COMMUNIST ORGANIZATION

This philosophy evolves jointly from the position of the proletariat in the class struggle and from the interpretation which is given to it by the most "conscious" representatives of this proletariat. Thus the Communist party is formed by this dialectic of action and interpretation, of struggle and ideology. The "correct" interpretation of the movement of the masses and of their potentiality supplies a political "line," a temporary expression of Marxist doctrine applied to the necessities of the moment. This "line" is elaborated in the name of the masses by the militants, who are in turn "guided" and "enlightened" by the theorists, who are the trustees of the pure Marxist-Leninist ideology. This implies a two-way circulation: the thinking, the intellectual level, of the masses and their possibilities are appraised and discussed by the militants, who live in contact with the masses; information and conclusions are then transmitted from the "base" to the "summit"; the summit fixes the line, which is communicated and explained to the base; and the base must in its turn adapt it for use by the masses. A stream of information and suggestions moves from the base to the summit; a stream of directives for propaganda and action returns from the summit to the base. "The party educates the masses and the masses educate the party."[1]

The structure of the organization is therefore adapted to the maintenance of two dialectical relationships: one established by Marx between theory and practice, the other established by Lenin between the vanguard and the masses. The line must be determined on the basis of "objective" information and "broad" discussion, but its implementation must be rapid and efficient. This has created the double preoccupation that, principally because of Thorez' influence,[2] has dominated the problem of party organization:[3] how to arouse interest and encourage free discussion among the rank and file and at the same time prevent this discussion from degenerating into conflicts likely to create factions which would hinder the application of the line — something which occurred in the early days of the party between 1921–1934.

The internal discipline of the Communists is not blind discipline; it is a discipline freely agreed to, a discipline consciously undertaken by each one of us. Once the discussion has been completed, the decision arrived at is obligatory for all, for the minority as well as for the majority. The party does not permit, and rejects as incompatible with party unity, the organization of tendencies, of groups, of factions, which would lead to the formation of several groups of leaders and which would result in the relaxing of discipline and in the division and disintegration of the party.[4]

The principle of organization adapted to this double task is called by the Communists "democratic centralism."

Before determining the party's orientation, each Communist discusses it within his basic group, the cell. When the discussion is

[1]Maurice Thorez, *Rapport au Xe Congrès du PCF* (Paris, 1945).

[2]Before becoming secretary-general of the party in 1932, Thorez was both director of the Nord Region and secretary of the Organizational Bureau, a national body which has since been abolished.

[3]"The work of organization is getting men to implement a political line" (Auguste Lecoeur, in *Cahiers du communisme*, 1949, no. 8).

[4]Thorez, *Rapport au Xe Congrès*.

completed and it is necessary to move into action, each member accepts and applies the decision of the majority. The whole party acts as a single man. The elected central organ supervises the execution of the decisions. The Communist members of the National Assembly, the Council of the Republic, and the departmental and municipal councils apply the party's policy under the direction of the Central Committee. This is democratic centralism.[5]

THE STRUCTURE OF THE PARTY

It is on these principles that the party's "apparatus" is founded and functions. The echelons of the party are, moving from the base to the summit, the cell, the section, the federation, the central committee, the secretariat. (See Figure 2.)

The Cell

The cell is the basic unit of the Communist party. It is composed of a minimum of three and a maximum of sixty members, but when a cell grows larger than thirty, it is generally subdivided.

FACTORY CELLS, LOCAL CELLS, AND RURAL CELLS

While other parties organize their members on a territorial basis, the Communist party groups its members, in principle, by their place of work. According to Article 12 of the French party's statute, "The cell is the basic unit of the party's organization (in the factory, in the mine, in the workshop, in the office, in the store, on the farm, etc.)." If the Communist party accords "fundamental importance" to the factory cells, it is because it depends essentially on the working class, on the proletariat, which, as Marx and Engels said in the *Manifesto,* is the "only truly revolutionary class." "But how can it be closely tied to the working class except by organizing in the very place of work itself?"[6]

It is obvious that large groups (women, workers in small businesses, tradesmen, peasants) cannot be organized on this basis. Therefore, the Communist party has established *local cells* (mu-

[5]Thorez, *Fils du peuple* (Paris, 1949), pp. 250–251.
[6]Léon Mauvais, "La cellule d'entreprise, organisation de base du parti," *Cahiers du communisme,* 1948, no. 5.

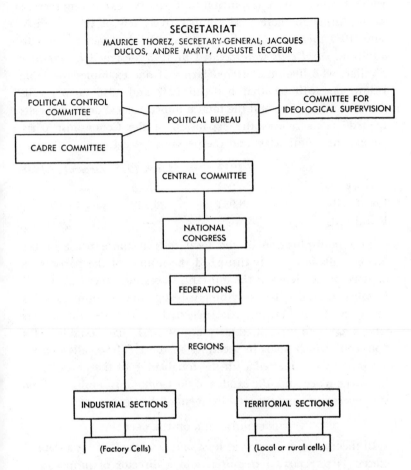

Figure 2. Structure of the French Communist party, 1951.

nicipal, neighborhood, street, or even apartment house cells) which have grown in proportion to the party's expanding recruitment. Although there were comparatively few of them at first, since 1937 there have been more local cells than factory cells. In addition, *rural cells* were created in 1945, designed for country dwellers who live on scattered farms. If one examines the table below, one will see that between 1937 and 1946 factory cells doubled in number, and the total number of local and rural cells tripled.[7] This reflects the expansion of the Communist party among the middle class and the peasants since 1936.

	1937	March 1945	December 1946
Factory cells	4,041	6,145	8,363
Local cells	8,951	20,702	15,860
Rural cells	—	—	12,060

This multiplication of the local cells at the expense of the factory cells has greatly disturbed the leaders of the party, who deplore the tendency of the militants to organize themselves comfortably in local cells. Everything is being done to counteract this tendency. Léon Mauvais has suggested as a model the miners who, unable to meet in their place of work, have established a "bus cell" which holds its meetings en route. These calls to arms are evidently connected with the toughening of the party which has taken place since the exodus of the Communist ministers from the government and the establishment of the Cominform.

THE FUNCTIONING OF THE CELL

In theory, the cell meets at least once a week. It elects a slate of officers, a secretary, a treasurer, and a director of propaganda, and it assigns most of its members to some specific activity. Its meetings are private and surrounded by some secrecy; however, some sympathizers or even some "good faith" adversaries may be invited for a discussion.[8] The officers are elected by the members

[7]Figures furnished at the eleventh congress of the P.C.F., 1947. In 1945 a certain number of local cells became rural cells.

[8]See the account of a visit by a Socialist to a Paris cell meeting in "Réunion de cellule," *La Nef*, October 1949.

of the cell, but they are not responsible to them. They are responsible to the section to which the cell is attached; that is, they can be removed by the decision of the section.

A cell has many activities:

1) It discusses the existing political and economic situation on the basis of the known facts and in the light of the directives that have been received, in order to train its members ideologically. All reports agree in acknowledging that cell discussions are vigorous and frequent.[9]

2) It conducts party propaganda and recruitment, distributes party publications, and spreads directives according to techniques to be examined later.

3) It intervenes in the life of the factory or town on all possible occasions and with all possible means: union elections, factory committees, strikes, the struggle against poverty, the struggle against unemployment, the defense of tenants, and the defense of the aged. Communists have a mission to take part in all movements based on grievances, no matter how unimportant, in order to lead them and at the same time explain them, linking them to the Communists' general conception of the class struggle and to their thesis of the moment (defense of peace, struggle against the Marshall Plan, and the like).

The Section

The section is a grouping of cells, sometimes on the basis of one or more factories, sometimes on a geographical basis. The delegates elected by the cells hold section assemblies in which they elect a section committee, which in turn elects its officers. This system of indirect election readily permits the screening of leaders

[9]See note 8 and the report of a Catholic published in *Esprit,* 1948, no. 7, p. 58: "I have attended cell meetings lasting until two in the morning, in which men and ideas, opinions and proposals, were fighting for supremacy. I can say that these were tempestuous sessions, in which everyone fought it out face to face on such issues as: Should the factory collaborate with the new R.P.F. municipal government for certain ends? What type of propaganda should be adopted? In recruiting, should one aim for quality or quantity? No outsider ever had any inkling of these disputes."

and the elimination of those who do not manifest complete orthodoxy.

The Section Bureau, consisting of the officers of the section, meets each week. It has a dual role:

1) It "controls" the action of the cells. Each of its members is a specialist in one branch — youth, unions, army — and supervises from his point of view the activity of the militants. Each night the section secretary takes part, if possible, in a cell meeting.[10]

2) It co-ordinates the information collected by the cells and transmits it to party headquarters just as it passes on to the cells instructions from headquarters.

The Region and the Federation

All the sections of a department constitute the federation. If there are many sections, an intermediary body, the region, may be interposed between the sections and the federation. In this case, the federation consists of several regions. One of the present problems of the French Communist party is to avoid creating overly large units which escape effective personal control.

The delegates from the sections or regions meet in a federal assembly, elect a federal committee, which elects its officers, the federal Bureau, which is the permanent instrument of direction and control of party activity in the department. This federal committee names, with the agreement of the Central Committee, a federal secretary, who is the party leader for the department. He is a person with considerable responsibility, and his selection is often difficult.[11]

The Congress, the Central Committee, and the Secretariat

The delegates from the federations should meet every two years[12] in a national congress. This congress hears a certain num-

[10]Thorez, *Rapport au Xe Congrès.*

[11]Thorez, "Le rôle du secrétaire fédéral," *Cahiers du communisme,* 1949, no. 4.

[12]The other parties hold their national congresses every year. After the war congresses were held in 1945 and 1947. Another should have been held in 1949 and no valid reason has been given for its postponement to 1950. However, a sort of little congress called the national conference meets each year.

ber of meticulously prepared reports on the life of the party, its successes, its deficiences. The discussion generally reduces itself to citing a certain number of facts to illustrate the orator's thesis, which often includes a detailed self-criticism. One never hears conflicts between tendencies, criticisms of the leaders, or contradictory speeches, which are customary at the congresses of other French parties: the political line is not criticized unless the party chiefs set the example.

The congress elects a Central Committee, a permanent executive organ which includes about eighty members and meets at variable intervals. The Central Committee itself names two bodies:

1) The Secretariat, a permanent supervisory body composed of a secretary-general and three secretaries (since April 1950, Maurice Thorez, Jacques Duclos, André Marty, and Auguste Lecoeur).

2) The Political Bureau, the organ of political leadership which each week specifies the line according to circumstances and furnishes the propaganda themes to be used during the week. The Political Bureau was made up in 1950 of the members of the Secretariat and of the following other members: Marcel Cachin, François Billoux, Charles Tillon, Raymond Guyot, Etienne Fajon, Waldeck-Rochet, Laurent Casanova, Victor Michaut, Léon Mauvais, and Jeannette Vermeersch.

Several committees assist the Secretariat and the Political Bureau in their tasks. The principal ones are:

1) The Central Political Control Committee. This committee, in theory, handles all controversial cases involving dissension, reinstatement, and so forth. Its role was decisive when the party went underground in order to prevent "infiltration" by the police and the disappearance and arrest of militants. Some people think that this committee continues to play a large role and even supervises the activity of the Secretariat. This is difficult to confirm, since its meetings are conducted in absolute secrecy.

2) The Central Cadre Committee, headed by Marcel Servin, has charge of encouraging and controlling the development of party cadres.

3) The Committee for Ideological Supervision, whose presidency recently passed from Laurent Casanova to François Billoux, directs the work of Communist intellectuals and adjusts its operation to the ideological and cultural activity of the party's adversaries.

This structure appears to satisfy the exigencies of a Marxist-Leninist party as we have stated them:

1) To assure through widely scattered cells the omnipresence of the party among the masses.

2) To determine, after discussion, a political line which must never, from that point on, be contested by the rank and file. The vertical organization of the party and the system of indirect election on all echelons (the assembly elects a committee, which elects a bureau, which elects a secretary, and so on) avoid the formation of opposing factions within the party.

3) To act in a variety of ways, legally as well as illegally. The rigorous separation of units is an essential element of security in those periods of clandestine operation for which the party, in conformity with the advice of Lenin, must always be prepared. The different cells and sections do not communicate with one another except through the intermediary of a delegate. In the event that one of these bodies becomes suspect or is contaminated by the police, it suffices to break off contact with this delegate — a procedure which the non-Communist Resistance movements ended up by adopting.

4) To ensure the rigorous and permanent control of each unit by another.[13] This control is not carried out by the rank and file but by the higher echelons, which see to it that no field of action ever outgrows their ability to supervise and administer it.[14]

The Communists, unlike the other French parties, passionately believe in the value of organization, repeating with Stalin, "The

[13] "To direct is not to write resolutions and distribute directives; to direct is to control the implementation of the directives" (Stalin to the Plenum of the Communist Party of the U.S.S.R., 1928).

[14] See Thorez, *Une Politique de grandeur française* (Paris, 1945).

political line once determined, it is the work of organization which decides everything, including the fate of the political line itself, its realization or its defeat."[15] When the party suffers defeats, they are automatically attributed to organizational deficiencies and not to political errors. These deficiences then supply the subject matter for vigorous criticism and self-criticism.

But this self-criticism, of which the Communists boast as one of their distinctive characteristics, is not applied by them to the political line itself unless they are urged to do so by the Communist party of the Soviet Union or by other Communist parties. This was the case when, after the foundation of the Cominform and the report of Zhdanov, Thorez gave the signal for self-criticism, which was then taken up, from summit to base, by all the party leaders and the party press. This famous self-criticism ordinarily deals with points of detail; it is not applied to basic problems except on the initiative of the leaders, who themselves are spurred on by Moscow. An isolated spontaneous criticism immediately arouses the suspicion of comrades and superiors. Indeed, it should not be forgotten that the French Communist party has established itself in spite of police repression; that it has seen almost all those who opposed its line and then left the party soon move into the service of its most implacable adversaries, when they did not go into the service of the police or even of the national enemy. (Doriot is the outstanding example.[16]) This is why all divergence appears as the beginning of opposition, and all opposition as the beginning of treason.

Thus "democracy" exists in the party, but within a sphere narrowly restricted in advance. On the occasion of some particularly

[15]Cited by Thorez, *ibid.*, and Lecoeur, in *Cahiers du communisme,* 1949, no. 8.

[16]Doriot, secretary of the party, appeared for one moment, in 1924, to be on the point of replacing Thorez, but, convicted of having organized a faction, he was expelled. He later founded the French Popular party and ended up, between 1941 and 1944, recruiting men for the police and the German army. A certain number of men who left the party at the time of the Nazi-Soviet pact also collaborated with Germany later. The best known of these is Gitton, former member of the Central Committee, who appears to have been in the service of the police even before 1939.

important about-face, however, a whole cell or the majority of a cell has pronounced itself opposed to the policy followed by the party leadership. But this opposition is circumscribed by the compartmentalization of the organization and has no effect on neighboring cells. A reliable section representative will try to persuade the opposition to retreat or else have it expelled. This is why, in periods of crisis, the dissenters, who know it is useless to vote "against" something with their hands, prefer to "vote with their feet": they leave the party.

PRINCIPAL AREAS OF ACTION

We will complete this study of the organization of the French Communist party by dwelling upon four areas which are especially important to it and to which it devotes much more attention and effort than do the other parties: youth, women, the formation of cadres, and the press.

Youth

The other parties, centering their activities on elections, concern themselves only secondarily with youth. The French Communist party, as the party of the class struggle, does not wait until a youth is qualified to vote before it takes an interest in him. It wants, on the one hand, to train in "the principles of Marxist Leninism" young people who will soon swell its ranks, and, on the other hand, it wants to influence youth as a whole.

Young people have always been a source of strength to the party. In 1936, of 330,000 members, 100,000 were members of the Communist Youth. During the Resistance, the party extended its influence over a very large number of young people, pushed into action by circumstances, and soon organized in Franc-Tireurs and Partisans of France. Profiting from this martial spirit, the party dissolved the Communist Youth and called upon its young members to work in the National Front organizations, the Union of French Republican Youth and the Union of French Young Women, which it, for all practical purposes, controlled. But the enthusiasm of the liberation rapidly declined, and the goals of these youth organizations appear to have been badly defined —

so much so that the number "of young people belonging to progressive organizations is still far from equaling the number of
young people who participated in the struggle."[17] The Union of
Republican Youth, which is more of a "political party"[18] than a
youth organization, is making only "very modest progress."[19]
Thorez has recently called the party's attention to this vitally important point and has urged the cadres "to guide the work of the
youth."

It is rather in professional organizations, unions, and student
groups that young Communists are active. Particularly in schools
and faculties, they often constitute the only organized and active
force. Communist youth played a considerable role in the great
strikes of 1947 and 1948; these young people are often almost
alone in responding to the party's call for the more dangerous
activities, where their dynamism and courage are impressive.
Young Communists are, to a large extent, recruited from among
the most vital elements of French youth; they are earnest, disciplined in their personal lives, and dedicated to sports.[20] War
and poverty have made them politically conscious at an early age.
But there are not many of them, and they do not exercise much
influence on the largely apolitical French youth.

Finally, even children have an organization, the Union of Val-
iant Boys and Girls (Union des Vaillants et Vaillantes). But it
is primarily in the vacation camps organized by the Communist
working-class municipalities that the very young are initiated into the party mystique by songs and stories. Many libraries and
even movie clubs are run by Communist women for the use of the
youngsters; a Communist children's literature has been started;[21]

[17]Léo Figuères, "Problèmes actuels de la jeunesse." *Cahiers du communisme,* 1948, no. 4.

[18]*Ibid.*

[19]Thorez, *Speech before the Central Committee at Ivry,* Oct. 7, 1949.

[20]These judgments are obviously personal and result from observations
made at the time of the demonstrations of November 1947 and the miners'
strike of November 1948, as well as from contacts with young Communist
workers and students.

[21]See Simone Téry, *La Vie de Danielle Casanova.*

and a Committee for the Defense of Children's Literature has been organized on Communist initiative to fight against the influence on the children of American-style comic strips.

Women

The participation of women in French political life is very recent, as woman suffrage dates from the liberation. But even before the war, the French Communist party was practically the only party that had a significant feminine membership. Communism has always struggled against "the reactionary conception of the woman in the home" and has demanded political equality and equality of wages for women.

Women participated in Communist activity even more during the resistance. At the first congress held after the liberation, in 1945, the party was called upon to "mobilize itself to aid in the mustering of women, on the basis of their rights and their duties, in democratic and mass organizations." Among the most important of these organizations is the Union of French Women, an organ of the National Front, directed by a Communist majority but including, especially in the provinces, an important minority of nonpartisan and even Catholic women. Thus in this area the party follows the same policy it follows among youth, but it appears to have been more successful here since the Union of French Women is a more lively organization than the Union of French Republican Youth. This activity has been fostered by the campaign for peace, a slogan to which women are particularly responsive. The party seeks to convince women of "a direct relationship between their daily difficulties and the war policy."[22] Food scarcities, the high cost of living, the shortage of schools, bureaucratic red tape, all are used to "agitate" the housewives. Women Communist workers are organized in groups by the General Confederation of Labor. In the past year Communist women have organized some rather significant demonstrations; they obtained signatures for the "peace ballot" and paraded on Joan of

[22]Yvonne Dumont, "La riche expérience du mouvement des femmes," *Cahiers du communisme,* 1949, no. 7.

Arc Day and Mother's Day. It is to be noted that the Communist party is not content with political agitation but seeks to give to women, whom it considers to be especially "alienated" by capitalism, a consciousness of their importance and of their social and political role. This is an innovation in French bourgeois society, where the education of girls did not begin until 1860.

The French Communist party wishes to exploit to the limit this still fresh source of power. It has thoroughly grasped the decisive importance of the attitude of women to any grievance movement: a wife can force her husband to strike, as she can, by her complaints, make him give it up. It seeks in every way to endow women with a political consciousness, which is still very rare in a nation where politics is traditionally the business of men. The Communist party glories in being the party which has the most women in the elected assemblies — 26 of 163 Communist deputies in the 1946 National Assembly were women — and, before the electoral reform which in 1948 diminished the representation of the Communist party, there were 2,000 Communist women on municipal councils. In addition, the Central Committee includes eight women, of whom some, such as Marie Claude Vaillant-Couturier and Jeannette Vermeersch, Maurice Thorez' wife, have outstanding abilities.

However, this movement is being inadequately supported. As Thorez said in 1949:

The party committees, the militants on different echelons, do not devote sufficient attention to work among women. Some consider it to be an inferior type of work. Too many comrades — under the influence of petty bourgeois prejudices — still demonstrate a lack of comprehension of, or sectarian scorn for, the necessary work among women.

Indeed, women represent only 11 per cent of the membership of the party.

The Training of Cadres

All Communist parties attribute decisive significance to the activity of the cadres, that is, as Stalin pointed out in *Questions of Leninism,* of the "men who understand the political line of the party, who consider it their own line, are ready to apply it..., without whom the correct political line is in danger of remaining on paper." This is clearly tied to the Leninist conception of the Bolshevik party. The formation of new cadres is all-important, for "three-quarters of the party is composed of members who have joined since the liberation."[23] It is necessary to ensure an adequate ideological and administrative training for these men, who are often young.

These, according to Thorez,[24] are the considerations that must guide the party in the choice of its cadres:

1) The most absolute devotion to the cause of the workers, to the cause of the French people.

2) The most intimate connection with the masses.

3) The spirit of initiative and responsibility.

4) The spirit of discipline.

How can these cadres be selected? By placing good men in the leading positions and constantly supervising their work. Thorez notes in this connection the usefulness of subdividing the organization in order to multiply the number of responsible posts. In his report to the National Conference on April 9, 1949, the secretary of the Cadre Committee, Marcel Servin, denounced the obstacles which retard the proper selection of cadres — scorn toward women and youth — and the shortage of working-class cadres.[25]

Once the cadres have been selected, it is necessary to train them. For this there are "cadre schools," institutions not possessed by other French political parties. From the beginning of 1947 to the middle of 1948, three schools with four-month training periods operated to train national officers. During the same period, eleven schools with four-week training periods were created for Communist militants in the trade union movement, in peasant organizations, in women's groups, and in youth movements. At the federation level, 129 schools, in session for two weeks, assembled

[23]Marcel Servin, "La conception léniniste de la montée des cadres," *Cahiers du communisme*, 1948, no. 4.

[24]*Rapport au XIe Congrès*.

[25]*Cahiers du communisme*, 1949, no. 5.

2,071 leaders of federal and section committees. In the first six months of 1948, 6,344 militants took courses in 777 schools. We must add many study centers intended for members of parliament, editors of newspapers, and others.[26] The program of theoretical courses consists of the study of the works of Marx, Lenin, and Stalin, including the latter's *History of the Communist Party (b) of the Soviet Union.*

The educational effort is therefore considerable. All opportunities are exploited: for example, during the miners' strike of November 1948, which lasted almost a month, every other day was dedicated to schooling the Communist miners. However, if we compare the number of students with the total party membership, we can see that this effort has still affected only a minority.

The Press

Following Lenin's dictum "without a press no mass movement is possible in a civilized country," the Communist party has made of the press its major propaganda instrument.[27] No other French party has as many newspapers as the Communist party.

Its central organ is *Humanité.* In the provinces after the liberation the party operated at least one daily paper in each department. But most of these newspapers were unable to continue, and by 1949 only twenty Communist dailies were left. Some of these have a relatively large circulation, such as *Les Allobroges* in Dauphiné (180,000) or *La Marseillaise* at Marseille (140,000). The Communist party possesses several weeklies, of which the most important are *France nouvelle,* the official organ of the Central Committee, with a circulation of 88,000, and *La Terre,* aimed at the peasants, with a circulation of 200,000. In the provinces the federations which no longer possess daily papers publish weeklies. The total number of Communist weeklies is about one hundred.

The Communist press has seen a decline since the liberation.

[26]Information supplied by Victor Joannés in the Cominform organ, *For a Lasting Peace, for a People's Democracy,* 1949, no. 5.

[27]For Communist data on the press, cf. the articles by Kriegel-Valrimont in *For a Lasting Peace, for a People's Democracy,* 1949, no. 27, and in *Cahiers du communisme,* 1949, no. 5.

Not only have newspapers disappeared, but the circulation has dropped greatly: *Humanité* is down from 460,000 in December of 1947 to 220,000 in July 1951; *Ce soir,* the Paris evening daily published by the party, has suffered a comparable decline from its 1947 peak circulations of 433,000. It should be noted that the total circulation of all morning Parisian dailies is 2,300,000 and of all evening dailies 1,500,000.

It is true that the party press is not limited to these large papers; it also includes a myriad of factory and neighborhood bulletins, both printed and mimeographed. It is also necessary to include union publications such as *La Vie ouvrière,* literary papers such as *Les Lettres françaises,* and publications devoted to sports and other special subjects. While not officially Communist, these papers reproduce the essential elements of Communist propaganda. But this abundance should not conceal the grave crisis which the party press is undergoing in spite of the fanaticism with which some militants dedicate themselves to the distribution of its product. (There are, for example, Committees for the Distribution of *Humanité,* which sell the paper in the streets.) This crisis certainly has general causes — the decrease in purchasing power and the lack of interest in politics — but it also has specific causes: the Communist papers, with some few exceptions, are badly edited and are written in such a sectarian manner that reading them becomes unbearable even for militants who are already convinced but who want nevertheless to be well informed.

The Finances of the French Communist Party

The French Communist party, as we have seen, possesses an important and complex organization. To round out this description, it would be useful to know the manner in which the party finances its administrative machine, its press (which is often in the red), and its costly propaganda posters.

Unfortunately it is impossible to give exact information on this subject. Speaking before the National Assembly on November 17, 1948, the Socialist Minister of the Interior, Jules Moch, accused the Communist party of possessing in a foreign bank in Paris, the

Banque Commerciale pour l'Europe du Nord, several accounts which, when considerably overdrawn, were abruptly and mysteriously covered. Moch stated his conviction that the "solidarity payments" made by the workers of the "people's democracies" during the 1947–1948 strikes had really been "disguised subsidies" supplied by the governments of those countries.[28]

In his reply, Jacques Duclos accounted for the party's resources derived from salaries turned over in their entirety by the Communist members of various political assemblies. Thus, in the month of October 1948, the Communist members of the National Assembly paid 12,456,939 francs into the party's account; those of the Assembly of the French Union, 1,830,860 francs; of the Council of the Republic, 6,329,712 francs; of the Paris Municipal Council, 968,500 francs; and of the General Council of the Seine, 795,-551 francs — making a total from these sources of 22,383,562 francs.[29] In the first ten months of 1948 the Communist members of these various assemblies supplied the party's account with a total of 219,525,626 francs. Of this sum, the party returned the contributors a little over a third, that is 86,856,450 francs, as their salaries for these ten months, leaving the party with a net 132,-669,176 francs. To these resources it is necessary to add the dues of members. The entire sum obtained from this source is unknown but it must surpass the figure given above. Finally the numerous contributions which the Communist militants are called upon to make must be included: it is known that collections are always being taken in the cells.

No matter what the total amount derived from these regular sources may be, it appears improbable that it is sufficient to support the offices of the party, and especially to maintain its propaganda. Thus it is possible that the French party receives financial aid from the Communist parties of the Soviet Union and eastern Europe. Proof of this was not, however, supplied by the Minister of the Interior and it is to be regretted that he, as well as the government majority, did not want to appoint a parliamentary

[28]*Journal officiel*, 1948, no. 135, Assemblée Nationale, pp. 7,005 ff.
[29]*Ibid.*, pp. 7,129 ff.

committee to inquire into the resources of the party, a step demanded by Jacques Duclos. In any case, this refusal demonstrates that proof of this foreign aid, if it exists, is not in the hands of the French police.

MILITANTS AND LEADERS

After having studied the organization, one must devote some space to the men — militants and leaders — not only because it is the men who give life to the organization, but also because the Communist party, which is not a "party like the others," claims to be less concerned with achieving electoral successes than with forming a new type of man, the Communist man,[30] a conscious combatant in the class struggle and a future citizen of the classless society. Finally, the personal qualities of the Communist militants and chieftains are a decisive element of action and propaganda, without which it is impossible to explain the enormous role of the party in French life during the Resistance and the role which it continues to play.

THE MILITANTS

Number and Distribution. Unlike the other parties, which possess "bastions" in certain regions and which have no members, or almost no members, in certain others, the Communist party has members everywhere. True, it is stronger in industrial regions than in rural areas: at the end of 1946 it had 37,000 members, or 5.6 per cent of the registered voters in Pas-de-Calais, and in the Paris area (Seine and Seine-et-Oise), 147,000 members, or 3.9 per cent. On the other hand, the agricultural department of Calvados had but 3,200 Communists, or 1.2 per cent. If one totals the members of the departments of the Nord, Pas-de-Calais (industrial and mining regions) and the Parisian region, one gets a total of 220,-000 members, or about a quarter of the party's strength at that time.

The proportion of members in industrial regions to total party membership has, however, considerably diminished since the war.

[30]*L'Homme communiste* is the title of a collection of stories by Louis Aragon glorifying Communist activities during the Resistance.

For example, in 1937, the Paris region had 115,000 members out of a national total of 370,000, or almost a third of the total. Ten years later with its 147,000 members, the Paris region represented less than a fifth. On the contrary, in the Vendée, a rural, clerical, and conservative department, the number of members grew from 179 in 1937 to 3,000 in 1947. Thus the Communist party has recruited, relatively speaking, more members outside than in the industrial centers, a phenomenon which we will examine more closely in the subsequent discussion of the distribution of Communist voters. It is emphasized at this point, however, since it has modified the internal equilibrium of the party and created a grave problem for a proletarian party, in which, in contrast to the prewar period, nonproletarian elements are today in the majority. Servin has emphasized that "before the situation was remedied in the course of recent federation conferences, the proportion of workers on federation bureaus and committees was *hardly one third.*"[31] He cited, among other examples, the departments of Ain and Aisne, whose forty-member federal committees included only nine and fifteen workers, respectively. Aisne did not have a single agricultural worker on its committee though it is a department with some 30,000 agricultural workers. In the department of Seine itself, too many sections were made up of students, professors, engineers, and accountants.

This is obviously the result of the recruiting done between 1941 and 1946, the years which preceded and followed the liberation. A great many Communist militants, at least 60,000, died, either by execution or in concentration camps,[32] and these militants were naturally among the most devoted. The gravity of the loss sustained by the Communist party can therefore be appreciated, as well as the difficulty that it is having in filling this

[31]"Choisir, promouvoir, former hardiment les cadres," *Cahiers du communisme,* 1949, no. 5.

[32]This number is difficult to determine. The Communists talk of 75,000 "executed." Among the 250,000 who died in concentration camps and the 100,000 civilians and members of the French Forces of the Interior who were executed by the Germans, there must have been more than 60,000 Communist militants.

void. The influx of new militants combined with the disappearance of many of the old ones has led to another serious disequilibrium: "Ninety per cent of our members are new, and do not know, or inadequately know, not only the methods of working with the masses, but often and above all the fundamental principles of party organization."[33]

This influx of new militants, who have often come from nonproletarian social strata, has presented the party with an internal problem which was acutely felt in 1947, when Zhdanov in his report to the Cominform "Conference of the Nine" called upon the western Communist parties not to underestimate the capacities of the working class. But, under the influence of the appeals for greater production launched by Thorez in 1945 and 1946, a good many Communists had let themselves slip into a position of "class collaboration" in industry. The party took advantage of certain weaknesses noted during the miners' strike in the fall of 1947 to weed out several local leaders convicted of "softness." Gaston Monmousseau, one of the Communist leaders of the General Confederation of Labor, attacked the militants "who sometimes allowed themselves to believe that everything could be taken care of from above, without the active participation of the working masses, without struggle, without making constant demands," and Thorez, speaking before the Central Committee,[34] after having emphasized the "progress of mass consciousness," complained about the complacency engendered by the liberation. "The liberation was followed by relaxation,...habits of easy life were acquired, while allowing the spirit of struggle, the class spirit, to weaken....A fighting spirit is lacking in some of the militants."

This is why the "party of the French renaissance" has remembered, on Zhdanov's cue, that it was primarily the "party of the working class" and has begun to reform. This reform means a new "bolshevization" of the party, marked by repeated exhortations to "raise the ideological level" and to "develop the fighting spirit." This clashes not only with the complacency denounced

[33]Mauvais, in *Cahiers du communisme*, 1948, no. 5.
[34]At Ivry on Oct. 7, 1949.

by Thorez but also with the traditional tendency of the French workers to become artisans or small shopkeepers as soon as they find it possible to do so.

Members and Militants. The expansion of recruitment is in principle facilitated by the party statute, which sets only these three conditions for membership:

1) Acceptance of the program of the party.
2) Payment of dues.
3) Work in one of the "base" organizations.

Aside from these restrictions, the Communist party "opens its ranks to all those who, even if they do not share its philosophical conceptions, respect party discipline and do not expound, within the party, philosophical conceptions other than those of the party." Thus it is on the bases of a common discipline and common action that the members of the party are recruited.

Here, however, more than in any other party, it is necessary to distinguish between the *member* and the *militant*. Many hold the party card who are only periodically active and who are scarcely even organized.[35] Raymond Guyot recently denounced[36] the delay in dues payments (in some sections the money collected is only 60 per cent of what it should be), and complained that some sections were doing nothing to bring back to the party this mass of wavering members.

Hundreds, thousands of Communists are outside of the party because of this. The activity of the cell is reduced to the work of a few comrades, always the same ones, and is therefore jeopardized. The very connection between the party and the masses is endangered. The correct policy of the party is being undermined.

But between the vanguard of militants and the bulk of the members one finds the same leader-follower relationship established by Lenin between the Bolsheviks and the masses. The party possesses a solid framework of two to three hundred thousand mili-

[35]For example, Mauvais in *Cahiers du communisme,* 1949, no. 2, pointed out that the strike in the Renault factories brought to light a thousand Communists who were not members of the factory section.

[36]*Humanité,* Oct. 18, 1949.

tants who can withstand any test. It is this framework that constitutes the real strength of the party, its "gold reserve"; it is on
these militants that it tends to rely during periods of crisis or
underground activity.

Mere members are attracted to the party by some aspect of its
policy and leave it if this policy changes. In this way the party
swelled from 1934 to 1936, only to diminish from 1938 to 1940
and to swell once more between 1941 and 1946. A decline started
again in 1947, the year of the foundation of the Cominform and
the return to an accentuated class position. But the true militants
do not let themselves be affected by the about-faces in party policy;
they are completely faithful, with a fidelity nourished by their
Marxism.

Portrait of the Militant. Indeed, they have the double conviction
that "Marxism goes in the direction of history" and that the
Communist party, "party of the working class," retains the exclusive privilege of "correctly" interpreting Marxism, so that party
errors can never be more than temporary and can be redressed by
appropriate self-criticism. This certainty that the class struggle in
the world proceeds infallibly to the destination which Marx
assigned to it and that the triumph of communism is only a question of time is the most authentic characteristic of the Communist
militant. The psychology of the Communist militant is singular-
ly comparable to religious psychology: it involves absolute certainty, a direct and exclusive relationship with the truth. "History
is in communion with him in a way that it never is with you."[37]
We must add — another religious trait — that the optimism of the
Communist is increased by the consciousness that his struggle is
connected to that of other Communists throughout the world and
that he thus benefits from the progress made elsewhere. The
French Communist consoles himself on the failure of a strike by
thinking of the advance of communism in Asia. Finally, other
men, the men of Soviet Russia, wait for him at the threshold of

[37]Jules Monnerot, *Sociologie du communisme* (Paris, 1949), p. 467.

paradise and his confidence in the proximity of the goal is reinforced by this belief.

Like a believer, this disciple of a materialistic religion is capable of giving his life for the triumph of his cause. All the last letters of Communists shot by the Nazis during the Resistance bear witness to this assurance of the value of their sacrifice and the triumph of their cause, whether they were intellectuals like Jacques Péri, who "dies for the happiness of tomorrow...and in order that France may live"; or Jacques Decour, who considers himself "like a leaf which falls from the tree to make humus"; or the metal worker Pierre Timbaud, who cried out before the firing squad: "Long live the German Communist party!"; or the mass of those who awaited execution alternately singing the "Marseillaise" and the "International."

This certainty based on faith makes the Communist militant more dynamic and more efficient than the militants of other parties. In calm periods, however, this is also the source of his shortcomings. Convinced of holding the true doctrine, the Communist is often better at condemning and insulting others than in debating with them. Situated in a world apart, he withdraws into his system of thought and uses a vocabulary which appears to the non-Communist stifling and boring. Sectarianism, hermetism, doctrinal frenzy are the products of a superiority complex which many Communists possess; they often render ineffective the party's propaganda, which appears convincing only to the already convinced. The Communist press, sermonizing, monotonous, frenzied, appears to non-Communists as a monument of bad faith and boredom.

Party discipline channels and utilizes the capacity for sacrifice of the militants. Once a decision has been made, as we have seen, it must be accepted by all. It will be applied with a devotion that no other political, social, or religious organization displays to such a massive degree. To his religious qualities, the good Communist adds military qualities; he moves in step, he executes orders and accounts for them. The jobs are distributed according to ability, but any militant must be prepared for complete dedication to the "cause." One sees important intellectuals now and then devote themselves with a quasi-mystical enthusiasm to inferior jobs — handing out leaflets, writing on walls.[38] This absolute devotion doubles or triples the real strength of the party;[39] its militants, its members of parliament, all work hard and always carry out their assigned tasks, no matter how great the difficulties may be or the amount of time needed. Thus they frequently succeed in imposing their will, either by rallying the most easily influenced as in the case of strikes and propaganda activities, or by profiting from the absence of less active adversaries, as is often the case in parliament and in the mass organizations animated by the Communists. Finally, this tenacious activity impresses the hesitant, who tend to judge favorably a cause which engenders such devotion.

The corollary to this quasi-religious certainty is the absence of all spirit of compromise. The Communists "extend their hands" to the Catholics and the Socialists, they invite them to "argue," but they never yield except on points of detail. This intransigence is also a source of strength as it makes the Communist party appear, in comparison with the other French parties which are accustomed to compromise, as a pure party which abandons none of its objectives. The Communist militant is alone in possessing this "sense of the enemy" which German sociologists have recognized as an essential element of political feelings — the desire to discover the enemy and ferret him out everywhere, to feel a hatred for him that, in the words of Duclos before the National Assembly, "can be sacred."

One would understand nothing of the psychology of a Communist if one did not begin by seeing that he is in a state of *total war* with present society. Dialectically, the proletariat is the negation of the bourgeoisie, and this negation is not only mental, but real; for him to deny it is to destroy it. The struggle must be implacable,

---

[38]Thus it is that university professors, eminent scholars, and even a former vice-president of the National Assembly, Madeleine Braun, sell *Humanité* in the streets every Sunday morning.

[39]"All party militants are permanently on call" (Lecoeur, in *Cahiers du communisme*, 1949, no. 8).

since long experience has demonstrated that all human relationships with capitalism weaken this struggle.[40]

THE LEADERS

The structure of the French Communist party gives to its leaders a more important role than other parties give to their leaders. And yet, the chiefs and the followers are more closely associated than they are in other parties. As a non-Communist observer writes: "Nothing resembles a Communist militant more than a Communist minister. Only the type of work or intelligence distinguishes the one from the other. This is not always true elsewhere, where success is often due to cunning, to accident, or to money."[41] It is true that the Communist chiefs have all "come from the ranks"; they have served as militants on all echelons of the party, whereas, most of the time, the leaders of other parties have been rapidly raised to positions of responsibility by their personal, electoral, or financial positions or by their literary culture or technical abilities. Communist intellectuals are rarely promoted to positions of political leadership, in contrast to what takes place in other parties. The intellectuals have a place of their own. The political leaders of the party are generally men who manifest to the highest degree the qualities of the Communist militant. While the leaders of the other parties do not include any workers, about half of the Communist leaders have been workers, such as Thorez, François Billoux, Charles Tillon, Benoît Frachon, and Léon Mauvais.

A classification of Communist deputies by occupation is interesting: of the 166 deputies that the party had at the beginning of 1947, 61 listed an occupation that can be included under the general heading of "worker." These included 25 metal workers, 12 construction workers, 11 railroad workers, and 5 miners. A certain number of them have not worked in these occupations for a long time. But it is important to point out the working-class origin

[40] Jean Lacroix, "L'homme communiste," *La Vie intellectuelle,* August 1947.
[41] Jacques Fauvet, *Les Partis politiques dans la France actuelle* (Paris, 1947). p. 67.

that is characteristic of an important part of the Communist group, in contrast to the other groups in the Chamber where deputies of working-class origin are very few in number: there are only seven in the M.R.P. group and four in the Socialist group, and these are exclusively skilled workers.

The "best-loved" leaders of the party are certainly Marcel Cachin, André Marty, Jacques Duclos, and, above all, Maurice Thorez.

Marcel Cachin, born in 1869, is the only representative of the older generation to survive the expulsions and resignations which characterized the history of the French Communist party between 1921 and 1934. The son of a policeman and the grandson of a peasant, Cachin became a teacher of philosophy. A Socialist party militant, he took over the direction of *Humanité* in 1912, a job which he still holds, in spite of his eighty-two years, in an attempt to prove the continuity between the pre-1920 Socialist party and the Communist party. He has in the party the prestige of a patriarch, of a veteran who symbolizes "fifty years of struggle."

André Marty, born in 1886, is the son of a worker who was condemned to death *in absentia* for having participated in the Commune of 1871. He completed secondary school, then enlisted as a seaman-machinist in the navy. Finding himself in the Black Sea in 1917, he took the lead in a mutiny in favor of joining the Soviets and was sentenced to twenty years in prison. Subsequently pardoned, he became one of the chiefs of the French Communist party and was sent to Spain to organize the International Brigades. Tight-lipped, brutal, he is the insurrectionist figure of the party.

Jacques Duclos, born in 1896, was a pastry maker. He is today the second man of the party. An excellent orator, a genial and friendly person, he leads the Communist parliamentary group in the National Assembly.

But the popularity of these three men is clearly inferior to that of Maurice Thorez. There exists in the party a real "Thorez *mystique,*" consisting of a very special sentiment in which adoration is mixed with affectionate camaraderie. This is symbolized by the use of his first name; there is not a militant who does not speak with enthusiasm and deference of "comrade Maurice" or simply "Maurice." All consider the secretary-general of the party less as a chief than as a friend, competent to guide, to counsel, to straighten things out, and as one who, coming from the people, has always remained faithful to them. The sentiment borne toward Thorez is at the same time fraternal and filial.

His statesmanlike qualities have been acknowledged in private by many of his opponents. He has told of his life in *Fils du peuple*.[42] Born in 1900 in a miner's family in the north of France, Thorez awoke very early to class consciousness in an atmosphere of poverty and strikes. Returning to the Pas-de-Calais after the upsetting experience of mass flight before the German invasion in the first World War, Thorez worked in the Socialist party. He pressed for the adherence of the Socialist Federation of Pas-de-Calais to the Third International; then in 1923 he became secretary of the Federation. By 1927 he was a member of the Political Bureau of the Communist party and in 1932 he became its secretary-general. From that date on, his history is the history of the Communist party, which he has led in two directions. On the one hand, he has reinforced and strengthened the machine, eliminated "factions" and oppositionists; on the other, he has advocated a policy of broad agreement with other sectors of opinion.

When Thorez took control, the French Communist party abandoned all vestiges of the Social-Democratic tradition, such as the toleration of struggle and compromise between factions within the party, and acquired the structure, simultaneously authoritarian and flexible, that it has since retained. From this moment, appeals for union have been unceasing. In 1924 Thorez advocated agreement between Communist and Socialist workers, frequently divided by the bitterness of the schism. His triumph was the unity-of-action pact between Socialists and Communists and the Popular Front of 1935, which was even joined by the Radical Socialists. In 1939 Thorez, who was drafted, rejoined the army; then, "on the order of his party," he deserted it. Condemned to death, he

---

[42]The latest edition, revised and augmented, appeared in 1949.

was pardoned by General de Gaulle, who at the time of the liberation took Thorez into his government.

Although one cannot talk of two "wings" in the party, two tendencies certainly exist: one, strictly proletarian and internationalist, is the "tough" tendency which stresses above all direct action, preparatory to an insurrection of the Bolshevik type — a tendency that is personified in André Marty. The other is the "open" tendency, attracted more toward alliances and to united action by diverse groups, tied to the French Socialist tradition, that is, more humane and patriotic — a tendency embodied by Maurice Thorez.

If in spite of this Thorez has retained until now the confidence of the Russian Communist chiefs, it is certainly because he has given proof of unquestionable intransigence in the realm of ideological orthodoxy, as well as of his fidelity, often proclaimed, to the Soviet Union. It is apparent, however, that the policy of the Popular Front and patriotic defense, which was that of the party from 1934 to 1939 and from 1941 to 1947, corresponds to the temperament of Thorez. From 1927 to 1949 all the party's campaigns have carried the personal mark of Maurice Thorez: "Open your mouths" – "No puppets in the party" – "No sectarianism" – "The hand extended to the Catholics" – "Popular Front" – "We love our country" — "The struggle for national independence" — "A broad democratic union." These slogans are unquestionably the expression of a tactic, but of a tactic followed with too much persistence not to be the expression of a deep desire in Thorez to make the Communist party a center of unity for the pursuit of broad national objectives. This man who spoke, one day in 1947, of "western communism"[43] could have become a French Tito, if he had remained on national soil and had been able to take the leadership of the French Resistance. Since the fall of 1950 Thorez has been in the Soviet Union, to recover from a stroke which half-paralyzed him. The party, to reduce the loss, tries to keep alive

[43]This formula, launched by Thorez at a banquet of Anglo-American journalists in France, has never since been used in the vocabulary of the Communist party.

the *"mystique* Thorez" through the regular publication of optimistic convalescence bulletins. Duclos, who is officially replacing Thorez, is far from having the same qualities or the same influence.

In spite of their differences the chiefs of the French Communist party are apparently solidly united with one another and with their party. No dissensions and no resignations have been recorded since 1940. And all the many efforts of the anti-Communists to discredit the "false prophets" in the eyes of the "deceived masses" have been futile in spite of the fact that the attacks against the "deserter" Thorez have been extremely violent, and that there has been no dearth of the classical accusations of corruption and depravity against the Communist chiefs.

It is notable that no Communist deputy has been implicated in any of the scandals which periodically erupt on the French political scene, and this is a weighty argument in Communist propaganda. The Communist leaders lead simple lives, generally with their families, and in all cases exempt from flagrant immorality. Thorez willingly lets himself be photographed in front of his pleasant but modest house in the Paris suburbs, together with his "companion,"[44] Jeannette Vermeersch, and his four young boys. The staff of the French Communist party is very poorly paid. The members of parliament, who are considered as members of the staff, give their salaries to the party chest, as we have seen, and are given as a monthly compensation the equivalent of the salary of a skilled worker in the Paris region, which is much below their parliamentary salary (actually what they get back is not much more than a third of what they give).

As all have known what it means to be outside the law, and almost all have been in prison, the Communist chiefs are proven militants in whom the party has confidence. Nevertheless, it is certain that, in spite of the enormous role played by Thorez and the prestige he enjoys, his disappearance or the revelation of a "betrayal" like that of Lazlo Rajk, while it would weaken the par-

[44] Thorez has been married to Jeannette Vermeersch since 1948.

ty, would not alone disorganize it. The militants put their "confidence in the party" above confidence in their chiefs. Moreover, it is difficult to estimate the degree of autonomous leadership Thorez enjoys. Alongside the official Communist leaders are generally found more or less secret ones. André Marty seems to have played an outstanding role in the organization of the 1947 strikes; and Laurent Casanova, a former lawyer of Corsican origin and a ponderous and obstinate theorist, appears to exercise a great influence on the party.

It is no more possible to refer to a standard type of leader than to a standard type of militant. Between Thorez and Marty there is as much difference as there is between a miner brought to the party via the trade union struggle and a young intellectual well armed with Marxist ideology; between a fanatical devotee of a tough policy and a young idealist charmed by "revolutionary romanticism." The French Communist party, to use a phrase attributed to Thorez, is "a vast range of humanity."

One can simplify, however, by distinguishing two categories of militants. One is made up of workers who continue within the Communist party a struggle commenced before 1914 in the Bourses du Travail and in the Socialist party of Guesde and Jaurès. They are motivated by a long tradition, but above all by poverty; they demand better wages and the "dignity" that is inseparable from a higher standard of living. For these men, the Communist party is no more than the party of the poor and oppressed, the party that always defends the workers.

The other category is composed of men who have the class struggle, not in their stomachs as do the others, but in their heads. They are first the disciples of Marx-Lenin-Stalin. They usually manifest a passionate and rigorous logic. Primarily recruited among the intellectuals, they are infinitely less numerous than the first category, but they do not lack influence because they teach the ideology. Thus at the side of Thorez, the former miner molded by poverty and the workers' struggle, we find Laurent Casanova, the lawyer-theorist whose cold intransigence is well known, standing as a gray eminence and perhaps as the future chief of the party.

All these men pass little by little into the mold of the same doctrine and the same organization, which isolate them in a totalitarian belief and discipline and tend to make of them a type new in France, a type whose dynamism attracts but whose fanaticism terrifies.

The bolshevization of the French Communist party has permitted the creation of a new type of Frenchman, previously almost unknown in the history of our country. This accomplishment is far from representing solely a positive value: it simultaneously involves the elevation and degradation of man and includes, among the new qualities which it brings, a principle of death. But the victory over the dominant mores is clear in a France where the upper bourgeoisie is often without grandeur and where the working class itself borrows from the petty bourgeoisie its tastes and its ideals. . . . The existence of such cadres, trained and hardened, poses one of the most serious problems of the France of tomorrow.[45]

[45]A. Rossi, *Physiologie du parti communiste français* (Paris, 1949), pp. 320–321.

XI

The French Communist Party and the Masses

Having examined the operation of the "motor," which is the party itself, its organization and its militants, we must examine more closely what this motor is trying to move, that is, the composition and extent of the masses that submit to its influence; and then we must examine how the "transmission belts" that connect it to these masses function: the party's diverse means of influence and its propaganda.

THE COMMUNIST ELECTORATE

The Communist party is the exact opposite of some parties, such as the Radical-Socialist party, whose whole existence is built around the preparation for and exploitation of elections. For the Communist party, the elections are only way stations; however, they are very important way stations, first because the party finds particularly favorable conditions for its propaganda at election time, then because elections furnish the Communists with evidence of the party's influence. If we interpret election results in the light of historical and geographical facts, we can actually deduce the broad social or psychological tendencies corresponding to the distribution of the votes obtained by the Communist party.[1]

[1]François Goguel has devoted his attention to these problems and we cannot do better than rely upon his studies of electoral geography published in

Numerical Growth

In the national parliamentary elections, the Communist party received 1,487,336 votes in 1936; 5,024,174 in October 1945; 5,489,000 in November 1946; and 5,038,587 in June 1951. Between 1936 and 1945 the electorate was doubled by the participation of women; the progress of the Communist party has, however, been considerable since it went from 14.9 per cent of the votes cast in 1936 to 26.5 per cent in 1951.

Communist Party Strength in Metropolitan France
Chamber of Deputies and National Assembly Elections
(In thousands)

	1936	October 1945	November 1946	June 1951
Registered voters	11,768	24,623	25,052	24,973
Communist voters	1,487	5,024	5,489	5,039
Communist party members	329	546	819	787

Communist voters were nearly 3.4 times more numerous in 1951 than in 1936, but the party's membership increased only by 140 per cent in the same period.

Geographical and Sociological Distribution

This growth has been accompanied by a remarkable geographical extension of Communist votes.

1) In 1936 the Communist party was very successful in working-class regions (the suburbs of Paris, the coal basin of the north, the Alès basin) and in certain departments where it profited either from a tradition of voting to the extreme left (Var, south of the Drôme, and a few other regions) or as a result of the strength of individual leaders. Elsewhere the votes were much less numerous, and they were nonexistent in some rural departments. But in the November 1946 elections the Communist party

Esprit since 1947 and upon the course given in 1948–1949 at the Institut d'Etudes Politiques and published as *La Vie politique de la société française contemporaine* (Paris, n.d.).

was the only one to poll never less than 6 per cent of the registered votes, and the one to poll more than 24 per cent in the
largest number of districts. Thus the electoral expansion of the
party has even surpassed the expansion of its recruitment. To cite
a striking example, in Vendée, a rural and conservative department, while the number of Communist members climbed from
170 to 3,000 between 1936 and 1946, the number of Communist
votes increased from 2,600 to 26,900. We can thus draw, with
Goguel, the first conclusion: "The importance of this geographical expansion, which is progressively overtaking the most diverse
regions, is that the Communist party is not only the first party of
France, it is also the one whose foundations are most clearly
national."[2]

2) Certainly the party has retained a strong hold on the voters
in the industrial regions: in all the Paris suburbs it won more
than 30 per cent of the vote, and it almost reached 40 per cent in
the northeastern suburbs. However, if one considers the total
number of Communist votes in the departments of Seine and
Seine-et-Oise (Paris suburbs), Nord, and Pas-de-Calais (mining
basin), one sees that in 1936 these regions supplied 38 per cent
of the national total of Communist votes, while in 1946 they did
not supply more than 28 per cent.

Moreover, in other industrial regions like those of the east
(Moselle, Bas-Rhin) and of the southeast (Rhône, Loire, Isère),
the party has won smaller proportions of the vote than in some
rural departments like Ardèche and Corrèze. Thus it appears that
the electoral strength of the Communist party is not always proportional to the degree of industrialization and of urban concentration. The Communist party is certainly the party which receives the most workers' votes, but it is far from receiving all of
them and may not even be able to win half. On the other hand,
it has progressed enormously in some regions where agriculture
and small-scale skilled artisanship prevail.

If one searches for the basic cause of this distribution, one is

[2]Goguel, "Géographie du référendum du 13 octobre et des élections du 10
novembre 1946," *Esprit*, 1947, no. 2.

led to think that the party has achieved its principal success, outside certain industrial regions, in the departments that traditionally vote to the left. Even before the war, this transfer of Socialist
votes toward communism had started, and it is this evolution
that was accentuated after the liberation and that was revealed
in the elections of November 1946. Professor Goguel had the
happy idea of pointing out the permanence of this evolution by
comparing the map of the *montagnard* (extreme left) vote of 1849
with that of the Communist vote. With the exception of certain
regions, such as Alsace, which have for special reasons moved
from the left to the right, there is a striking analogy. Languedoc,
the southeastern Mediterranean region, and the Massif Central
have remained the bastions of the extreme left. The progress of
industrialization has now added to them several departments
north of the Loire and especially the industrial region bounded
by Paris, Rouen, Lille, and Sedan. Thus we can distinguish the
two principal sources of Communist electoral strength: on one
hand, industrialization, which has created the proletariat and
class warfare; on the other, a leftist tradition that, in some departments, goes back to the revolution and which has successively
sought to affirm, through the Republican, Radical-Socialist, Socialist, and Communist parties, a desire for democratic freedom
and social justice.

The foundation of the French Communist party is economic on
one hand, ideological on the other. The Communists of the Nord,
of Pas-de-Calais, or of the Paris suburbs certainly want society
organized on a collective basis: this is a normal attitude for industrial workers. But in Corrèze, for example, where more than
70 per cent of the heads of farming families are also farm owners,
it is doubtful that the collectivistic aspiration is as clear: there
communism appears to be more democratic than collectivistic.
In spite of all the doctrinal trappings of Marx, Lenin, and Stalin,
communism is purely and simply the successor to the "mountain"
of Ledru-Rollin. It owes its strength to the fact that it is the
"farthest to the left" of the French parties, the successor to the
socialism of twenty years ago and the radicalism of fifty years ago,

more than to its position as the promoter in France of the social revolution achieved by Russia.[3]

The electoral position of the French Communist party takes us back to the ambiguity that has been noted in the discussion of the party's history and recruitment. This party's Marxist, Stalinist, internationalist, and proletarian aspects must never let us forget its national roots; it is a party "unlike the others" which nonetheless appears at certain moments and for certain strata of the population to be a party "like the others."

Current Trends

The weakened popular support for communism, which had been noted ever since the partial cantonal elections of March 1949, has been confirmed by the general elections of June 17, 1951. The Communist vote dropped from 5,489,000 in 1946 to 5,039,000 in 1951, or from 28.4 per cent to 26.5 per cent of total votes cast. This decline of about 8 per cent takes the Communist party back to its 1945 positions.

The non-Communist parties, which had all oriented their campaigns against the Communist party and had succeeded in isolating it entirely, had perhaps expected more. Nevertheless, this loss of strength is significant especially when compared to the gains obtained at the same time by the Communist-Socialist Popular Front in Italy. It seems clear that the advance of communism in France has been stopped and that a saturation point has been reached which cannot be exceeded under present conditions. The answer to future developments lies in the policies of the new government to be organized as a result of the elections. A government of the right would tend to strengthen the Communist position, while a government of reform and social justice might lead to an acceleration of its decline.

In the 1951 elections the Communist party suffered rather severe losses in many of the agricultural areas where it had established itself after the liberation. Also, communism lost ground where it had been accepted because of its patriotism during the

[3]Goguel, *op. cit.*, p. 256.

Resistance period. The new Communist policies of violent and systematic opposition, of unconditional attachment to the Soviet Union, and of favoring a return to an "internationalist" and "classist" position have undoubtedly been the main causes of Communist losses. Thus we find once more verified the law which controls the history of French Communism and according to which the transition from a soft to a hard policy results in a loss of votes.

On the other hand, in a few agricultural departments communism was able to strengthen its position, between 1946 and 1951, as a party of the left in the historical sense of the word. In the Creuse the Communist vote increased from 38 to 40 per cent and in Corrèze from 40 to 41 per cent of votes cast. The loss of votes has been generally small in the industrial regions except in the east and in the Paris area. The Communists consolidated their positions in the mining fields of the north as well as in the southeast (Marseille, Grenoble). It is important to note that the three Paris "arrondissements" where the Communist party got the highest vote (from 37 to 38 per cent of the total) are at the same time the areas where housing conditions are the worst. Finally the Communist vote has tended to increase where it was already strong (Dordogne, Indre, Pas-de-Calais), while it declined where it was weak (in the department where it was weakest, the Vendée, the vote declined from 14 to 9 per cent).

The 1951 vote shows that the electors lost by the Communist did not go back to the Socialists. Rather many of them seem to have gone over to the other extreme, the RPF. This might show that many Communist voters see in the Communist party a party of opposition determined on change, rather than a doctrinaire Marxist-Stalinist movement faithfully supporting the Soviet Union.

This electoral analysis leads us to think that there is a much greater difference between the Communist militant and the Communist voter than there is between the Communist militant and the party member. Not only are four-fifths of the Communist voters not party members, but they vote Communist for reasons which often have little to do with the special nature and aims of the French Communist party and which can even be the very opposite of those aims. It is significant, moreover, that the party itself most frequently seeks to present its lists of candidates to the voters not under the "Communist" label, but under some such name as "List of the Republican and Resistant Union Presented by the French Communist Party." The party knows that the great majority of its voters live outside the Communist sphere of influence during nonelectoral periods. One party leader recently remarked:

At the last general elections, the party received more than 35 per cent of the votes in the Seine. But the daily sale of *Humanité* in this department represents only 12 per cent of the total sales of morning papers. That means that on the whole two-thirds of the Communist voters in Paris read some other paper than *Humanité,* most frequently one of the reactionary organs aimed at the workers and "little people," such as *Parisien libéré* or *Franc-Tireur.*[4]

The party is presented with an essential problem: How to operate on the non-Communist masses to get them to vote Communist? And how to maintain Communist influence over the masses that have voted Communist? This raises the problem that we must now analyze: the methods of spreading Communist influence, the organizations and the propaganda themes designed to rally the non-Communists.

TACTICS AND PROPAGANDA

One would get an erroneous conception of the aims of the Communist party by defining them only in terms of programs, legislative proposals, and parliamentary positions; to do this is to treat the Communists as a party like the others. While the other parties desire reforms without wishing to challenge the principles of society or the foundations of the regime, the Communist party wishes to modify these principles and these foundations radically. This is why in a "capitalist" society, under a

[4]Etienne Fajon, in *Humanité,* Oct. 31, 1949.

regime of "formal democracy," all the party's proposals and attitudes go beyond the stated objectives and form part of a strategy whose end remains the transformation of the "bourgeois" democracy into "socialist" democracy through the agency of the dictatorship of the proletariat.

Lenin, on the basis of the Russian situation, defined in his *Tasks of the Russian Social-Democrats* the double role of Communist parties. One phase is on the economic level and consists of guiding the proletariat in the struggle for its demands. The other, on a political level, consists of creating agitation "based on the political needs of the moment" for "democratic ideas." But, he added, "in the economic struggle, the proletariat is absolutely alone..., while in the *political* struggle for democracy the Russian working class is not alone: all the elements of political opposition come to align themselves at its side." We shall examine separately this economic struggle and this political struggle, while never forgetting that the Communists pursue them simultaneously and are always ready at any time to replace one with the other. As Lenin stated in *Left Wing Communism: An Infantile Disorder*, "The revolutionary class, in order to fulfil its task, must be able to master all forms or sides of social activity without exception.... [It] must be ready to pass from one form to another in the quickest and most unexpected manner."

The party, operating in a bourgeois democracy, works on two levels. It utilizes the technique of "double power," aligning itself against the state in the name of the oppressed proletariat, which has already been declared the legitimate sovereign of tomorrow, while demanding the freedom of action permitted other parties and using against the bourgeois state its own democratic principles, thus exploiting, in order to maintain its freedom of operation, what Raymond Aron has called the tactic of "maximum democracy."

The play of these two tactics is particularly clear in France. After the departure of the Communist ministers from the government, the party exploited to the utmost the demands of the General Confederation of Labor and the great strikes of the fall of 1947 and 1948 against the Third Force majority. At the same time, it never ceased to present itself as the defender of liberty, to call for a "government of broad democratic union," and to protest against the ostracism imposed on a party that represents "one-third of the French population."

One can see what an error can be committed by reducing Communist policy to the dimensions of the parliamentary arena. The Communist International, at its second congress, had already reminded each Communist deputy that he was not "a legislator seeking a common language with other legislators, but a party agitator sent among the enemy to apply the decisions of the party." Parliament constitutes for the party a platform for privileged propaganda. The speeches of the Communist deputies[5] always contain the central Communist propaganda themes; the laws they propose, their resolutions, their orders of the day, are designed to support this propaganda by apparently concrete proposals. In this they are following instructions which were laid down as early as 1924 by the Political Bureau: "Those elected must make purely demonstrative proposals, conceived not with a view to their adoption, but for propaganda and agitation."

The French Communist party battles vigorously in parliament, as it does everywhere, but the parliamentary front is only secondary. It carries out its activities and propaganda constantly among all strata of the nation. The propaganda themes worked out by the Political Bureau are taken up by the Communist press, adapted to social and regional conditions, and then echoed by the satellite organizations. This propaganda is not planned and carried out in a purely Machiavellian fashion, for the phenomenon of an echo is actually created: the Communist masses repeat their slogans to the leaders, who end up by being themselves impressed with them and by really believing in what they had originally said. In this way, after Zhdanov's remonstrances, the leaders of the party appeared to believe, during the fall of 1947, that the French working class was capable of triumphing, and

---

[5]The selection of Communist candidates is made by the Central Committee, which also names the president and officers of the parliamentary group.

today they proclaim the possibility of a "government of demo-cratic union." This self-persuasion can become, depending on the circumstances, a source of weakness or a source of strength.

The Communist propaganda machine, in any case, functions remarkably well. It uses fully all the classic resources of propa-ganda: the press, posters, meetings, and the like, but its true strength resides in the systematic use of person-to-person propa-ganda, practiced in conversation or by the door-to-door tech-nique. Thorez has never ceased to object to brutal methods of propaganda and to repeat that it is necessary to "explain, explain again, always explain." This immense effort of explanation and persuasion is amplified by the utilization of organizations which, without being Communist, include an important group of Com-munists; even if this group is not a majority, it generally suc-ceeds in imposing its point of view because it possesses cohesion, superior political education, and often superior devotion. These organizations give Communist propaganda a kind of "broad de-pendable base"; by taking up Communist themes, they enable the party to prove that these themes are not strictly Communist but that they correspond to the interests of a great number of non-Communist Frenchmen.

Although the final aim of the French Communist party is a radical revolution, its propaganda and its activities are special-ized, flexible, and varied, as they apply to different social classes.

THE FRENCH COMMUNIST PARTY
AND THE SOCIAL CLASSES

The Working Class

The Communist party, as we have said, considers itself the agent of the working class. In its eyes a fundamental identifica-tion exists between the working class and the party, an identifi-cation which is both doctrinal and mystical; and the result is that, to the Communists, no other organization or workers' party can be anything but an intolerable scandal and the temporary product of treason. The Communist party promotes working-class unity as it promotes its own existence. The offspring of the

Socialist party at the congress of Tours,[6] the Communist party considers the present Socialist party as a "fragment." The Communists "want unity of action at any price"[7] and hope to merge with the Socialists in a future "French Workers' party," which would be the party of all French workers.

THE APPEALS FOR UNITY

Unity of action, which the Communist party has proposed twenty-six times to the Socialist party, was achieved against fascism in 1934. The collapse of the Popular Front and the Nazi-Soviet pact again widened the breach. In the first election after the liberation, the Communists and Socialists received 51 per cent of the votes; together they held a majority in the country and in the Constituent Assembly. At that time the Communist invitations to unity became more pressing, but the Socialists resisted. The Communist party maneuvered so well, however, that the draft of the constitution was supported only by the Socialist and Communist parties. But this draft was rejected and the two parties lost the virtual majority that they had held.

The favorable moment had passed. However, the Communist leaders continued to invite the Socialist workers to join in the "common struggle." But the roads were too divergent, and even the menace of de Gaullism did not promote unity of action. The Communist party, moreover, always rejected any direct agreement between the parties, urging instead unity at the level of the rank and file, all the while continuing to denounce the Socialist leaders. But this distinction between the leaders and the led is sometimes difficult to recognize, and the Central Committee had to call upon the Communists "to eliminate the tendency to confuse, in too many cases, the Socialist workers with their leaders and instead to aid the Socialists to see clearly, to convince them patiently in order to create the conditions for unity of action."[8]

[6]"The party is the continuation of socialism," the Communist leaders kept repeating in the period from 1921 to 1925.

[7]Maurice Thorez at the national conference at Ivry in 1934.

[8]Resolution of the national conference of Montreuil, April 10, 1949.

The same tactic has been followed, with the same obstinacy, with respect to Catholic workers. April 17, 1936, on the eve of the election, Thorez pronounced over the radio the appeal that has become famous: "We, who believe in a secular state, extend our hand to you, Catholic, whether worker, employee, artisan or peasant, because you are our brother, and because you are crushed by the same burdens as we."[9] This invitation, which has been constantly repeated ever since, reached the initial stages of realization in the Resistance, where the Communist militant and the Catholic militant, "he who believed in heaven and he who did not,"[10] had many opportunities to collaborate with and to judge each other. The resolution of the national conference of Montreuil urged the Communists to apply the policy of the outstretched hand toward Catholic workers and, while defending the secular state, to respect Catholic opinions and beliefs. Above all the party wishes to withdraw the Catholics from the political influence of the clergy. "The Catholic workers are subject to the spiritual guidance of the clergy but they do not acknowledge the clergy's right to dictate their political conduct. As for us, we will continue to extend a brotherly hand to them."[11]

This attitude is new for the French left, which is traditionally anticlerical. But the Communist party has succeeded in maintaining it at the same time that it has fiercely defended the lay state, and even while making the lay state its principal electoral propaganda theme in some regions.

Among the many Socialists who have left their party, the number who have later joined the Communist party is quite small. As for the Catholics, very few have joined the party. If, however, the appeals for political unity have, up to now, miscarried, one cannot say the same of unity on the union level.

[9]Some of the force of Thorez' statement is lost in translation as he employed the second person singular, *tu,* which in French implies a close personal relationship.

[10]The refrain of a poem by Louis Aragon.

[11]Speeech by Thorez at Mulhouse, Oct. 9, 1949.

UNION ACTIVITY

The French Communist party has always given unconditional support to union demands, except in 1947 when it participated in the government; and we have seen that in 1947 it soon thought better of it and that this was the cause of the departure of the Communist ministers. But this support is not limited to wage demands: "We are concerned with the slightest needs of the workers," Thorez has said.[12] It is impossible to enumerate all the demands that the party has raised or sustained concerning the aged, youth, women, soldiers, pensioners, the sick. The strongest factor in the success of the party is that it has systematically gone to the defense of the "little man" against the "privileged," and not only in words but also in acts. Communist-controlled municipalities have established all sorts of institutions for unemployment relief, old age assistance, legal and social advice, and vacation camps. These achievements have been developed especially in the famous "red belt" that surrounds Paris.[13]

It is particularly through the unions that the Communist party influences the working class. The General Confederation of Labor, reorganized after the liberation, was the trump card in the Communist party's hand. But the Communists, as generally occurs in the organizations they colonize, ended up by alienating the non-Communists, most of whom left the General Confederation of Labor after the failure of the big strikes in the fall of 1947. But the C.G.T. has reconquered a large part of the lost ground. The continuous rise in prices has been a weighty argument in its favor. The C.G.T. includes the great majority of unionized miners and building trade and metal workers; in other occupations, the Christian unionists have frequently reached understandings with the C.G.T. Only the Socialist unions remain hostile. The gap

[12]Speech at the Salle Bullier, Dec. 2, 1932.

[13]Communist-controlled municipalities have a triple function: (1) to give concrete assistance to the working class; (2) to serve as a fulcrum for strikes and insurrections; and (3) to train administrative cadres (A. Treint, in *Cahiers du bolchévisme*, Feb. 15, 1925). In 1948 the coalition of Socialists, Popular Republicans, and Gaullists took many municipalities from the Communists and drove wedges into the "red belt."

between wages and prices, the poverty of many workers, and finally the clumsiness which the government has often displayed in putting down strikes are rallying the majority of organized labor to the General Confederation of Labor. This confederation, although it includes a certain number of non-Communists, has as its secretary-general Benoît Frachon, former secretary of the Communist party, who is on "detached service" as leader of the C.G.T., where he applies Communist directives through a staff three-quarters of which are Communist.

Certainly the C.G.T., which had five million members in 1946, has lost half of its strength as the outcome of the 1947 split and because of the lassitude of the non-Communist segment of the working class. It is, however, the strongest workers' organization, and it is capable, in spite of its only too visible political attachment, of setting almost the whole working class in motion behind it in moments of crisis. Thus the Confederation represents the most valuable mass of man power at the disposal of the Communist party. If the appeals for unity have not produced spectacular results, the party is convinced that the fall in the workers' purchasing power and the threat of unemployment are leading the working class to unity in fact if not in form. On October 7, 1949, Thorez said to the National Conference at Ivry:

Yes, there is an irresistible current towards unity that resembles on a higher level the situation we knew in 1934–1935. We are unquestionably moving toward great class struggles, toward great battles for widespread masses of the people, in which the united working class will carry the banner of the struggle for progress and liberty, for peace and national independence.

The Peasantry

For Lenin the peasantry was the indispensable auxiliary of the proletariat in the conquest of power. It is an invariable characteristic of Communist parties that they seek to achieve an alliance between these two groups.

Until the war the Communist party had hardly set foot in the French countryside, in most of which a balanced agriculture prevails and which is inhabited by peasants whose prudent and con-

servative mentality is proverbial. However, the Resistance operated as a diffuser of communism; technical progress has brought
the cities and the country closer together; and Communist propaganda has coincided with a development dangerous for French
peasantry. For the last twenty years, the number of small agricultural holdings has tended to decrease in favor of large ones:
from 1929 to 1946, 880,000 small holdings, about a third of the
total figure, disappeared.[14] And, contrary to general belief, land
is unevenly divided in France: 383,845 farms of more than 26
hectares, or 10 per cent of all farms, include 19,944,825 hectares or
50 per cent of all cultivated land. Thus, out of every one hundred
French farmers, the ten largest owners hold as much land as the
other ninety. Finally, the number of agricultural workers, tenant
farmers, and *métayers* is equal to the number of farmers who own
their land. One can therefore see that, even if there is no agrarian
problem in France at the moment, the position of small land-
holders in France is nevertheless menaced.

In its agrarian program, which was worked out in 1921 and
augmented by several suggestions from Lenin and which has been
maintained ever since, the Communist party promises:

a) The confiscation of all land belonging to those who do
not cultivate it themselves, with indemnity only in the case of
the smaller owners.

b) The transfer of these lands and equipment to the working peasants (tenant farmers, *métayers*, agricultural workers,
and small proprietors who have insufficient areas at their disposal).

c) An absolute guarantee to small farm owners of continued
and hereditary enjoyment of their lands.

d) A ban on the sale and purchase of lands in order to prevent their falling into the hands of capitalists and speculators.

e) The transfer to the community of large estates having
great economic importance, with a view to transforming them
into modern socialist enterprises.

[14]Figures from the *Bulletin de la statistique générale de la France*, Suppl.,
July-September 1948.

f) State aid for the electrification of the countryside and the mechanization of agriculture.

g) Support for agricultural co-operation in all its forms, including producers' co-operatives that, developing on the basis of the initiative and free consent of the masses of working peasants, will open the way toward modern socialist agriculture, which is alone capable of bringing prosperity and social progress.

h) A pension for all old peasants.

It is apparent that this program is radical insofar as it relates to the expropriation of large landowners and, at the same time, cautious with regard to the establishment of collective farms. It was conceived with a view to dissipating the fears that Soviet socialization arouses in a peasantry strongly attached to private ownership of the land. It appears to engender only mild enthusiasm in a peasantry with an instinctive distrust for all political programs. However, the Communist party has won many votes among agricultural workers, who are generally poorly paid and poorly housed, and among tenant farmers and sharecroppers *(métayers),* who expect the Communists to give them the land they work. It is probable that these votes will diminish if the party continues to appear far from actual power, that is, incapable of keeping its promises.

The penetration of the Communist party into the countryside has been helped by the Communist weekly *La Terre,* which is aimed at the peasants and has a circulation of 200,000. But the influence of the party has less of an ideological nature among the peasants than among any other group. Its influence is due to the concrete demands that are part of the party's vocabulary. It is due especially, as we have seen in our analysis of the election results, to the reputation that the Communist party has of being the party farthest to the left, a reputation that is profitable in certain sections of the countryside that have not forgotten the pre-1789 domination of the "lord and the priest" and which fear a return to this condition under other forms.

The Middle Classes

Many businessmen and artisans profited from the period of scarcity and the black market. The less merchandise there was, the more the intermediaries flourished by reselling it at high prices. The multiplication and enrichment of tradesmen are essential elements of the postwar French picture.

A proletarian party might naturally be expected to denounce this situation and to exploit the discontent of the producers against the unproductive middlemen. The Communist party has been very careful not to do this. Actually, in Marxist doctrine, the middle class is forced by the necessity of things to ally itself with the proletariat. While the *Communist Manifesto* stated: "The middle classes become revolutionary as a result of the prospect of their impending transfer into the proletariat," the history of the period between the two wars has shown, however, that this prospect could lead them to become Fascists rather than revolutionaries. In the eyes of the Communists, the middle classes are the pivot of the political situation; the victory of the Communists depends on the orientation of the middle classes, at least under the legal conditions of a democratic regime. The Popular Front represented more than an interparty cartel: it represented the alliance of the working class with a petty bourgeoisie that felt itself to be equally menaced by the crisis.

The Communist party remembered this lesson. It opposed, soon after the liberation, a new currency issue combined with a ceiling on the amount of currency which could be redeemed, an operation that would have cut into the cash reserves accumulated by the peasants and businessmen. It vigorously denounced in January 1948, for the same reasons, the withdrawal from circulation of all five-thousand franc notes, as well as the Mayer withholding tax which hit businessmen, artisans, industrialists, and taxpayers whose taxable income exceeded 450,000 francs. At present the party connects wage demands with the interests of businessmen by showing them that an increase in the volume of their business depends to a large degree on an increase in the purchasing power of the working class.

It does not appear that this Communist solicitude for the middle classes has been reciprocated. The tendency to emulate the upper bourgeoisie, the discontent aroused by the strikes, the fear of a Communist insurrection prevail among most middle-class people. On the other hand, the favor shown toward businessmen has sometimes put the party in a bad light before working-class opinion and has opened it to charges of demagogy and of playing a double game.

THE CURRENT SLOGANS OF THE FRENCH COMMUNIST PARTY

We have already emphasized the decisive importance of Zhdanov's report to the meeting in August 1947 that formed the Cominform. This report accused the Western Communist parties of following a policy of conciliation and of not having been able to discern in time that American imperialism,[15] under the façade of the Marshall Plan, was threatening the national independence of the peoples and the peace of the world.

As a result of this conference the slogans of the French Communist party were radically changed, and the struggle began under new auspices. There was no longer any question of conditionally accepting American aid, which had been the position of the French, Italian, and Czechoslovakian Communist parties: it was to be rejected *in toto*. From this perspective, the departure of the Communist ministers from the government in May 1947 assumed a new meaning: they had refused to associate themselves with a policy of capitulation before American demands. The struggle for national independence and the defense of peace were mingled in a single attitude of hostility to the Marshall Plan, "the plan of enslavement and war." The French governments

[15]For simplicity's sake we will use in this section expressions borrowed from the Communist vocabulary without putting them in quotation marks each time. We are attempting here to condense as clearly as possible the Communist themes without confusing them with our own point of view. Cf. H. Chambre, "Pourquoi les communistes sont-ils opposés au Plan Marshall?" in *Travaux de l'action*, 1948, no. 26, and "Le PCF dans les six premiers mois de 1949," *ibid.*, 1949, no. 33.

were the slaves of warmongering American capitalism. For convenience in explanation we will separate these two themes which are always interwoven in Communist propaganda.

The Struggle for "National Independence"

In the eyes of the Communists, the Marshall Plan has a triple aim: to ward off the eventuality of a production crisis in the United States; to thwart the industrialization of the countries aided; and to establish a block of states subservient to the United States and directly dependent on a Germany well on the road to recovery.[16]

The first of these three points concerns only the United States. But the second involves French industry, the foundation of national independence.[17] Local difficulties are effectively used by the Communists as French governments, with expansive optimism, have too often presented the Marshall Plan as providential largesse that would immediately restore prosperity. The Communist tactic in such cases consists of interesting the personnel in the fate of the threatened branches of industry by founding Committees of Republican Defense, which have been successful only in the motion picture and airplane industries, that is, in industries that are, by definition, unstable.

The bilateral agreements of the European Recovery Program furnished the party with other arguments:

These agreements, fruits of the Marshall Plan, are resulting in the curtailment of French national sovereignty, in making our country an American commercial agency. American citizens will not be subject to the jurisdiction of French courts in case of conflicts with the French government. The International Monetary Fund will be able to fix the exchange rate of European money. Americans will be able to intervene when a raw or finished product becomes scarce in a Marshallized country. The most-favored nation clause will be extended to the states under military occupation by the United States, that is, to Germany.[18]

[16]See Thorez' report to the Central Committee, April 14, 1948.

[17]See Charles Tillon, "Le Plan Marshall, abandon de l'indépendance française et de la défense nationale," *Cahiers du communisme*, 1948, no. 5.

[18]François Billoux, "La lutte pour l'indépendance nationale," *Cahiers du communisme*, 1948, no. 7.

The second threatened sector is, according to the Communists, that of national defense. The Brussels conference, then the Atlantic Pact, have integrated the French army in a military framework directed by the United States. This structure is not designed for national defense, but (1) to defend a reactionary political system against the proletariat; (2) to stifle the colonial peoples' aspirations for freedom; and (3) to prepare for a war against the U.S.S.R., a war in which the French army would play the role of a sacrificed pawn.

This policy of national resignation is reflected in the abandonment of the reparations owed by Germany and the halt in the dismantling of German factories. The denazification and the demilitarization of Germany have not really been carried out, and Germany, once again given priority by the United States, will soon be capable, thanks to its superior industrial equipment, part of which was stolen from occupied countries, of imposing its wishes on France. Federated Europe is only the "ideological camouflage" for this policy; it is the means of establishing a political and economic unity which will be easier to govern from Washington.

It does not appear that this theme of national independence has had the reverberations among the masses that the party anticipated. If the Communists have not succeeded in arousing national feeling against the "American party," however, their criticisms of the Marshall Plan have been taken up in quarters that have been disturbed by its military consequences. The January 15, 1949, issue of *Le Monde* stated: "The themes that were, several months ago, the appanage of America's bitterest enemies have become commonplace. Accusations or suspicious with respect to the Marshall Plan that were sacrilegious last May are now quite common."

But above all the exploitation of the "German danger" has found a considerable echo in a country three times invaded and pillaged. The Communists are fighting bitterly against the proposed rearmament of Germany, and have found some allies among conservatives and anti-Fascists who cannot forget the memory of nazism.

The Struggle for "Peace"

Since the beginning of 1949 the theme of the struggle for peace has tended to be integrated with that of national independence.

According to a Marxist, the contradictions of capitalism lead to war. The Communists are convinced that the United States is moving toward an economic crisis from which it cannot hope to escape except by armament and war. To support their thesis they cite the statements of Americans, who are described as influential, proclaiming that a depression would be worse than war. In contrast, the U.S.S.R. can only be pacific since, being socialist, it has eliminated from its midst the very germs of war. Thus, in the face of an imperialistic country threatened by economic crisis, a country in which some businessmen have profited from war, stands a nation that has never ceased to offer peace and that, after having lost seventeen million men in the last war, seeks only to build socialism in peace.

That is why the French must join the peace camp against the war camp, the peace camp being led by the Soviet Union with which, moreover, France signed a friendship pact in 1945. The defense of peace is thus identified with defense of the Soviet Union. The signing of the Atlantic Pact, the "war pact," strengthened even more the party's determination to do everything to prevent "aggression" against the U.S.S.R. Thorez had already hurled at the imperialistic and warlike clan his sensational declaration that "the people of France will not, will never, make war on the Soviet Union."

This campaign is supported by those non-Communist Frenchmen who fear that their country, hardly recovered from one invasion, will be ravaged again. The point in the Communist argument that is most frequently taken up by others is the heavy burden of military expenses. Frequently one hears compared the sum voted for the war budget and that for alleviating the poverty of the workers, the scarcity of housing, and the shortage of schools. Several municipalities, ones in which the Communists

are in a minority, have voted resolutions on this point. The unpopular and costly war in Viet-Nam is also a point of contact
between the Communists and numerous non-Communist Frenchmen.

Communists and some non-Communists, particularly former
members of the Resistance, are linked for the "defense of the
peace" to the Combatants for Peace and Liberty, led by Yves
Farge (a former Resistance chief), the Abbé Boulier, and Charles
Tillon (former chief of the Franc-Tireurs and Partisans and
former Communist minister). The movement, which has no
membership as such, calls on all Frenchmen to organize into
councils for peace and liberty on the local level. These councils
have the mission of agitating by demonstrations and pressure on
the deputies against any curtailment of liberty and especially
against the "policy of preparation for war." While on the whole
Combatants for Peace and Liberty works in the same direction
as Communist propaganda, its platform is broad enough and its
structure sufficiently flexible to enable it to include, along with
the Communists, former members of the Resistance who were
their comrades in arms, Catholics, Protestants, and nonpartisans.
The struggle against the Atlantic Pact, the "peace ballot," and
the campaigns for atomic disarmament and against the German
menace furnish activity for the four thousand "municipal councils" that make up this movement. However, a certain reticence
has appeared on the part of non-Communists who have been upset by Russian provocations against Tito and by the creation of
the German People's Republic.

A Government of "Democratic Union"

The Communist party proclaims that the peace can be definitely saved and national independence recovered only by a change
of policy, and a "government of democratic union," that is, a
government "in which the working class and its Communist
party would have the place they deserve" alongside other democrats "who are sincerely dedicated to justice and liberty."

The objection has often been made that no parliamentary

majority for such a government exists. The party has replied through the mouth of Thorez that "the action of the masses, by asserting themselves, will cause the triumph of a government of democratic union."[19]

Such a government, as the Communists conceive it, would bear no comparison with the tripartite coalitions that characterized the government after the liberation. It would be composed, in addition to the Communists, of Socialist or Christian groups; it would actually be led by the Communists and would resemble the first governments in the "people's democracies." But this resemblance is not something that inspires confidence even in those who would be prepared to participate in such a government. The Communists wish to govern with others, but these "others" do not want to work with the Communists; so, in the eyes of non-Communist observers, in spite of the assertions of the Communist party, this government of democratic union signifies nothing but a Communist government.

A few days after the June 1951 election, the Politburo of the Communist party issued a declaration calling for a program which reflects the essential tactics and themes we have just analyzed:

The French Communist party, conscious of defending the interest of the nation, calls upon all Frenchmen and Frenchwomen who are against war and poverty to unite and battle in common in order to achieve a peace program conforming to the interest of the French nation and its people:

1. Conclusion among the five great powers (United States, U.S.S.R., People's Republic of China, Great Britain, and France) of a peace pact open to all nations.

2. Repudiation of all agreements which weaken national independence and departure of American occupation forces from French territory.

3. Conclusion of a treaty of peace with a demilitarized, unified, democratic, and peaceful Germany.

4. Immediate peace in Viet-Nam; return of the expeditionary forces employed in Viet-Nam and in Korea.

5. Passage of a law forbidding war propaganda; outlawing of atomic weapons and of all other instruments of mass destruction.

[19]Speech of Oct. 9, 1949.

6. Progressive reduction and control of armed forces and of armaments; utilization of the sums thus saved for the development of the country, and for the social and economic needs of the people in order to ameliorate the living conditions of the laboring masses of town and country.

7. Protection of democratic liberties against all factious groups. The French Communist party appeals to all Frenchmen and Frenchwomen who care for the independence of France, for liberty and peace, to oppose, with their united strength, the policies of war, poverty, and fascism of the lackeys of imperialism. It appeals to them to labor with all their strength to create the conditions permitting the formation of a government which will be a true French government, a government of social progress, of liberty and of peace.[20]

This program is certainly more "demonstrative" than practical. If it is undeniable that in its attitude towards the wage and the peace problems, the Communist party has successfully played its role of agitator of the masses, it is no less true that it has not been able to expand its success to the point of creating a political coalition capable of holding a majority and governing. Even before the election, perhaps aware of the limitations of their approach, Jacques Duclos repeated the earlier declaration of Togliatti and affirmed that the French Communist party was ready to support any government which took the initiative towards a political program of "national independence," defined essentially as the denunciation of the Atlantic Pact, the end of the war in Viet-Nam, and the support of attempts to find a peaceful solution to the Korean conflict.

[20]For the complete program see *Humanité*, June 23, 1951.

XII

The French Communist Party
in the French Nation

How can a Frenchman be a Communist, many foreigners and even some Frenchmen wonder. These people see the Communist party only as a revolutionary organization in the pay of Moscow. The facts have demonstrated that many Frenchmen, coming from diverse social classes, are Communists or vote Communist for a variety of reasons. But this coalition of interests from which the Communist party cleverly profits is insufficient to explain the place that the party occupies in French life. Other questions remain to be answered: How can anyone belonging to the French intellectual tradition see in the Communist party the incarnation of the future of France? And how can Frenchmen with widely differing ideological beliefs place their hopes in the Communist party? How is it that one finds in the party, or in the marginal areas around the party, patriots at the side of internationalists, Christians alongside marxists, and, with the proletariat, many bourgeois, industrialists, doctors, students, professors, writers, artists, who stand to gain no material benefit from a Communist revolution?

Before concluding, we must examine the hopes and the myths that five million Frenchmen project into the French Communist party. We must be excused here for leaving the realm of pure description to refer to psychological data that are less verifiable than facts, and with regard to which personal evaluation inevitably plays a greater role.

THE PRESTIGE OF THE FRENCH COMMUNIST PARTY

One cannot reply to the questions that have just been posed without first referring back to the years of war and occupation which were, as we have seen, decisive for the expansion and growth of the party.

The military defeat and the Resistance shocked the consciences of many Frenchmen, especially the young people. A seventy-year-old republic had collapsed against a background of incompetence and treason. This resulted simultaneously in a profound disgust for the men and the regime responsible for this collapse and in an aspiration for something radically new, for a revolution. The Radical-Socialist and Socialist parties were compromised by their negligence in preparing for war; the parties of the right had furnished the foundations of the Vichy regime and numerous "collaborators." Only the Communist party, outlawed after September 1939, existed as an organized political force in the Resistance.

We have mentioned the courage which its militants showed at that time. But even more than from this personal valor, communism drew its strength from the confirmation which events seemed to give to its thesis. After having failed in its task, the bourgeoisie, the ruling élite of the country, rallied to the Vichy government; in the face of this class resignation, the "working class alone," in the words of the Catholic writer Mauriac, "remained faithful in its entirety to the cause of the profaned fatherland." This fact produced the sentiment that was most favorable to the spreading of communism, the belief that the bourgeoisie was condemned by history and was impotent to reassume the leadership of a country that it had lamentably abandoned, and that the working class, excluded from power but nonetheless faithful, was alone capable of giving France a future. The Communist party contained the most numerous and most dynamic elements of the working class. It appeared then as a strong, disciplined organization, supported by a powerful International and capable of leading the working class, at last, to something else than the bloody defeats that had marked its history since 1848.

France had just been conquered, and by a defeat so brutal that thinking Frenchmen suddenly realized the distance that separated the Jacobin myth of French power, entrusted with guiding humanity toward liberty, from reality. This resulted, especially among young people, in a serious crisis, one of the most obvious results of which was the vogue of existentialism. But this crisis led a much larger number of young people to communism, young people sickened by the decadence of a bourgeois country; convinced that the proletariat, a new force, bore the values of the future; and happy finally to have found in the ranks of the French Communist party a call to devotion and sacrifice and those opportunities for action that seemed to be disappearing in their humiliated country.

In the replies to a broad inquiry among youth on the "temptation of communism," initiated by the magazine *Esprit*,[1] one recognizes these psychological explanations of Communist prestige. We will cite only one of the published replies that clearly sums up most of the arguments presented in favor of the Communist party. It is that of a student at the Ecole Normale Supérieure and a former inmate of a concentration camp:

I think that I should sign up with the French Communist party:

1) because Marxism seems to me to explain in a satisfactory manner the present political situation;

2) because the ruling classes in France have arrived at the point where, in every sphere (political, economic, administrative, judicial, colonial) their interest is directly opposed to the national interest; because their policy, which is determined by fear and composed simultaneously of obstinacy, hesitation, and violence, is the most disastrous possible; and because revolutionary action is indispensable for eliminating these ruling classes;

3) because, amid the timidity of some and the bad faith of

[1] *Esprit*, 1946, nos. 2 and 4.

others, the Communist party alone has the power, the cohesion, the boldness, and the self-confidence necessary to conduct this revolutionary action.[2]

It appears undeniable that the will to survive and to be absorbed in a great collective project, which was exploited by European fascism, appeared at that time in France in the form of communism. If the Communist party profited from it to the extent of being the beneficiary of so much dormant energy and devotion, it was because historical circumstances made it possible at that one moment for the party to be the embodiment of the most diverse virtues. It was at one and the same time the party that had been right, the party that held the future in its hands, the party of patriotism, the party of internationalism, the party of the renaissance, and the party of youth. This was the moment when the Communist poet of the Resistance, Aragon, sang the merits of the party, in "La Diane française."

> Mon parti m'a rendu mes yeux et ma mémoire.
> Mon parti m'a rendu le sens de l'épopée.
> Mon parti m'a rendu les couleurs de la France.

Certainly the circumstances have changed, but one cannot understand the present strength of the Communist party if one does not take into consideration this extraordinary psychic "crystallization," which brought together more or less conscious aspirations that, logically, appear contradictory.

PROGRESSIVISM

This prestige extended well beyond the party itself. It was such that after the liberation not only did almost nobody dare to attack the Communist party, but many Frenchmen, especially those who came from the traditional left and the Christian Resistance movements, collaborated with the Communists in the National Front and in innumerable other organizations led or supported by the party. "A complex" was created "in which Communist party, peace, liberty, country, social justice are

[2]*Ibid.*, no. 2, p. 197.

closely associated and evoke one another reciprocally."[3] Writers, scholars, and artists, often among the greatest, such as Aragon, Eluard, Langevin, Joliot-Curie, and Picasso, gave an intellectual guarantee, so important in France, of the sincerity and importance of this curious complex. Carried away by the double seduction of legend and capability, a great many Frenchmen, particularly intellectuals, created around the Communist party the marginal zone of aid and sympathy that is called progressivism.

Intellectual Progressivism

In many ways this is a specifically French current that one may call revolutionary humanism, a legacy of the revolution of 1789 through the intermediaries of Michelet, Quinet, and Anatole France. This tendency, Jacobin, "forty-eightish," *Dreyfusarde*, sees in a revolution the climax of an immense popular drive for justice. This tendency was represented by writers like Martin-Chauffier, Vercors, Cassou, Friedmann, and Aveline, who in 1947 published a collective work entitled *L'Heure du choix*, in which, with reservations, they declared their support for the activities of the Communist party.

How could such a sentimental tendency, so essentially contrary to the implacable logic of thought and action of Marxism, have been able to unite with the ideology and practical action of communism? We see two reasons:

First, the history of France in the nineteenth century was marked by terrible class conflict in which the working class in 1830, 1848, 1871, and at the time of the Dreyfus affair was always found on the side of justice, progress, and human freedom. The class struggle in France has acquired the mythical aspect of a conflict of values in which the working class necessarily takes its position on the side of the Good. This sentimental Manichaeism thought it had found its theoretical expression in Marxism and, especially, its concrete expression in the Communist party, which claims simultaneously to defend the working class and to struggle for human progress.

[3] A. Rossi, *Physiologie du parti communiste français* (Paris, 1949), p. 381.

Second, the traditional parties of the left (Socialist and Radical-Socialist) were, after the liberation, stripped of their prestige and pushed toward the right The defense of the innocent and the oppressed, which was one of the most important factors in the success of these parties, was monopolized by the Communist party, which consequently acquired the most precious heritage of the French left. In addition, it happened that the policy followed by the Third Force governments furnished the Communists with numerous opportunities to rally to their support individuals belonging to the Christian or Socialist left: for example, the use of torture and the military excesses in the colonies and in Indo-China.

A certain number of Christians have also given their support, more or less conditionally, to the party. Many of them are in the Union of Progressive Christians, which does not include more than a thousand members, both intellectuals and workers, but which influences quite a broad sector of French Catholicism. For them also the cause of social justice cannot be separated from the rise of the proletariat and from its struggle for a better life.

If the influence of the Communist party is particularly strong among many left-wing intellectuals, it is because intellectuals are more sensitive than others to the prestige of a doctrine that allies rigorous orthodoxy with concern for effectiveness, and thus satisfies the two basic nostalgias of intellectuals. "An aspiration toward orthodoxy is projected on a real and vital phenomenon that is a doctrine, a church, and an army all combined. This phenomenon possesses the attraction of completeness and of unity."[4]

True, one can be astonished with Raymond Aron that "the merits of the Communist solution are in exact contrast with the ideologies that lead the western intelligentsia toward it,"[5] but this paradox disappears if one considers, on one hand, the old tradition which carries so many French intellectuals toward a sentimental and quasi-mystical "left" and, on the other hand, their present ardent desire, which appears contradictory but

[4]Jules Monnerot, *Sociologie du communisme* (Paris, 1949), p. 274.
[5]Raymond Aron, *Le Grand Schisme* (Paris, 1948), p. 150.

which is actually complementary, for effective action. In the influence of the party on the intellectuals we again find the ambiguity that we observed in the influence of the party on the electoral body: the Communist party represents simultaneously the "tough" revolutionary party of the proletariat and the party of progress and social justice.

Political Progressivism

Progressivism, as it has been described by André Mandouze, one of the leaders of the Christian progressives, "is something that in its dimensions exceeds the numerical limits of the Communist parties, and in its content is not subject to all the prejudices of Marxist doctrine."[6] This progressivism constitutes for the party an "aura" from which it gains prestige and, at the same time, a reserve on which it can draw and which it can maneuver.

An editor of *Le Monde,* stressing Mandouze's comment, wrote:

The number of members of the General Confederation of Labor, like the number of Communist voters, is many times greater than the party's membership. In the same way, a progressive fringe has now detached itself from every party, for example, the Unitary Socialist party, the Radicals of the Left, the Progressive Christians, and others. These organizations of varying importance exercise on the movements from which they came an influence that it would be a mistake to underestimate.

These diverse progressive fringe groups are generally very small. The Unitary Socialist party, which detached itself from the Socialist party, does not have more than 2,000 members. The Progressive Union, which includes eight deputies, is only a parliamentary group, without roots in the nation. However, these groups possess a daily paper in Paris *(Libération),* a review *(Les Cahiers internationaux du travail),* and, above all, some politicians such as Pierre Cot and intellectuals such as Paul Rivet whose prestige is great. While these organizations are numerically of little importance, they are extremely active and constitute cores of influence that must not be underestimated. Around them one

[6]*Les Chrétiens et la politique* (Paris, 1948), pp. 61–62.

day the latent progressivism of the non-Communist masses could crystallize, and this possibility is by far the most important element of progressivism. Actually, the Socialist party's abandonment of its class position, its collaboration with the center and right in the government, and its attitude in the strikes and on the colonial question have made of it, in the eyes of many Frenchmen, a sort of new Radical-Socialist party. This evolution removed the party from a whole sector of the left that the Communist party is trying to occupy. Nevertheless, in spite of the electoral benefits that the party has derived from this situation, the Communists have not succeeded in creating on their right a progressive party capable of supporting them and confirming their campaign propaganda.

THE ISOLATION OF THE FRENCH COMMUNIST PARTY

In fact, in spite of the existence of the phenomenon of progressivism, the isolation of the party has continually increased since 1944. Shortly after the liberation the party, for its profit, sought to unite the Resistance movements. This attempt failed. The year 1945 saw unity of action with the Socialist party. But this did not last long, and a majority of the Socialist leaders have become, since 1946, the bitterest adversaries of the Communists. Today the Communist party seeks, by depending upon the progressive fringes that have come from socialism, radicalism, and Christian democracy, to establish a union capable of giving substance to the slogan "government of democratic union." But here also, the defeat is certain: this progressive union has not been realized.

The political isolation of the party is thus an accomplished fact. During the life of the first National Assembly, on almost all votes of major political importance the 184 votes of the Communists and their allies have been found alone in opposition. Occasionally, on some subjects, a small number of M.R.P. deputies voted with the Communists. Likewise in administration, the party has progressively lost the greater part of the key positions it occupied when it participated in the government. In contrast, in the country the party is making contact with large masses of people through trade union activity and the so-called defense of peace. But these masses do not appear to be ready to support all the objectives of the Communist party and to consummate these partial unions in common political action.

In spite of the fact that it is the party's tactical objective, the realization of this broad union is impossible for several reasons: political struggles have tarnished the prestige with which it gleamed in 1944; the Machiavellianism and sectarianism of certain Communist militants have disgusted a great many non-Communists who have quit the common organizations, tired of being perpetually exploited without being in a position of responsibility. But the principal cause is essentially the new policy initiated by Zhdanov in September 1947 at the conference of the nine Western European Communist parties.

On the one hand, the new exigencies of a ruthless struggle have eliminated many of the timid and the hesitant; the defeat of the great strikes in the autumn of 1947 was, from this point of view, decisive. At the same time, the party has appeared less and less tolerant; nonconformist opinions have been condemned and harsh prosecution has been opened against all intellectuals and artists guilty of making concessions to liberalism or of friendliness toward America. Several Communist intellectuals have been forced to self-criticism. Others have redoubled their "vigilance." A review, *La Nouvelle critique,* founded in 1948, specializes in denouncing everyone who does not submit to the most absolute conformity. The result of this has been a sort of intellectual emaciation of Communist publications, which are becoming incapable of attracting the interest of non-Communists; and most of the intellectuals who were at first sympathetic have left the Communist zones of influence.

But this new policy again throws the spotlight on the subjection of the French Communist party to the Soviet Union, a subjection that the dissolution of the Comintern in 1943 seemed to have transformed into voluntary co-operation. In the summer of 1947 it became apparent that the French party determines its policies according to the requirements of Soviet policy; Zhdanov's report and the formation of the Cominform reinforced this impression. At the same time, the "people's democracies" began to eliminate the allied Socialists and then the Communist chiefs who were connected with national Resistance movements. From then on the myth of a French Communist party achieving the union of the popular masses for a revolution simultaneously proletarian and patriotic, in the tradition of the French revolutions, was eclipsed by the dictatorial and police state reality of the East.

Anticommunism, compromised by Hitlerite and Vichyite propaganda, found this situation a useful weapon and regained its vigor. In the course of the last four years, the tone of the press, of parliament, and of the salons has been radically transformed, and the vogue of communism has been succeeded by anti-Sovietism. This anti-Sovietism, however, is confronted by obstacles and above all by the belief possessed by a majority of French Communists that their country is strong enough to prevent a Communist revolution from resulting in France's subjugation to the U.S.S.R., and that it possesses so firm a humanist tradition that it would be impossible to implant in it the police methods of the East. The Communists to whom one points out the present situation in the "people's democracies" almost invariably reply: "Our country is very different, and things would work out much better among us."

If the Communist militants as a whole have not been affected by this growing subjection to the U.S.S.R.[7] and remain impervious to anti-Soviet propaganda, numerous sympathizers have, on the other hand, been troubled by the systematic eulogy of life in the U.S.S.R. and the continual dithyrambs addressed to Marshal Stalin. These sympathizers are today seeking methods of distinguishing themselves from the party sufficiently so as not to appear as lusterless satellites.

Since 1947 the position of the Communist party in the French nation has changed greatly. The party has lost prestige. It has

---

[7]The sentimental formulation of this subjection is: "Fidelity to the Soviet Union is the touchstone of proletarian internationalism."

not succeeded in establishing the progressive union that is the condition of its success. Today it is clashing with a reinforced anticommunism that unites against it all the other political parties. Yet this anticommunism that blocks and isolates the party is at the same time an element of its strength. In effect, this anti-Communist feeling divides France between communism, which appears as the opposition, and anticommunism, which, by a sort of internal logic, moves progressively toward the right. The dialectic of communism and anticommunism makes impossible the existence of a non-Communist left which will not be either absorbed by the Communist party or forced toward the right. This dialectic has greatly facilitated the Communist party's effort to monopolize the forces of the left.

XIII

Conclusion

THE French Communist party seems to have achieved its greatest success in 1947, when it could boast of a million members and of the support of nearly 30 per cent of the electors. Since then it has been isolated and it has lost members. This decline is not, however, as considerable as the circumstances and the history of the party would lead one to expect.

What are the reasons for the fact that the Communist party has been able to "limit the damage"? Some of these apply to the party itself, which emerged from the Resistance rejuvenated and consolidated. Thorez has listed them as follows:

1) A clear and precise program which responds to the needs of the era and to the generous democratic traditions of the French people;

2) The organization of the party, the atmosphere that prevails within it, its magnificent optimism and its confidence, the virile fraternity that unites all its members, their devotion to the cause, the seriousness and the dignity of their lives, the quality of its leaders, both old and young, Marcel Cachin, Jacques Duclos, André Marty, and so many others;

3) The concrete achievements of the Communist party wherever it has been able to display its creative activity and exercise its authority, notably in the administration of Communist municipalities;

4) The clairvoyance of the party in the prewar years, its incessant struggle against the so-called "nonintervention" policy, against the Munich betrayal, against the activities of the fifth column, which opened the way to war and to Hitlerism;

147

5) The exemplary attitude of the party in the war against the German invader and against the traitors of Vichy; the courage, the abnegation, of its militants, who sacrificed themselves by the tens of thousands for the salvation of the fatherland and for the triumph of their Communist ideal.[1]

To these reasons Thorez added one more: the integrity of Communists elected to office.

It is certain that the organization of the party, the devotion of its militants and its chiefs, its sense of the concrete, its reputation for historical infallibility, and its attitude in the Resistance have weighed and continue to weigh in its favor.

The second cause of Communist success lies in that ambiguity that we have found at each point in our analysis: the party simultaneously presents itself as a new party, a Marxist party of the dictatorship of the proletariat, and as the heir to the old French left. On the electoral level it thus gains the votes of a large part of the working class and, at the same time, the votes of all those who, attached to the leftist tradition, give their votes to the only party that appears really revolutionary. The prestige of the Communist party rests on the same ambiguity, especially with respect to the intellectuals who have committed themselves to it either out of revolutionary romanticism or out of an appreciation of the potentiality of the proletariat. Raymond Aron has analyzed well the psychological bases of Communist influence:

Communism in France is nourished above all by a double conviction: that of the working masses who, faithful to Marxist ideology, identify the power of the party with their victory; that of the idealists who continue to interpret Stalinist despotism as a stage in the liberation of humanity. At the same time, all those who despair of France and dream of participating in a greater destiny, all those who are tired of the weakness and inaction of the democracies, move toward the party that puts devotion and energy at the service of European unity, if not of world unity.[2]

The French tradition, as we have said, facilitates the junction of these two elements. It happens, however, that the demands of

[1]*Fils du peuple* (Paris, 1949), pp. 249–250.
[2]*Le Grand Schisme* (Paris, 1948), p. 252.

Soviet policy dissolve this unstable compound; at such times the Communist party tends to become again the Bolshevik party, specifically proletarian, that it was at its origin: this was the case in 1939. But at other moments, when international circumstances are altered, the party, profiting from all the advantages which we have analyzed and which are due to its own organization and the peculiar characteristics of the French scene, becomes the great party to which different classes confide their interests and in which a large number of citizens place their hopes for their country. The French Communist party is a complex reality which succeeded in allying a foreign method and a foreign ideology with the French mentality, and its wide and diverse recruitment gives the party an incontestably French substance. The Communist party is like an accordion that contracts when it plays a Russian air and expands when it plays a French one.

Certainly the Communist party has, since 1947, entered a period of contraction, although not quite so great as that of 1939. It is politically isolated. The membership itself is diminished. It seems, on the basis of apparently reliable information, which is, however, difficult to verify, that expulsions and resignations have multiplied since the beginning of 1949. The Federation of the Seine is supposed to have lost 9,000 members, of whom 1,500 were expelled. Some cells are supposed to have refused to meet for the purpose of approving the trial of Rajk. Without overemphasizing these accounts, one must regard them as straws in the wind. The French Communist party has reached a crisis, especially since the campaign against Tito redoubled in violence and since Rajk was condemned in Budapest. While the brutality of Communist methods in eastern Europe still appears to trouble but few of the mass of Communist militants, some progressive writers have publicly expressed their disapproval,[3] and a certain number of Communist intellectuals (students in particular) are beginning

[3]Almost all of these progressive writers whom the Communists call "fellow travelers" have disapproved of the methods employed in the Budapest trial and in the struggle against Tito. See especially the declarations of Vercors and Jean Cassou in *Esprit*, 1949, no. 12.

to hesitate and even to leave the party. In fact, leaving aside the employment of methods that are repugnant to the French mentality, the Soviet attitude toward Tito poses directly the central problem of the French Communist party. French Communists feel more or less consciously that their obedience to Russia constitutes the greatest obstacle to their success; they feel that their advent to power in a country whose national consciousness is the oldest in history would put them in the same situation as Tito in Yugoslavia. While a national communism of the Titoist type would assure the French party of great success, this development can hardly take place within the French Communist party so long as the cold war continues.

The present policy of the U.S.S.R. can only accentuate the decline of the French Communist party. This decline, however, will not go very far and will leave the party well above its prewar position. The basic strength of the party results from the situation of a France that two wars have morally and materially exhausted. On the material level, the burdens of these wars are not being shared equally. The purchasing power of the workers has diminished in relation to 1939, while others have been enriched. Often badly paid and badly housed, French workers do not even have the consolation of feeling that they are making sacrifices for their future. The present system, even if they accommodate themselves to it, does not in their eyes contain the least promise of improvement. We allude here to that inarticulate despair that is the fundamental psychic element of the European crisis. Europeans have seen the agony of capitalism as a result of wars, fascism, and concentration camps. This regime appears to them to be condemned, and they expect nothing good to come from its artificial resurrection. This is why the Marshall Plan, of itself, has aroused so little enthusiasm among the European masses. In contrast, communism profits greatly from this feeling that European capitalism is doomed, a feeling that leads non-Communists to a sort of inertia. Only a profound structural change can restore hope and confidence to European workers. Until such time the Communist party holds a monopoly of revolutionary expectations. Without this structural change, without a revival of European hope which can find outside of communism its objectives and the will to realize them, the French Communist party will continue, with its ups and downs, to be a powerful force, because it is intrinsically and, so to speak, physiologically connected with the European crisis, the crisis whose symptoms France, as always, displays most violently.

Part III by Aldo Garosci

THE ITALIAN COMMUNIST PARTY

>>>>>>>>>>>>>>>>>>>> * <<<<<<<<<<<<<<<<<<<<<

XIV

Italian Communism between the Two World Wars

THE Italian Communist party is, or at least was at the moment of the Cominform's foundation, the largest Communist party in Europe as far as membership is concerned. It is, therefore, one of the most important organizations through which international communism acts. Certainly, with the French Communist party, it is the most important outside the "iron curtain." Up to 1947 it held key positions in several ministries and furnished Italy with ambassadors and functionaries; until 1951, it ruled, with Communist mayors, several of Italy's largest cities, notably Turin, Genoa, Venice, Bologna, and Florence. It directs the policy and controls a majority of the members of the largest and most active labor organization, the Italian General Confederation of Labor. It has an active and widely read press as well as its own publishing houses.

Yet this party had no legal existence during the long years from 1926 to 1943. In the six years between its founding and dissolution (January 1921 to October 1926), it suffered from all kinds of legal as well as illegal persecutions, ending with the enforced emigration of many of its leaders. Also during this period its membership never rose above 50,000 while its influence within the labor movement, though substantial, was not a determining one, since it was never able to assume control of the most powerful labor organization, the General Confederation of Labor, then in Socialist hands.

Thus, the Italian Communist party of today is not the outcome of a long political struggle in a democratic state as are, in varying degrees, the Communist parties of France, Germany, and Czechoslovakia, but of a long period of underground battle against Fascist dictatorship. This has had a decisive effect upon the development of both the negative and the positive characteristics of the party, which had to form and reform its ranks in the underground. The early combative posture into which the Italian Communist party was pushed by fascism made acceptance of its rigid structure a spontaneous and natural process. Finally, the great turning points of international communism (the rise of Hitler, the Moscow trials, the Hitler-Stalin agreement of 1939), which elsewhere had immense repercussions and produced deep crises within the various national parties, affected only a few individual members in Italy.

FROM THE FOUNDING OF THE PARTY TO THE FASCIST REPRESSION, JANUARY 1921 TO NOVEMBER 1926

Founding of the Party

The Italian Communist party was formally established at the congress of Leghorn (January 21, 1921) when a minority decided to split from the Socialist party and form a new party. This was the outcome of a movement which had started within the ranks of Italian Socialists during the war and had reached great proportions after the Russian revolution and in the postwar period.

The Italian Socialist party, unlike its French and German counterparts, had not been in favor of Italy's entrance into World War I but had assumed a neutralist position. This was due to the fact that the Italian working masses had made their entrance on the political scene only since 1900 as a result of the work of moderate leaders of socialism such as Turati, Treves, Bissolati, and Prampolini. This made them reluctant to subscribe to international policies in the formulation of which they had not participated. Further, Italian intervention in the war had not appeared linked to immediate national interests, as it had in

France, Belgium, or Germany, and had come about under the pressure of minorities of the right and of the crown, rather than through the free decision of parliament. Even Giolitti, the greatest statesman Italy had had from 1900 to 1914, was against the war, as were the masses and the Catholic hierarchy.

The slogan "neither acceptance nor sabotage," coined by Costantino Lazzari to define the Socialist position during the war, was susceptible of various interpretations. A group resolutely against the war and insistent upon putting an end to it in revolutionary fashion soon developed within the Socialist party. This group found a response even among party leaders, and high-ranking Italian Socialists who did not subsequently join the Communist party did attend the meetings held in Switzerland at Zimmerwald (1915) and Kienthal (1916), at which Lenin and other extreme pacifists were present. At these meetings very firm positions against the war were taken, and reaffirmation was given to the principle, common to all Socialists of all countries before the war, that international solidarity among workers should be considered more important than the national bond among citizens.

On December 30, 1917, orders sent out by Lazzari, secretary of the Socialist party, read: "All should follow with confidence the developments in Russia where, thanks to our comrades, peace and socialism are being achieved." The fifteenth congress of the Socialist party was held in September 1918 in an atmosphere of high revolutionary hopes and sympathy for Russia, and, when the Third International was founded in Moscow in March 1919, the Italian Socialist party was the first to join. Thus, it was as a member of that organization that the Socialist party held its next congress in Bologna in 1919 and won 156 seats in the Chamber at the general elections of the following month.

Nevertheless, currents directly opposed to communism still controlled the party. The bulk of the party supported the Russian revolution in a sentimental fashion and, taking hope from the increasing agitation throughout the country, looked to the day when a collectivistic regime controlled by workers and peasants would replace the bourgeois liberal state. At the same time, the majority, including men such as G. M. Serrati, the editor of *Avanti!,* Costantino Lazzari, and Adelchi Baratono, also preserved the sentimental and apocalyptic frame of mind of the old socialism and opposed the introduction of the military discipline advocated by the revolutionary wing. On the party's right, respected for services rendered to the working classes in the past, a group of leaders including Turati, Treves, and Modigliani called for democratic methods.

But the resolute group headed by Amedeo Bordiga of Naples was already emerging, preaching the necessity of abstention from all parliamentary activity in order to concentrate the party's forces on organizing the workers in "soviets" and in revolutionary military formations. No less important was the Turin group led by Gramsci, Terracini, Tasca, and Togliatti. In 1919 it started a weekly, *Ordine nuovo,* which was to become the most important organ of Italian communism. It drew its inspiration from the experiment of worker's councils set up in the large factories of industrialized Piedmont not for the purpose of dealing with such old-fashioned issues as wages and conditions of work, but for the purpose of gaining control over the management of the factories. Thus, the group came to dream of founding a party leading to the creation of a new state and of a new civilization. It emerged from an environment that had traditionally stressed order and technology, and its aim was to get rid of the sentimental, humanitarian, and vaguely romantic elements of earlier socialism.

The old Socialist leader Costantino Lazzari confessed at the Leghorn congress of January 1922 that he could not find in the *Ordine nuovo* the words "brotherhood" and "humanity." What he found instead was an almost "protestant" emphasis upon the responsibility and seriousness of labor's task in creating the new civilization and upon the need of assimilating the better intellectual abilities of the new generation.

The strikes of the postwar years reached their climax in September 1920 with the workers' seizure of the factories. This was accomplished not by the Socialist party or the Confederation of Labor but by the young revolutionary workers grown to maturity during the war and supported by the intellectuals of the *Ordine nuovo*. Here, in the first issue of the journal as a daily, on May 1, 1921, Gramsci called for a state based upon workers' councils in which the "working class would be organized as a productive class and in which a spontaneous and free flowering of worthy and capable individual energies would be possible."

Bordiga and the *Soviet* in Naples, Gramsci and the *Ordine nuovo* in Turin, Giuseppe Tuntar and the *Lavoratore* in Trieste — these were the groups that pushed toward the break with the old Socialist party. To give full effect to the break and to take with them the masses who still believed in the possibility of a workers' and peasants' revolution, Russian style, in Italy, they had to place themselves within the fold of the Third International. To have a reason for the break, they had to adopt the Twenty-One Conditions that the second congress of the International had laid down for its member parties. One of the principal conditions was that parties belonging to the International must expel those who had been labeled "reformists." In Italy this meant having to reject leaders who were not only still respected and loved by the masses but who were still in control of the main labor unions. Another burdensome condition was that requiring the abandonment of the old and glorious name Socialist party in favor of the new one of Communist party.

The Italian delegation to the second congress of the Third International, made up of Graziadei, Bombacci, Serrati, and Bordiga (three of whom were to join the Communist party at the Leghorn congress), had accepted the Twenty-One Conditions and assumed the additional task of submitting them to the Socialist party convention. In a preconvention meeting of the Communist group at Imola, Bordiga's intransigent motion prevailed and the Communists decided that either the party would eliminate the "reformists" or they would form a new party of their own.

The seventeenth congress of the Socialist party met at Leghorn on January 15, 1921. Upholding the Communist position for expulsion of the reformists were Graziadei, Terracini, Bordiga, Bombacci, and Gennari. The right, led by Turati, held out for freedom of interpretation of the International's directives. The center, led by Serrati, who was to accept the Moscow conditions two years later, opposed the expulsion of the right. Kabakchev, Bulgarian representative of the International, read a message from that organization, signed by Zinoviev, Lenin, Bela Kun, and Bukharin, categorically declaring that, even "before knowing what will be the majority opinion at your congress, [we declare that] those who refuse to accept the separation from the reformists violate an essential order of the Communist International and, by that alone, place themselves outside of it." The message closed with an open call to secession: "The Italian Communist party must, one way or another, be created. Of this we have no doubt. To this party will go the sympathies of proletarians throughout the world and the warm support of the Communist International. Down with reformism! Long live the true Italian Communist Party."

In the final voting, the majority remained with the so-called Serrati "unitarians," who obtained 98,000 votes. The Communists won 57,000 votes, and the reformists had only 14,000. Immediately after the voting, Bordiga read the declaration of secession: "The unitary group, which has the majority, is now placed outside the Third International. Delegates who voted for the Communist motion will leave the hall, meeting at eleven o'clock at the San Marco Theater."

The causes for the schism were many and deep, and Italian communism had native roots. Nevertheless, the Italian Communist party was born through the direct intervention of the Communist International, which was already dominated by the overpowering weight of the effective power and "myth" of the Russian revolution. The party has preserved throughout its history this double nature of representative of certain historical traditions of the Italian working class and of agent of Soviet communism.

The Fascist Offensive and the Communist Struggle
against the Socialist Party

The Communist party was partly the product of resentment against reformist leaders who had not permitted a revolution. From this point of view it was born too late, for it appeared at a time when, in both Italy and the rest of Western Europe, the revolutionary tide was ebbing, retreating before fascism, which challenged not only the revolution but also the legitimate and recognized workers' institutions. Therefore, the first few years saw the party use its energies in a twofold struggle, on the one hand to win control of the workers and their organizations from the Socialists, on the other hand to protect itself against the assaults of fascism.

Fascism thrived upon the offense done to patriotic sentiments by the "neutralism" of the Socialist masses. It found support among the displaced war veterans, who had acquired a lust for power, blood, and reckless living, and among the great landowners and those northern peasants whose Socialist organizations left them still unsatisfied. Asking for and, to a large extent, receiving the support of the Italian judiciary, bureaucracy, and police, fascism began its campaign to destroy the "red citadels." By isolating the large cities and successively concentrating its forces on the many smaller provincial cities, it succeeded in destroying union headquarters in each of them and in forcing the better-known anti-Fascist leaders to leave town. The anti-Fascists were forced to resort to strikes, and in more than one region, particularly toward the end of the drama in the summer of 1922, the Fascists met with armed resistance from part of the population, including Communist groups. But the conditions for such resistance were extremely difficult, given the government's complicity with fascism.

The leaders of the Communist party did not fully recognize the Fascist menace. They thought of themselves as an army, but their attention was focused upon the ultimate conquest of the capitalistic system rather than upon mere defense from an immediate danger. Therefore, the Communist party had its most difficult moments and its greatest defeats in its early days. Its deputies decreased from eighteen to thirteen in the elections of May 1921. At the congress held in July 1922, the General Confederation of Labor remained in the hands of the reformists. Bordiga's attempt to create a military organization, the *arditi del popolo,* was abandoned when he discovered Masonic influences within the ranks. In April 1921 the Chamber of Labor of Turin, a center of revolutionary action, was burned; it went up in flames again immediately after the march on Rome. In the summer of 1922 the workers' strongholds were crushed, one by one, by Fascist "punitive" expeditions.

At this time the contradictions in the Communist position appeared greatest. On July 2, 1922, the party affirmed that "it is impossible to put an end to the slave regime imposing itself upon the greater part of the Italian masses" by relying upon a new "government ready to use the official forces of the state in the legal repression of fascism"; and so it called a "national general strike." It favored a "Workers' Front," which included labor leaders of every political opinion. But when every battle ended in defeat, the Communists would accuse their allies of treachery.

These tactics followed the "theses" approved at the party's second congress held in Rome in March 1922. Thesis thirty-five discredited the efforts of all non-Communist left parties to join in the resistance to fascism: "The Communist party will ask the workers to accept help from the left as an experiment, which will be described by party propaganda in pessimistic terms." Thesis thirty-eight discounted an anti-Fascist coalition government: "Another hypothesis is that the government will invite the proletariat to participate in an armed struggle against the assault of the right. This invitation can only be a trap.... In consequence, no 'loyalty' should be proclaimed or practiced in respect to such a government."

The Communists' attitude toward the democratic state, now threatened by the Fascists, was therefore one of extreme contempt, further contributing to the party's isolation. When the Fascist deputy Giunta pulled out a gun in the Chamber of Deputies,

Ordine nuovo of August 11 wrote, "It is a pity, Giunta, that you did not fire!... We have the honor to inform you that we think even less than you do of parliamentary rights and guarantees. and in seeing them torn to bits we have even more to gain than you." The Fascist attack upon the state, if successful, meant outlawing the Communist party. A circular letter of the Executive Committee on October 11 and a report made the same month by Togliatti to the fourth congress of the International give a clear indication of what was expected in this connection. Nevertheless, until the *coup d'état,* the party's high command continued publicly to describe fascism as not unlike the liberal regime.

On October 25, commenting upon the Fascist rally at Naples which was the prelude to the march on Rome, *Ordine nuovo* called it a comical incident, "the glories of Piedigrotta renewed by fascism." On October 28, with the mobilization of Fascist squads already under way, the paper hinted that "the proletariat cannot side with any of the bourgeois groups struggling for power." The following day an official proclamation of the party confirmed these policies: "In the present conflict... [the workers] cannot side with the so-called constitutional government, since it has shown its total incapacity, nor can they hope that the Fascist dictatorship, because it is the fruit of insurrection, will be able to carry out beneficial reforms for the proletarian and even the middle classes." Within twenty-four hours the paper which had printed these lines was destroyed along with all other legal organs of the party. But a later comment on the march on Rome made by Terracini in *Internazionale comunista* showed that the Communist party had not changed its position: the *coup* had simply been a cabinet change without importance to the revolutionary working class.

Later events led the Communist party to become more anti-Fascist, despite the tactical errors it had committed and despite its determination not to recognize the real meaning of the Fascist-democratic conflict. In the first place, while Communist resistance against fascism was weak and uncertain, communism was the only movement, apart from the small Republican party, which had an organization in which it put its trust rather than in legal institutions and guarantees. A circular letter of the Executive Committee dated October 11, 1922, listed all necessary measures for underground activities in the anticipation of a *coup d'état*. Continuity of party organization was to be assured; newspapers would continue to be sent even to those who, because of intimidation, returned them. "Apart from possible ordinary disciplinary measures," concluded the letter, "you are warned that every official announcement of the dissolution of party organs simply means that those organs are to continue to function illegally." In following this program, the Communist party was the first and for many years the only political party in Italy to adopt the idea that political life might continue underground.

The shift to underground action helped to heal the beginnings of a disagreement, already clearly revealed, with the International on questions of strategy, organization, and tactics. At the end of June 1921, the Communist International held its third congress, at Moscow, and new principles of even greater centralization were sanctioned: absolute obedience on the part of national groups was demanded, public discussion of decisions of both the executive bodies and congresses was proscribed. With respect to tactics, previous defeats suffered in Italy and throughout Europe forced Russia to adopt the policy of "united fronts" with Socialist parties, in the hope of strengthening the international position of the Soviet Union. In keeping with the position taken by Bordiga, the representative of the Italian party, Terracini, spoke against such a policy. Confronted by Lenin's firm stand, however, he yielded.

This congress of the International had also renewed its request to the Italian Socialist party to submit to the Twenty-One Conditions. Maffi, Riboldi, and Lazzari, Socialist delegates at the congress, accepted the task of advocating submission at the eighteenth congress of the Socialist party (October 8–12, 1921) and lost. But opinion in favor of ousting the reformists and conducting new discussions with the Communists prevailed at the next congress held in Rome on October 3, 1922, when, by a narrow majority, the right was expelled. A joint committee composed equally of Socialist and Communist representatives was immediately formed under the auspices of the Third International. Even though the Communist party of Italy[1] had submitted to the International, the arguments of Bordiga and others in favor of the substantial independence of the party within the framework of the International had prevailed at the second party congress in March 1922. The united-front idea was acceptable only within economic bodies: "Communists," they said, "while participating in the fight in economic associations directed by Socialists, syndicalists, or anarchists, will not refuse to follow their policies... but will show that at a certain point in their development such policies become impotent or utopian because of the incorrect methods chosen by the leaders."

The march on Rome was followed by systematic violence. In March 1923, 10,000 Communists were arrested. With the discovery of the Executive Committee's underground headquarters, its leaders, Bordiga, Tasca, Grieco, and Gramsci, were brought to trial. Since constitutional guarantees had not yet been suppressed, the trial was held before ordinary courts and the accused were acquitted on grounds of insufficient evidence.

The Communist Party in Semilegality

Once in power fascism did not suppress all democratic freedoms immediately. It continued the use of violence and transformed its black-shirted squads into a "voluntary militia for national security." It sought to secure for itself an absolute majority in the Chamber through a new electoral law. (This law gave two-thirds of the seats to the party receiving the highest number of votes; the remaining one-third was to be distributed proportionally among the other parties.) But freedom of the press, although greatly circumscribed through intimidation, still existed. In fact, *Unità*, directed by Antonio Gramsci, was able to make its first appearance in 1924.

[1] Such was its official title then. It was changed to Italian Communist party only at the fifth congress, after World War II.

The discussions held at Moscow under the pressure of the Communist International between the Italian Socialist and Communist delegates reached a conclusion favorable to the Communists with the formulation of the Fourteen Points published on January 18, 1923, in *Avanti!* But at the Socialist congress held in Milan in April 1923, Pietro Nenni succeeded in preventing the liquidation of the Socialist party. Some pro-Communist Socialists nevertheless deserted the party, and, thanks to this new gain and to public reaction against Fascist violence, the number of Communist deputies increased after the elections of April 6, 1924, from thirteen to eighteen, while votes were obtained for the first time in southern districts like Bari, Naples, and Palermo.

In June 1924 the Fascist party suffered a serious setback as a result of the nationwide reaction against the murder of the Socialist deputy Giacomo Matteotti. Traditional freedoms were effectively reasserted for the next six months. During this period the so-called "Aventine" came into being, when the opposition deputies, with the exception of the liberals, decided to leave the Chamber of Deputies and not to return until the Fascist government, responsible for the Matteotti crime, had resigned. But the hoped-for intervention of the king did not materialize. With 1925, fascism definitely entered its totalitarian phase.

The Communist party belonged to the "Aventine" but, refusing to look for the re-establishment of constitutional government through the action of the king, it advocated a policy of revolutionary opposition and the creation of a "republican assembly based on workers' and peasants' committees." Actually, this was simply a piece of propaganda rather than a goal sought through the tactical compromises which real aims usually require, and the party's policies at this time did not reveal any desire to move the masses to aggressive action. But the subsequent disintegration of the "Aventine" seemed once more to prove the validity of the party's more extreme position.

Meanwhile, a great transformation was taking place in the party's leadership and machinery. The organizational principles laid down earlier by the International for the "bolshevization of the party" (as a result of which the old section, in which all members of a given locality met, was replaced by the cell formed at the place of work) were being accepted by the Italian as well as by other Communist parties. In their early years, the French, Italian, and German Communist parties had not succeeded in supplanting reformist leaders in the unions; the cell was designed to permit Communist penetration into workers' organizations. In addition, the cell system was well suited to the times and was almost a necessity during the underground struggle. From 1925 on it was adopted without resistance and remained, with modifications, the typical Communist organization even after the recovery of democratic freedoms.

The cell system, unlike that of the section, prevents the formation of widespread factions within the party and entrusts the supervision of practically the entire organization to the hierarchy responsible for party policy. Discussions arising within cells are "discussions of work," of enforcement of orders. A division within a cell can easily be eliminated before it becomes widespread.

With this change went the liquidation of Bordiga's supporters and the rise of the Piedmontese group of *Ordine nuovo* to a commanding position. After the collapse of the "Aventine," the Communist deputies re-entered the Chamber, where they engaged in verbal battles with the Fascist majority. Their leader, Antonio Gramsci, declared during a discussion of the law on Fascist youth organizations that such organizations would one day be seized and employed for different reasons through the creation of a proletarian youth movement.

Now secretary of the party, Gramsci gave to it his own peculiar imprint. He was the principal author of the document known as the Lyons Theses. This was a motion approved in January 1926 at the Lyons congress, which was held in France in order to escape Italian police action. In it all traces of Bordiga's influence were once and for all eliminated.

According to the Lyons Theses, the party must not "abstain from supporting and joining in partial actions" even though it was convinced that in a capitalistic system such actions would not better workers' conditions in a "serious and lasting fashion." In particular, "the vindication of liberty offers the best ground for agitations and struggles having limited goals" and conducted in the name of the "workers' and peasants' government." The Lyons declaration warned, however, that this did not represent an "actual stage of development in the struggle for power," given the impossibility of "resolving the problem of the state in the interests of the working class in any form other than that of a dictatorship of the proletariat."

On November 9, 1926, the Communist deputies, with the other deputies of the "Aventine," were declared relieved of their parliamentary mandate. Between August and November of that year most of the party's Executive Committee, including Gramsci, Terracini, Roveda, and Scoccimarro, were arrested. Tried two years later, in May 1929, they were sentenced to terms in jail averaging twenty-three years. Almost all survived fascism, but Gramsci himself, broken by the long and painful ordeal of imprisonment, died in Rome on April 27, 1937.

The intellectual and moral strength of Gramsci, the significant role he plays in the drama of Italian communism, and his attempt to give a broader ideological foundation to communism, make him worthy of more than passing notice. Born of a poor Sardinian family, Antonio Gramsci migrated to Turin in 1915, where he later received a doctoral degree in letters. In Turin he saw the development of the revolutionary movement of the workers in the great industries of that city. He sought to give this movement the sweep of a great Italian moral, material, and intellectual revolution. Led to reinterpret Marxism in the light of postwar experience and of Italian historicist philosophy, he tried to be, at the same time, the political, moral, and intellectual creator of the bases of a new society. In politics, his works contain, besides the usual motifs of the proletarian revolution, his own original criticism of Italian society, condemned by him as weak and antiquated. In the "hundred cities" of Italy, haven of a "coupon-clipping" bourgeoisie, he saw the dead hand of a parasitic past. In the church he saw both a strong institution to be used as a model of the way in which intellectual agreement is organized and the symbol of all reaction. As for Italian intellectuals with their "disinterested" attitude, he saw them as a class no longer responsive to the needs of the people and the nation.

While rejecting the positivistic interpretations of Marxism and the simple-minded approach of those who wanted to change only the economic understructure without fathoming the complexity of the political and moral problems, Gramsci's social concepts remained tied to the view that the problem of understanding the world does not exist. There is merely the problem of changing it or of understanding only as much of it as is necessary to bring about the desired changes. He therefore called Lenin the greatest contemporary philosopher. This equal emphasis on revolutionary needs, with their elements of tyranny, and on intellectual life, with its requirements of criticism and of freedom, makes Gramsci a particularly attractive but also a deeply contradictory figure. He is both totalitarian (the word "total" is one of the fundamental motifs of his writings) and liberal —totalitarian in his reduction to action, and specifically to class action, of every aspect of life; liberal in his vivid conception of the variety of influences at work, in his dislike of Bonapartism, and in his perception of the opportunities that a "modernizing" revolution will offer to the peasant without whose active and conscious support that revolution would not be possible.

Gramsci's writing, which he continued after his arrest, is found in fragmentary and cryptic form in notebooks written in prison and in letters to his family as well as in articles and other material published before his arrest. Since 1945 these works have been made public for the first time in nearly complete form. But their publication has not led to a rethinking of these problems in Communist circles. The Communists have limited themselves to presenting Gramsci as a supporter of a great "national" Italian party and of a modernization of national life, and to exploiting and glorifying his literary battle with Benedetto Croce. Gramsci's departures from Communist orthodoxy have been veiled with the greatest care. Nevertheless, Gramsci's thought has not been without influence in shaping the "liberal" attitudes of the party toward intellectuals and their ideology, whenever Moscow orders are not in direct opposition. In particular, Togliatti, who is described as Gramsci's heir in spite of his nearly opposite temperament, tries not to lead the cultural life of his party into the stagnant waters of a too elementary and vulgar Marxism. Paradoxically, the existence of Gramsci has helped to make the Italian party more political than ideological, in keeping with the general trends of the last few years.

THE UNDERGROUND PERIOD

Political Positions

Driven underground or into exile, the party continued to develop lines of policy on the more important political events of the day and to indicate them through published or secret directives. Sometimes they were effectively applied and resulted in agitation or even political action. In other cases, they remained on paper and are of interest only as indicating the attitudes of party leaders and militants. Nevertheless, one must follow at least the general lines of Communist policy in this period.

In its broad aspects, the position of the Italian Communist party on European questions was not essentially distinguishable from that of the Communist International. Indeed, from the third congress of the International onward, Russia's grip on the party became stronger both in matters of theory and of organization. Furthermore, the intense struggle for power inside Russia gave a specific character to the first period of the Italian Communist underground.

Following united-front tactics, the Communist party between 1926 and 1928 sought to act as a "party of the masses" and to oppose fascism with the idea of an insurrection in favor of a "republican assembly of workers' and peasants' committees." In this period the fight was aimed primarily at fascism, less at democratic parties. If democratic parties were attacked, this was mainly on the ground that they had abandoned the anti-Fascist battle.

The Communist opposition to fascism took over some of the slogans made popular by fascism, such as disdain for those who believe that democratic and legal methods are valid at all times and in all instances.

But as a result of the decisions of the sixth congress of the International in the summer of 1928, the attack against non-Communist democratic parties increased in violence. According to the International, the world, after the revolutionary period of 1917–1921 and the subsequent period of stabilization, had now entered a third period, of violent revolutionary crisis. In this period, he who was not with the Communist International was against it and was a Fascist. In particular, the Communist attack was directed against social democracy, which was likened to fascism and called "social fascism."

The more thoughtful Italian Communists, and primarily Togliatti, apparently wanted, if not a milder form of attack, at least a continuation of the general anti-Fascist front approach.[2] In public, however, the Italian party conformed completely to the directives of the International, and Togliatti assumed responsibility for the attacks against social fascism contained in the official party journal, *Stato operaio*. The only ones to come out openly for a broad anti-Fascist alliance were the "opportunists," who were expelled in these years for just that reason.

After Hitler's rise to power and in particular after the attempted seizure of power by French Fascists on February 6, 1934, both the Italian and French Communist parties carried out the most decisive about-face in the history of Communist parties. A policy of "pacts of unity of action" with Socialist and democratic parties replaced the attacks against social fascism. A pact among the Italian parties was concluded on August 17, 1934; the French parties followed soon afterward. Official consecration was subsequently given the new tactic in Dimitrov's report of July 1935 at the seventh and final congress of the International.

[2]According to present party apologetics, it was not until the fourth party congress of 1931 that these policies were sought.

From this time until the outbreak of the war, the Italian Communist party identified its policy with that of the whole anti-Fascist movement. It was against the Ethiopian war and opposed Fascist aggression. It called a congress of the various Italian anti-Fascist parties at Brussels in October 1935, from which only the "Justice and Freedom" movement of Carlo Rosselli was absent. It opposed Fascist intervention in Spain and organized the Garibaldi Battalion, one of the most efficient groups of the International Brigade. In Spain it kept up resistance to the bitter end: Togliatti was arrested with other members of the International at Madrid during the *coup d'état* of Colonel Casado. Finally, shocking the republican consciences of the other anti-Fascist parties, the party called for "the union of all Italians" and extended its hand to Fascist workers in the struggle for specific social reforms and against Hitlerism. This policy, which, as we shall see later, had its first test among the emigrés, was but an anticipation of the program later followed in Italy from 1943 until the liberation.

Of all Western European Communist parties, the Italian party was the most clearly identified with the experiment of alliances and fronts. In France, because of the government's intervention in Spain, and in Spain, especially after the establishment of Communist hegemony, these policies either collapsed or met with serious difficulties. Given fascism's continuance in power and the party's lack of contact with problems of government, Italian Communists were able to continue the united- or popular-front policy until August 1939, and even then it was not formally repudiated.

The pact between Hitler and Stalin threw into confusion the leaders of almost every western party who had taken seriously the anti-Fascist about-face of the seventh International congress, but it affected the leaders of the Italian party in a smaller measure. The pact came at a time when the Italian organization was tied to international communism only through French connections. Communist political orientation with respect to the impending war was decided at a conference held August 11–13, 1939, at Paris. Togliatti, absent from such meetings since 1934, was present. The treaty between Russia and Germany was signed on August 12. Granting that Togliatti may have been informed of the "neutral" position of Russia, which had been decided upon months before, he probably did not know how far Russia would go. The agreements reached at Paris, therefore, restated the common anti-Fascist struggle.

The repression of communism in France that followed the change of party line as a result of the Nazi-Soviet pact forced the Communists into political inactivity. From September 1939 to March 1940, when he took shelter in Moscow, Togliatti too was inactive. Those of his party who had emigrated to France followed, even in this state of dispersion and outlawry, the defeatist directives so useful to Germany. But in Italy these directives, by supporting neutrality, opposed also Fascist interventionist policies and did not require any positive acts of alliance with Germany.

Italy's entrance into the war in 1940 coincided with the fall of France and also with the first break in Russo-German solidarity. Thus the Italian Communist party could resume its old anti-Fascist line even though in terms of an alliance of all proletarians against the bourgeoisie. Such was the meaning of the party's appeal to the Italians after the French-Italian armistice. With the invasion of Russia in June 1941, the Communist party returned to a policy of solidarity with all democratic parties against fascism. The goal of its political struggle was to be peace with the Allies, liberation of subject nations, and the reconquest of freedom. To this end, the Communists worked hard for an agreement with the Socialist party and the Justice and Freedom group, and then for the creation of united committees representative of all opposition parties. These took on various names, such as the Committee of Action for the Union of the Italian People, the Italian Committee for Peace and Freedom, the Provisional Committee for the National Action Front. On July 25, 1943, all were consolidated in the Committee of the Opposition, a name the "Aventine" had used in 1924. After September 8, 1943, the name Committee of National Liberation was adopted.

Organization

The Italian Communist party was for a long time the only Italian party to survive fascism's suppression of freedom, because it had prepared an underground organization in advance. During the early period of fascism this clandestine body functioned through a "domestic center" connected with a "foreign center" located in France. Local responsibilities were entrusted to regional and interregional secretaries. More than once the "domestic center," through arrests, expulsions, and defections, ceased to exist and had to be re-established. Nevertheless, such a center remained active until 1932, when the party Executive Committee gave it up as too dangerous and moved the entire high command abroad, though direct connections with the regional groups were still maintained.

Until 1927 the Communists were exceedingly active and succeeded in provoking strikes in the provinces of Vercelli, Turin, and Trieste. At the end of that year, however, the party was thrown into confusion by a wave of arrests, and at a meeting in Basle it decided that it had to "work at lower costs." But in 1929, in accordance with the International's belief in an impending crisis, organizational activity was again increased.

In the 1929 upsurge of organizational activity, the Communist party was no longer alone. Other political groups, of Socialist and liberal principles, had also established their own organizations. The very important Justice and Freedom group was among them. Nevertheless, because of its greater experience, longer preparation, and greater resources (always needed by an underground organization and in this case furnished by the International), the Communist party remained more efficient and active than the other groups which had to finance themselves independently. However, while the presence of other political organizations acted as a stimulus to the new Communist campaign, the crude policy of opposition to social fascism under which the campaign was waged limited its effectiveness.

After 1932, with the suppression of the "domestic center," the party intensified its activities among Italian emigrés in France through the so-called "language groups" of the French Communist party. After the formation of the French Popular Front, however, independent organizational work was developed, and the *Unione popolare* aspired to become the economic association of Italian workers in France.

The outbreak of war, the arrest of many Communist leaders in France, and Russia's foreign policy during the early months of the European conflict, led to the disintegration of the Communist organization. Only in March 1940 was the party's "foreign center" reborn, under the direction of Silvati, Novella, Massola, and, later, Negarville. And only on the first of August 1941, after Hitler's attack upon the U.S.S.R., did a Communist leader, Massola, return to Italy permanently for the purpose of rebuilding the party. Between 1941 and 1942 the party re-established its propaganda groups and cells in Milan and Turin. It succeeded in establishing a small press and in spreading, in the second half of 1942, throughout northern Italy, with ramifications as far south as Rome. April 1943 saw the return of "instructors" Clocchiatti and Leris and of "foreign center" members Negarville and Silvati, the escape of Roveda, a member of the first party Executive Committee jailed in 1926, and the return from France of Amendola and Novella. Subsequently the Italian underground Communist organization was reconstituted along the same structural lines that had existed at the beginning of the Fascist regime.

The Political Balance Sheet

The accomplishments of the Communist party in the years from 1926 to 1943 are relatively great, particularly since they were achieved against the strongest difficulties. A rough estimate would place active and responsible party members in Italy at between 1,500 and 3,000 at this time. The last published statistics of the special Fascist tribunal for the security of the state (the highest political court of the regime), reported in the London *Times* of January 6, 1933, show the following data: In 1927, 222 individuals were sentenced; in 1928, 641; in 1929, 158; in 1930, 210; and in 1931, 526. The peak must have been reached in 1935 in prepa-

ration for the Ethiopian war. It would seem from this that the
estimate given above for party militants is accurate if the following factors are taken into consideration: an underground
group cannot escape the police for more than six months to a
year on the average; a certain percentage of those sentenced belonged to Slavic groups or were persons acting independently
(no attempt on the life of Mussolini, for example, was made by
the Communists); not a few Communists let out of prison resumed political activity and were condemned for a second time.

Until 1934 the fortnightly or monthly publication of *Unità*
was seldom interrupted. The Communist party always managed
to be present at those few economic demonstrations which took
place in the twenty years of fascism: the 1927 strikes, the 1928
strikes of women textile workers, and the demonstrations of the
unemployed at Turin in 1930. When d'Aragona, Colombino,
Rigola, and other reformist leaders dissolved the old Confederation of Labor at the end of 1926, the Communist party took up
syndical activity on its own for the few months when such struggle was still possible and effective. Thus it earned the right to
present itself as the party of the working class when freedom was
finally regained.

Prison terms did not weaken the bond between those arrested;
rather, they strengthened it. Prison terms helped to turn workers,
who originally had generically thought of revolt against society,
into disciplined men trained in party doctrine, in its elementary
principles of philosophy as well as of action. In every prison
"party schools" worked in secret. Being the most numerous as
well as the best organized, the Communists could absorb the
younger or the less convinced members of other anti-Fascist
parties, who, isolated, did not enjoy a similar protective shield.

The party high command was molded in the underground and
in prison. With the exceptions of Palmiro Togliatti, of Luigi
Longo, who knew a long jail term only after having been condemned in Spain, of Mario Montagnana, and of a few others, all
the present leaders of the Communist party spent many years of

their lives in prison. While this may have damaged their physical health, it has tempered them against the outside world.

Perhaps the greatest service the Fascist regime did the Communist party was its cushioning of the repercussions and crises following the great reversals of the line of international communism. Russian direction was accepted not as something extraneous but as necessary and natural. The party's first crisis, known as the Bordiga crisis, developed at the Lyons congress of 1926. The second crisis began in 1929 with the liquidation of "opportunism" and saw men like Tasca, Boatti, Tresso, Ravazzoli, and Silone leave the party. Tasca was liquidated primarily because of disagreements concerning the International in which he had sided with Bukharin. The others were liquidated as a result of the dispute concerning the correctness of the International's estimate of an approaching revolutionary phase. The opportunists were both right and wrong. They were right when they foresaw the protracted nature of the struggle; right when they showed the folly of isolating the party through an indiscriminate crusade against social fascism. They were wrong in not foreseeing the great mass of new members who would join the party in the course of this desperate struggle. They were simply eliminated, however, and what would have produced a schism in other countries was limited to the loss of a few members.

The party also managed to weather the storm of the Soviet-Nazi pact of 1939. Young party militants like Lombardo-Radice, Natoli, and Buffalini, as well as old-timers like Umberto Terracini and Girolamo Li Causi, took positions at this time which carried them nearly outside the party or even beyond it. But once the critical moment had been surmounted, they were again taken back into the fold.

In summary, it may be pointed out that in its origins the Communist party was a small party with little control over the great economic and syndical organizations of the masses. It opposed rigid hierarchical party structures and the subordination of Italian national interests to those of Russia. But as fascism began to disappear, communism returned to open political life as a party representing the majority of the working class, with well-organ-ized cadres, a hierarchy clearly defined, and a devotion to Russia no longer merely sentimental but also organic. Throughout, it had eliminated its dissidents and overcome its various crises with the least possible harm to itself.

XV

The Communist Party during the War and after the Restoration of Democracy

THE Fascist regime in Italy was one of violence, but it was not a casual incident unrelated to Italian social reality. The Italian liberal state, the fruit of the will of an enlightened minority, had been created in the nineteenth century out of many backward states which had been politically weak, lacking a defined foreign policy, and at the mercy of foreign powers. It had had to build from nothing all the public services required by civilized nations. It functioned well enough despite its lack of modern organization and succeeded by 1914 in raising the Italian people to a level of development they had never known before.

Politically speaking, however, the state was considered the property of a minority. Organized parties in the modern sense, parties which proceed in orderly fashion from propaganda to power, did not exist until the dawn of the new century with the birth of the Socialist party. Under these circumstances, the first World War presented Italy with a grave crisis. The war had been forced on Italy by the necessities of national survival and it had been entered into without preparation and with grudging spirit. The Catholics, who had the strongest organization even though antiquated, did not enter political life until after the war when Don Sturzo organized the Popular party. The old parties of the pre-1914 period, more in the nature of currents of opinion, had governed the country largely by reliance upon the administration and the military forces of the state, and were now confronted with a crisis of their own when faced with the modern organized parties of the Socialists and Catholics. The failure to surmount the crisis in the relationships between the old parties representative of the liberal tradition and the new "mass" parties, brought about the victory of fascism.

Once in power, fascism exerted a continuous "party" action over and above its use of police methods and of state machinery. It affected the citizen at every moment of his life and forced him to active and open loyalty. Without doubt, figures on Fascist elections or plebiscites were falsified. The crowd, in reality apolitical or hostile to fascism, was driven to the ballot box by threats of hunger or loss of jobs. Thus the people learned the habit of being guided by propaganda and a ruthless political machine. It can, therefore, be understood how, out of the crisis of fascism, parties were born that tended to seek control of the whole of social life for their political ends, and it is not difficult to understand why the Communist party has been the one to win the greatest success. Furthermore, in a situation where the solution of the Italian problem depended to a large extent upon outside forces, it was the only party in contact with an international movement systematically exploiting the political factor.

ROLE OF THE COMMUNIST PARTY
BEFORE JULY 25, 1943

Towards the end of World War II, the role of the Communist party was chiefly that of stimulating and organizing the revolt among the working classes. Ten strikes, most of them at Turin and Milan, occurred in various factories between August and December 1942. Eleven more took place in the first two months of 1943. The strikes of March and April 1943, however, were the ones that gave control of the working masses to the Communists. Though the party organization was still weak, strikes broke out on March 6, 1943, at the Fiat Mirafiori plant in Turin and then spread throughout Piedmont and Lombardy, lasting through the first two weeks of April and ending in the arrest of many leaders. But economic concessions which threatened the Fascist war economy had been granted.

The *coup d'état* of July 25 revealed the strength of antifascism throughout the country. The notice of Mussolini's dismissal by the king showed how small the influence of the mass parties was, for the first demonstrations, except in the great centers in the north, were largely organized by monarchist supporters. Amid the general uncertainties, the first real result of Communist policy was the hard-won liberation of the majority of fascism's political prisoners. The release of these men put a trained high command already inured to battle at liberty for the coming anti-Fascist struggle. Secondly, the Communist party won the nomination of Giovanni Roveda as commissioner of the workers' confederations of industry, along with Bruno Buozzi, a Socialist, and Achille Grandi, a Christian Democrat. This nomination gave final recognition to the fact, already established during the underground and the great strikes in the north, that the Communists were now the largest working-class party. It also created the basis for the Communists' future control of trade unions by placing control of the single Fascist syndical organization in the hands of the new mass parties. When liberation finally came, the pre-Fascist Confederation of Labor was officially reborn, with participation of all workers' groups in a single confederation.

The conquest of the syndical movement by the Communist party was thus rapid and complete. At one stroke, the Communist were able to install themselves in a centralized organization to which all workers were accustomed to send dues and to look for support. More solidly organized and combative than the Socialists or Christian Democrats, the Communists could, in effect, take over the bureaucratic structure erected by Fascist corporativism at such heavy cost to the working class.

ROLE OF THE COMMUNIST PARTY AFTER THE ARMISTICE OF SEPTEMBER 8, 1943

For some time following September 8, 1943, the Italian Communist party worked on its own initiative without direct influence from Moscow. As was to be expected, there was great indignation among active anti-Fascists and patriots at the inability of a government composed of generals and supported by the monarchy to organize effective resistance against the Germans. In the Committee of Liberation even the more moderate elements were forced to face the obvious fact that if Italy was to be saved, an underground fight against the Germans had to be waged without waiting for government orders. In the provinces where the partisan movement became active, the determination increased to direct a revolution by the Italian people with its own forces and in its own name. In the eyes of the Italian people, Marshal Badoglio was a discredited leader, and the parties militarily and politically on the immediate right of the Communists refused to recognize him. The Italian Communist party was, on the whole, in agreement with this stand. Against the "government of the king," it proposed not a "republican government," but a "government of the Committee of National Liberation."

The parties which had only an embryonic existence on July 25 were reborn throughout Italy under the initiative or spell of the Committee of National Liberation. In the armed struggle against the Germans, the Communist party found a strong competitor in the democratic-republican socialist-tinged Action party, which had inherited the cadres of the Justice and Freedom group of 1929–1934. The Action party, by devoting itself to forming partisan units, prevented the Communist party from having a monopoly of the Resistance. Other armed units were created by young reserve officers. Even the Socialists and Christian Democrats, parties which had previously eschewed revolutionary organization and had entrusted their futures to the support of public opinion, now formed their own partisan groups.

Upon his return from Russia in April 1944, Togliatti, in his "report to the cadres of the Communist organization of Naples," did away with the noncollaboration policy of the Committee of National Liberation. He declared that one had to be "logical," and since the institutional problem could not be solved, one had to "move on to resolve the real problem: the creation of a government." The Communists laid down three conditions, later reduced to one, for this government. First, the Communists should participate in a government to be set up on "the basis of mass parties." The other two conditions were a call for a postwar constituent assembly, something already granted by the Allied powers, and a demand that the government should mobilize for war against Germany.

With this reversal, Togliatti annulled the mediating functions of the moderate left-center parties and came out in favor of a permanent coalition between the Communist, Socialist, and Christian Democratic parties. This was a coalition like those created in the countries of eastern Europe, where all democratic parties cooperated in governments and the Communist party later eliminated the other co-operating parties.

Generally speaking, conservatives in other countries praised the "realism" of the Communist party in contrast with the doctrinaire positions of the other parties. They did not see that by this move Togliatti could paralyze the whole party system and that he would assume the role of protector of all leftist parties. Nor did they realize that Togliatti might possibly reduce the "self-liberation" of the Italian people to a problem of relationship between a government holding the traditional instruments of power in its hands and mass organizations over which the Communist party was gradually extending its control.

In reality, the Communist party was never allowed to gain complete control of the situation. The other groups included in the Committee of Liberation showed notable vitality, and the Communists were never alone in the Resistance or later. During the Resistance period the Communists met with the competition of the Action party. In the months immediately following the Resistance, there was the expansion of the Socialist party, then the growth and consolidation of the Christian Democratic party.

Thus the political life of the new Italy was never reduced to a mere conflict between the old classes of bureaucrats and functionaries and the revolutionary people's forces organized and controlled by the Communists. Instead, the conflict was to be among a number of parties all having democratic programs.

The Italian Communist party remained loyal to the program drawn up by Togliatti. It endeavored to push Italy toward a people's democracy and to prevent any independent initiative by the Socialist and Action parties. It continued to participate in the government in order to reap all the advantages of operating within the legal framework. It sought to strengthen itself throughout the country in order to control, directly or through dependent associations, all political and economic life and all activities having social importance.

THREE YEARS OF PARTICIPATION IN THE GOVERNMENT: 1944–1947

The Italian Communist party participated in the government from April 1944 until May 31, 1947, when the third de Gasperi cabinet came to an end. Togliatti participated in all cabinets of this period, with the exception of de Gasperi's second cabinet.

Until the elections of June 2, 1946, the cabinets in which Communists participated were always made up of all six parties of the Committee of National Liberation. But for some time the Communists had been thinking of a coalition based chiefly upon the three great mass parties, around which the other parties would turn. Most assuredly, this Communist position accelerated the crisis of the smaller parties. To control and absorb the Socialists and to gain a majority by forming a bloc with them, to keep the Christian Democrats from their allies and voters on the right through a pact (a pact which the Christian Democrats always refused to sanction, knowing that it would have just this result) — such was the cabinet strategy of the Communists.

The Italian Communist party was never able to obtain the cabinet posts which would have given it decisive power in the state machinery. It should not be forgotten that the government was set up before the signing of the peace treaty and thus was supervised by an Allied Control Commission in which the Anglo-Americans had the effective power. The Ministries of Foreign Affairs, Interior, and Defense always escaped the Communists. The Ministry of Finance held by Antonio Pesenti and Mario Scoccimarro might have opened the door to an important reform program if the party had been interested in it. Finally, the Ministry of Justice held by Togliatti, aside from any ephemeral influence it might have given him over the judiciary, left him only with responsibility for the amnesty which put an end to the prosecutions for crimes committed by Fascists and Hitlerites. Indeed, this was an amnesty drawn up in such a way that it made possible the acquittal of high-ranking Fascist politicians as well as criminals responsible for Nazi repression, while it failed to prevent possible later judicial actions against Communist partisans guilty of common crimes in the course of the insurrection.

Why did not the Communists in power register any significant achievement, particularly in the economic and social fields? Why were the social reforms promised by all parties during the Resistance put aside during the work of the Constituent Assembly? The answer may be, as the Communists say, that more substantial social reforms were not effected because the Allied occupation and resistance of the parties of the right forced postponement from the time when they would have been relatively easy until the succeeding period when the social order was set on more conservative foundations.

That this explanation contains some degree of truth is unquestionable. In the period preceding the June 1946 elections, the conduct of the Communists and especially of their leader Togliatti, was one of moderation dominated by the fundamental aims of bringing about elections, the peace treaty, and the withdrawal of Allied forces. However, foreign bayonets or reactionary parties intent on sabotaging "progressive democracy" cannot alone explain why it was not possible to achieve more sweeping reforms, to steer the nation's economy away from the interests of privileged groups, and at least to outline a technically sound program acceptable to the various parties. What kept the Communists from achieving more, in a socialist sense, was the fact that their participation in government at that time sought to increase their own influence, with the conquest of power as the goal, and not to solve the problems of the country. In spite of having amended their classical position that "partial gains in capitalistic regimes are illusory," the Communists seemed to have preserved the essential point of their doctrine, that what is achieved in the bettering and stabilizing of society is meaningless if it does not lead to an increase in the power of the party.

We can find fresh proof of this principle by examining the activities of the Communist party in pursuit of "partial gains." The Communists asked for a more energetic purge of the Fascists, hoping to proceed to a "social purification," or the liquidation, of some of the leaders of big industry. But their criteria for such a task were uncertain and arbitrary. The Communists themselves had accepted a truce with the monarchy and the army, both of which were gravely compromised with fascism. How could they demand the prosecution of the less guilty? Besides, in order to swell their own forces, they were indulgent with the younger Fascists; but their responsibility for the defense of fascism, taken in a juridical and not a social sense, was not different from that of the hated industrialists, and sometimes was even greater. To be revolutionary, purification would have had to be conducted according to political standards such as might be set up by a committee of public safety. If its purpose was to achieve justice, it would have had to be based on precise, clear, and juridically sound rules. As it was, the Italian purge failed in either aim.

In the economic field, the Communist party advocated the continuance of restrictions, rationing, and controls in order to secure a more equitable distribution of basic necessities. But if this offered advantages to a party busy defending the interests of the urban masses, the system could not function without stern measures directed at the rural classes and the requisitioning of agricultural products. Could the party afford to arouse and anger the peasants before the revolution arrived?

The absence of a concrete economic policy was mentioned by Togliatti himself at the economic convention of the Communist party on August 23, 1945, after the liberation of northern Italy. Noting that "a certain disorientation" and a "very great divergence of opinion" existed with regard to economic problems, Togliatti declared himself "against any measure which consciously would lead to a catastrophic solution of the Italian crisis." He affirmed the necessity of a productivistic policy and said he was in favor of private initiative, deeming "utopian" the demand for a national economic plan. In asking for a "controlled economy," he carefully distinguished this concept not only from what the Bolsheviks had asked for in 1917, but also "from what we asked for in 1919–1920. . . [as an] element in the struggle of the working class for the conquest of power."

Instead, Italian Communists now called for "control over production and exchange of the type which existed and still exists in England and the United States"; in other words, they asked for a labor program. But a labor program implies an efficient bureaucracy, and here Togliatti could only say that progress was being made in the purification program. It implies rigorous and scientific collection of taxes, and Togliatti could only cite "the improved fiscal policy. . . [initiated] by some Communists in the north, by making a list of the rich profiteers of fascism and making them pay according to their wealth." Clearly, this was an example of the policy of direct class struggle best adapted to discourage private initiative and that regularity and impersonality of state action which is necessary for the success of the controls he had in mind.

Even the demand for workers' councils could not survive for long. After the liberation of northern Italy, almost all factories were taken over by commissioners aided by workers' committees. Public opinion felt that it was only right that those who had saved the plants from Nazi destruction should have the responsibility of managing them. But this situation required early clarification — either workers' committees everywhere, but with limited rights, or nationalization. In any case, the primary considerations should have been rationalization, the unfreezing of man power, and full employment policies. The Communist party, controlling the unions, looked only to the most pressing need, that of preventing job dismissals. For the rest, it had no policy, and, through weariness, lack of capital, and the legal restrictions on the commissioners in financial operations, the old industrialists soon came back everywhere.

Before the liberation of northern Italy, the Communists entertained the hope that the Committees of National Liberation themselves would be able to become the new government. This — as the Communists realized and Togliatti openly said — would have led to "the prospect of a violent clash, of an armed conflict between the organized forces of the anti-Fascist front and those of the police and the army." In order to avoid this, Togliatti said on April 7, 1945, at a meeting of the party's national council, "the advent of new men" was necessary. Later, when the victorious anti-Fascist insurrection had carried these new men to the top and Ferruccio Parri, of the Action party's partisan command, became a candidate for the premiership, Togliatti, who would have preferred a Socialist he could handle easily, regarded him coldly. A few months later Togliatti abandoned Parri to his fate and, with him, the program of the Committees of National Liberation, and worked directly for a de Gasperi government. He then consented to solve the question of the monarchy through a national referendum rather than through action by the Constituent Assembly.

Once a republic had been decided upon, neither he nor his party had a program whose realization was close to the people or which required the Communists' presence in the government. The Communists had taken under their protection certain rights of the lower classes whom they were organizing; but the protection of these rights was not a task requiring their collaboration in the government. This is so true that, despite the party's desperate efforts, its expulsion from the government came about by a simple cabinet crisis, and without the Christian Democrats having to come to prior agreement with other parties.

To secure their return to power the Communists created an electoral alliance with the Socialist party and a few small independent groups, called the People's Democratic Front (Fronte Democratico Popolare), which obtained 31 per cent of the votes in the national elections of April 18, 1948. This action had the result of consolidating the Christian-Democratic majority, previously only a relative one, into an anti-Communist bloc. The People's Front defeat was explained by Togliatti and the Communists as due to the intervention, under government pressure, of "intermediate masses politically oscillating and inactive," while "the majority of the politically active and productive population" had voted for the People's Front.

The Communists did indeed gain, directly or indirectly, control over many groups holding key positions on the economic, military, and political stage. The party thus has at its disposal an active, convinced, well-organized nucleus, as was demonstrated shortly afterward when, after the attempted assassination of Togliatti on July 14, 1948, communications between north and south were interrupted, factories occupied, several cities completely isolated, and, in Genoa, armored police cars disarmed. But these "active" groups cannot gain power through democratic means while two-thirds of the population are not with them. They might seize power through revolutionary means, although by now the police, army, and other armed corps are strongly reenforced and Communist control of the economy and of public services is much weakened. But the Communists are firmly opposed to any such revolutionary attempts before the outbreak of a new international conflict.

Finally, let us examine the foreign policy of the Communist party since the liberation. Until the end of the war it had supported a policy aimed at giving maximum military support to the Allies. Later, the Communist party, while intransigent in claiming the Alto Adige for Italy and the maintenance of the western frontier, was ready to abandon Istria and Trieste to Yugoslavia. This stand was perhaps justifiable from the point of view of Russian and Slavic policy, but it was unjustifiable from the point of view of the national policy which the Communists claimed to defend. To affirm that "from the eastern regions, if we except the period of the great barbarian invasions, an attack upon our country or an attempted invasion has never been made, above all by peoples of Slavic nationality," was to forget the whole course of the first World War. While the government worked to save at least western Istria and its predominantly Italian population for Italy, Togliatti referred to Trieste as an "Italian city with a Slavic hinterland"; its "Italian nature must be defended, though taking into account, among other things, the fact that it is a city which has ever aspired to govern itself in a democratic manner and, in addition, seeking above all a solution which will not open a permanent conflict between the Italians and the Slavs." This was Tito's solution. This was the time when, while the Italian Communist party was allowed to be rude to the French Communist party, Tito, advance outpost of Russia in the West, had to be obeyed.

This position on Trieste and Togliatti's later support of Tito's suggested barter of Gorizia against Trieste invalidated the sincerity and rationalism of the Communist views on other aspects of Italy's foreign policy: on the colonial problem, on the abandonment of nationalism, or on realism in dealing with the big powers. It revealed the Communists as nothing but instruments of Russian interests.

The same mortgage weighed on Communist policy after the party's exclusion from the government. The campaign against the Marshall Plan could not find support in a country so much in need of aid. The campaign against the Atlantic Pact and the new military commitments found a greater response in a country which, through the game of alliances, had been dragged into wars whose necessity the people had not felt. But even in the case of the Atlantic Pact, the impossibility of a Communist revolutionary campaign was clear. Having called the pact an "instrument of war" and having said that its acceptance by parliament would lead to war, it was not easy to control the masses in the face of a different reality.

XVI

The Italian Communist Party in Italian Society Today

THE RULING CLASS

The Italian Communist party is led by Palmiro Togliatti, secretary-general of the party. Between him and other leaders of the party, the Communist press and propaganda machine had made a clear hierarchical distinction even before Togliatti's return to Italy in 1944. At that time Togliatti was almost unknown except by the party militants: neither his underground name "Ercoli" nor that used for his broadcasts from Moscow, "Mario Correnti," meant anything in Italian political history. Yet, even before his return, it was apparent to all that Togliatti would become the leader of the organization, for he knew the secrets of the International and was the depositary of its will. On his arrival he abruptly changed the party line, then opposed to collaboration with King Victor Emmanuel, and led it to take the initiative in setting up the Salerno government. This act alone raised Togliatti above other party leaders, and upon the liberation of each city his visit was the party's first formal political manifestation. Soon Togliatti was one of the best-known men in Italy.

In developing the myth of the leader, which constantly appears in the Communist press, the traditional clichés have been used: Togliatti is a sage who without effort identifies the correct party line and who firmly combats "deviations." He is a fighter who is always on hand in the party's difficult moments. To make him stand out in these roles, some facts have been distorted and the dangers he faced at the time of the march on Rome have been exaggerated. Nor should it be forgotten that others were in command of the party in its most difficult moments and in the course of the partisan campaign and that Togliatti did not serve the long prison terms served by other party leaders. But all this has not affected the political stature of Togliatti, who is indeed a man of culture, endowed as well with many private virtues. As a whole, the myth of the leader has not been pushed to absurd lengths, and a certain awareness of the danger of exposing the party to ridicule has always been present. Appellatives such as "The Best" disappeared soon after they provoked the ironical reactions of anti-Communists.

A special feature of the Togliatti legend is the coupling of his name with that of Gramsci. To be sure, the relationship between Gramsci and Togliatti was certainly closer than that between Lenin and Stalin: Gramsci and Togliatti worked together on the *Ordine nuovo;* they had a common cultural background based more on the great liberal thinkers and critics than on Marxism, with slightly greater literary pretensions in the case of Togliatti. But it is clear that Gramsci's revolutionary and intellectual strength could not be transmitted simply through propinquity. In the early years of the Communist party in Piedmont, there were other *Ordine nuovo* writers who enjoyed greater prestige than Togliatti: men like Terracini, who is still in the party, and Tasca (as A. Rossi, he has become the nonorthodox historian of the French Communist party) who was later expelled. To reduce a complex movement like that which founded the *Ordine nuovo* to a mere Gramsci-Togliatti relationship is obviously a mythological simplification for propaganda purposes only.

But mythology aside, Togliatti has undoubtedly been the leader of the Communist party since 1926. From 1934 to 1943 he was also a member of the Executive Committee of the Third International, and as its secretary, Togliatti was among the signers of the resolution dissolving the International in June 1943. In the clandestine period he executed and applied the orders of the International, although it appears that on more than one occasion he was inclined to "opportunistic solutions," that is, to take into account the actual circumstances in which party action had to develop. But his diplomatic skill in applying the orders of the International saved the Italian party from those great crises which beset Communist organizations elsewhere.

These diplomatic qualities must have earned him the trust of the Russian leaders, for during the Spanish civil war the International put him at the "disposal" of the Spanish party. Without doubt he helped to pick the strategy by which the very weak Spanish Communist party succeeded in gaining a monopolistic position within the Popular Front. This must have been an interesting experience, for the Spanish Communist party had initially tried to win over the old ruling classes, such as army officers, by reassuring them about their ultimate fate. In the light of the Spanish experience, Togliatti's policy upon his return to Italy and his decision to put his party into the Badoglio government acquire new perspective.

Since the liberation Togliatti has aimed to govern the country with the help of the Socialist party and, if possible, of the Christian Democrats, establishing a government chosen through free elections and based upon a parliamentary majority, but controlled by the masses. At first Togliatti thought, in the period of exhilaration at the end of the war, that this government could be created as part of a plan of general co-operation between the western democracies and communism. This plan, despite the discontent of the purists among the Communists, was not abandoned until after the Communists' elimination from the government and until after Italy aligned herself with the western powers through the Marshall Plan and the Atlantic Pact.

Togliatti himself had believed it possible to return to power after the 1948 elections. The Popular Front's defeat was a genuine surprise to him. In spite of the increasing violence of his language, however, he was always cautious not to throw the party into an open battle in which it would surely be defeated. The only time that the Italian Communist party has risen in revolt and showed the strength of its military organization was after the attempt on Togliatti's life on July 14, 1948.

As early as 1924 Piero Gobetti, a keen observer who had seen Togliatti at close range, described him as "a victim of his own restlessness, of an indecision which may appear an inexorable and tyrannical cynicism, and is often regarded as equivocation but is, perhaps, the result of a vainly repressed critical sensibility. No final judgment is possible." Presumably many Italians today agree in this suspension of judgment. While he has seemed to act with tolerance, he has rigidly forced both the Italian and foreign Communist parties to follow the policies of Moscow. He has never shown any indication, at least publicly, of desiring to embark in new and vital directions. More than the other party leaders who are endowed with greater apparent orthodoxy, Togliatti is the incarnation of Italian communism: flexible and shrewd, and by now shorn of all the idealism, the mythical impulses, and the millennial sentiments which were strong at its birth thirty years ago.

Pietro Secchia and Luigi Longo, as vice-secretaries of the party, are nearest to Togliatti. They too rose to leadership after the first World War. Both were organizers rather than politicians. Longo comes from the extremist Socialist Youth Foundation. A member of the underground "domestic center," he was a commissioner in the International Brigade in Spain, where he appeared as a man of common sense in contrast with the violent Frenchman Marty. He also fought with the partisans in Italy. Secchia has known the Fascist jails and has been a leader in the underground. In temperament he is even more rigidly orthodox than Longo. Neither Secchia nor Longo, because they are more extreme in their views than Togliatti, can aspire to succeed him, for they could not fill his position without disrupting the delicate party balance between fanaticism and liberalism.

In addition to Togliatti, Longo, and Secchia, the party directorate elected at the sixth congress of January 1948 was composed of Giorgio Amendola, Girolamo Li Causi, Celeste Negarville, Teresa Noce, Agostino Novella, Giancarlo Pajetta, Giuseppe

Rossi, Antonio Roasio, Giovanni Roveda, Mauro Scoccimarro, Emilio Sereni, and Velio Spano. Ruggero Grieco, Rita Montagnana, and Umberto Terracini were elected "candidate members." Later, Eugenio Reale, Italian ambassador to Warsaw when the congress was held, was added to the directorate. At the seventh party congress of April 1951, all were reappointed with the exception of Reale and Rossi, while four new members were included: Arturo Colombi, Giuseppe de Vittorio, Edoardo d'Onofrio, and Ruggero Grieco (the last promoted from the position of "candidate member").

An analysis of this leadership from the time each of its members joined the party will be useful in understanding the forces predominating in the Communist high command. First of all, there is the large group of Piedmontese origin, not all of them coming from *Ordine nuovo* but all linked to the origins of the party. To this group, along with Togliatti, belong Longo and Secchia; Roveda, older than the others and a party member since the Leghorn congress; Teresa Noce, wife of Longo; Rita Montagnana, former wife of Togliatti; Negarville, who went from Socialist activity in Turin to work in France during the exile, later to the underground, to prison, and finally to Moscow from 1935 to 1938; Roasio, an exile in Russia for a long time; and Giancarlo Pajetta, a much younger man who did not live through the creation of the party but accepted it as a fact. As against eight pre-Fascist leaders belonging to the Piedmontese groups, there are only three non-Piedmontese: Li Causi, a Sicilian emigrant to Venice, the only member of the present directorate who did not side with the Communists at Leghorn; Scoccimarro, a Venetian, a member of the party command after the Lyons congress; and Grieco, who has been a member of the Executive Committee of the Communist party since the congress of Leghorn and is the only one to come from the old group of Bordiga's *Soviet*. Amendola and Sereni represent the younger generation who joined the party during the underground period.

Grieco and Terracini, both mere "candidate members" up to 1951 when Grieco was promoted, are the only ones in the history of the Communist party who have the right to stand on a level with, if not above, Togliatti. Grieco was among the founders of the "foreign center"; for years he was secretary of the party and during the war he broadcast from Moscow. When Togliatti appeared isolated, he was one of those who most quickly supported him.

Even more impressive is Terracini's record. Apart from the role he played in the party when it passed from the influence of Bordiga to that of the *Ordine nuovo* and apart from his qualities as a diplomat and jurist, Terracini is the Communist who was sentenced to the longest jail term by the Fascist courts. Yet, against him weigh his opposition to the Third International's decision against social fascism at its sixth congress and his opposition to Russian policy at the time of the pact with Hitler. In fact, this latter position forced him to leave the party temporarily. In 1948 he gave an interview in which he favored a Truman-Stalin meeting and saw a certain parity between the opposed interests of the Soviet Union and the United States. This interview met with severe criticism by the party, criticism to which Terracini was forced to submit. If we can speak of minority groups within the directorate, it is due to Terracini, who has indicated their existence to the public. He has been president of the Constituent Assembly and is certainly the leader of the party in the Senate if not in parliament. He is a typical example of the "possibilism" and complexity of Italian communism.

The men of the directorate are not the only Communist leaders with great influence. Giuseppe di Vittorio, secretary-general of the General Confederation of Italian Labor, and Edoardo d'Onofrio, trained in Moscow and director of the Communist men's federation, were added to the directorate in 1951. Others include Renato Bitossi, second in command in the labor confederation, who spent fifteen years in prison; Giuseppe Berti, one of the leaders of the "foreign center" under fascism; Mario Montagnana, also one of the "foreign center" leaders and now one of the editors of *Unità;* Antonio Cicalini, Battista Santhià, and Giovanni Parodi, who were among the organizers of the first workers' councils; Umberto Massola, the first to reopen the "domestic center" in 1943; Ilio Barontini, an outstanding figure in the Spanish war and the partisan campaign; Maria Maddalena Rossi, president of the Communist women's organization, Unione Donne Italiane; and Concetto Marchesi, a professor of the classics at Padua, the party's most brilliant intellectual.

Only a minority of these Communist leaders are of working-class origin; more often they come from the borderlands between the *petite bourgeoisie* and the proletariat. Those nearest the working class joined the party before fascism; those who joined later, such as Pajetta, Spano, Amendola, Reale, and Sereni, were all university students with middle-class backgrounds. Almost all, however, spent long years in jail; all were kept from normal life and personal careers. All are professional revolutionaries who have paid a personal price for their politics and are not thinking of any career outside the party.

Are there factions within this high command? The question might also be asked if there are factions in the party as a whole. No easy answer is possible. Organized blocs or even independent groups such as are found in democratic parties are certainly not to be found in the Communist party. Their existence would be contrary to the very nature of the party. But personal groups or cliques do exist, and there are people to whom certain specific activities seem to be reserved and who come to the fore whenever the current political situation requires that these activities be pushed into the limelight. For example, it seems clear that Longo and Secchia, as organizers and veterans of the partisan war, are the men who handle especially difficult situations and who take firm doctrinal stands. If the Cominform were to tell the Italian Communist party to abandon the static maneuvering of today, Longo and Secchia might be called upon to do the job. To Longo fell the task of attacking, in September 1948, the "cultural liberalism" of the party that seemed to be based upon a logical interpretation of the clause in the 1946 party statute which grants members freedom of philosophic and religious opinion. But it was

Sereni who had the task of making available for Italian consumption the cultural formulas of Zhdanov. Then, in November 1949, Togliatti, in a brief declaration on the nature of artistic content which contained an abundance of materialistic orthodoxy, rose to the defense of the party's humanists and said that "the content of art is, for a Marxist, nothing but reality in its development."

Factions in the party are then simply groups which form when the party has not decided on the line it wants to take on specific issues. It can happen that a person who follows one group on one specific question will not follow it on another. The only political position within the party which can be called distinct is that of Terracini. However, to regard this as an omen of heresy and schism would be wholly arbitrary in the light of the party's organization. Only political conditions different from those of today would give such a position more significance than it has at present.

ORGANIZATION OF THE PARTY

The main traits of the top leadership are reflected in the several strata of leaders forming the party hierarchy. In general, one can speak of a triple tier: first, those whose communism dates from the formation of the party and whom we are surprised not to find in positions of control, men such as Ottavio Pastore or Felice Platone, both newspapermen; second, those who go back to the first years of the underground and were reared in party schools, in prison, or in Russia; and last, those who became Communists during the second World War. Typical of this last group are sons of eminent personalities of the pre-Fascist Italian political and cultural world.

In general, for parliamentary tasks, the party chooses new men or those who are not too clearly identified as Communists. In any case, proportional representation in Italy removes any glory there might be in being a deputy as it makes all deputies mere puppets of party machines. Particular care is taken in the selection of mayors, almost all of whom are forced to pursue largely nonpartisan administrative policies owing to the strong control exercised by the central government. On the other hand, the old guard is used within the machine, to which newcomers cannot have access.

The Communist ruling class today controls vast masses of people, almost all of whom entered the party immediately after the liberation. At Florence on October 3, 1944, Togliatti laid down the principles which must govern the party: it must be a party of control over society and not merely a party of opinion. The masses came to the party; they came borne by enthusiasm and still required firm integration into the party framework: "If there develops a situation where only a group of comrades works, our party. . .will not be a real mass party but merely a vast grouping of sympathizers alongside a few active elements." We must realize, continued Togliatti, that the party is no longer the small revolutionary party of its origins:

When we met at Leghorn in 1921 there were 42,000 Communists in all of Italy. Today we have 35,000 members in the province of Naples alone, 30,000 in the Rome federation, and so on. . . . We have to create unions, co-operatives, mutual societies; we have to maintain relations with friendly parties, . . . and to take into our hands, wherever possible, local administration. . . . We have to organize the young people, have to do a job among the women.

There must be many cells and capillary organizations which can penetrate deeply into the life of the country. "I suggest that we decentralize our organization as much as possible and *create the greatest possible number of small organizations.* If a cell has more than a hundred members, it will be difficult for only three comrades to make it function."

Togliatti explained this penetration of the party into every vital center of the nation more clearly in a speech at a Communist women's conference:

A party that is truly a people's party is present wherever the people meet and are active, in the factories, the fields, the offices, the ships, the unions, the co-operatives. But the people are first of all at home where the women are, and the women are the ones who set the tone of family life. As long as we do not succeed in establishing ourselves in the homes, in the markets, wherever the life of most of the people goes on in its elementary forms, we shall not be able to say we have succeeded in establishing a people's party.

Thereafter, the success of the party was measured against its penetration into the so-called "elementary" forms of life. A year after the Togliatti speech to the Communist women, their leader, Rina Picolato, said at the second organizational conference of the party: "Our women's cells in many cases hardly function; they have not become active political organisms.... The influence of our 400,000 members is not yet felt everywhere." What is the remedy? As usual, to try different forms of organization, to attempt to parallel as much as possible the structure of the country, to subdivide activity into smaller and ever more innocuous-appearing associations.

The habits and conditions of the workers of Turin and Milan are too different from those of the peasants of Sicily and Apulia.... We cannot think of putting a woman of Sicily or Campania, for example, into the regular sections along with the men.... Again, in some places we have been able to mobilize the women only through trade union programs. For example, there are the "jasmine pickers," the "olive pickers,"...and the "associations of homeless women," of "friends of the peace," of "friends of the school."

The women's organizations are typical of the whole party. The effort is to reach all strata and centers of social life. A party so organized is a party oriented toward conquest and control of society, busy, of course, in discussing, but in discussing the application of orders, not the political program of the party itself. In an apartment house cell, still more in a factory cell that meets at the place of work, a member who might want to raise the issue of party deficiencies with respect to the great problems of renovating Italian life or who might want to criticize the party's general policy would be considered a disturbing element and would be removed, with the approval of the others.

What has been the postwar numerical strength of the Communist party? According to the official figures, at the end of 1945 there were 1,700,000 members paying dues; at the end of 1946, 2,150,000, a number which became, after a huge membership drive, 2,215,000 in June 1947. On January 25, 1949, Scoccimarro, commemorating the foundation of the party at Leghorn, declared that it had "more than 2,300,000 members." At the seventh party congress in April 1951, the figure of 2,580,765 members, including 463,000 members of Communist Youth, was announced. However, this group is not homogeneous, nor can it be compared, as is often done, with the 45,000 or 50,000 of 1921.

One of the reasons is the relatively low price of the membership card. On August 31, 1947, the party secretariat announced: "To spur the membership campaign, the party has decided to reduce the price of the 1947 card. For all who join the party after September 1, the price will be reduced to ten lire." This sum, equivalent to half the price of a newspaper, is clearly a mere symbol and cannot be compared to the high dues asked of party members in the pre-Fascist period. This does not mean that in the course of its activity the party does not obtain a substantial total revenue through income from newspapers, books, and magazine subscriptions. It means simply that without continuous activity on the part of trained personnel, the party would disintegrate into a body of generic sympathizers.

At the organizational conference of 1947 Secchia said that there was "too much disequilibrium in the numerical strength of the party from region to region, from federation to federation.... We must openly recognize that a strong residue of workers' party tradition remains, accompanied by unjustifiable suspicions of intellectuals." Amendola added that "the data given by comrade Secchia show that 80 per cent of the members come from northern and central Italy and only 20 per cent from the south."

Since 1947 more members have been acquired in the south thanks to dogged work in agricultural co-operatives and peasants' leagues. But Communist penetration of the south remains confined almost exclusively to the poorest peasants, the *braccianti*.

While the swollen figures of the north have contracted in some areas, the Communist party has been successful in keeping most of those who joined the party after the liberation. Other parties, like the Socialist, which had similarly benefited from the postwar rush to join the new political parties (a habit developed under fascism when one's livelihood depended upon the party card), lost quite heavily.

The large influx of young people into Communist ranks which characterized the period of anti-Fascist struggle halted abruptly after the liberation. The trend was toward nonparticipation in political life, or toward the right. In the more backward zones of Italy, even Christian Democracy is considered leftist. At the organizational conference of 1947, Enrico Berlinguer, the Communist youth director, indicated that the lack of success affected other parties even more than the Communist party: "The youth groups of the Action party, of the Republicans, even of the Socialists, are depleted or facing difficulties which they are unable to overcome."

Yet the party did not then decide to create a youth federation of its own. Perhaps it recalled that out of the old Socialist Youth Organization, whose members in an overwhelming majority had joined the Communist party, had come not only such Communists as Longo, Santhià, Negarville, and Teresa Noce, who formed the backbone of the revolutionary party in the underground period, but also not a few heretics, such as Silone and Spinelli, who had later aimed the most damaging criticism at the party. It is more likely that the party continued to favor an apolitical youth front in order to capture Italian youth on a wider area. In the spring of 1947 at the party's youth conference, Berlinguer cited the success of this mass organization containing "400,000 young Communists." He recalled the "establishment of 3,000 training courses, the convention for the fight against tuberculosis, the creation of youth councils in many Italian cities, the conventions of young metallurgical, textile, and agricultural workers," and ended by calling for the strengthening of all mass youth organizations.

The conclusion must be, however, that such tactics did not recruit too many Communist party members. Thus, two years later on April 15, 1949, after all hope of establishing a people's democracy in Italy had been given up for the moment, the Central Committee of the Communist party decided to revive the Communist Youth Federation. Longo's report on the subject notes the contrast between the immediate postwar period and the situation in 1949. "In the face of the postwar decline of youth movements, Catholic organizations have improved their positions and today count, thanks to a capillary program, 13,000 men's and 18,000 women's groups, with about 1,300,000 organized members." Longo sought a remedy in the multiplication of youth cells: "Where they have already been created, they have given good results and have re-inforced the youth movement. . . . But the execution of this policy has been only partial. Only a fourth, or at most a third, of what could have been done has been done."

The creation of a Communist youth organization corresponds to a shift, which has been accentuated since 1949, away from the postwar "open" phase, in which the party adapted itself to democratic coalition methods, even if only in the interests of Russia, toward the "closed" party, which prepares itself for a protracted struggle. Among the aims of the new youth federation is the "conquest of young people to the idea of socialism and Marxian Leninism"; among its activities is "the more intense and systematic education in the theoretical knowledge of Marxian Leninism of those youths who already feel that they are with communism but who do not yet have clear notions about it."

In the same vein, a development, or rather an about-face, has occurred in the interpretation of the ideological clause of the 1946 party statute.[1] The official party daily, *Unità,* had said then that the clause proved that "(1) the Communist party is not an atheistic party, for it accepts within its fold the faithful of every

[1] Article 2 of the statute reads: "All honest workers of both sexes who have reached 18 years of age may join the Italian Communist Party, independently of race, religious faith, and philosophical convictions. Every member of the Party is obliged to accept the political program and the statute of the Party, to work in one of its organizations, and to pay dues regularly."

religion; (2) membership in the Communist party does not imply acceptance of the philosophical doctrine of materialism." On October 23, 1946, Secchia added, "It is the statute of a national party,...of a democratic party,...of a workers' party,...of a party of militants,...of *a new type of party,*...of a unitary party." But, two years later, on September 23, 1948, Longo declared that

on the ideological level, the article which permits party membership independently of religious faith and philosophical convictions has in practice been interpreted as a directive in favor of neutrality, of indifference to enemy ideologies, to non-Communist ideologies.... Ideological defense and attack have also been weak with respect to the great political problems of today, such as the antithesis between the U.S.S.R. and the United States.... Even worse, some have become supporters of "freedom of opinion," "freedom to commit errors."...On the political level we cannot accept a party where everyone goes his own way saying that later results alone will show who was correct. Similarly, we cannot tolerate such attitudes on the ideological level.

This intolerant statement has not, however, been followed by those drastic purges and large-scale expulsions which part of the press and the public expected as probable. It is to be suspected that, because of the influence of Togliatti, the method of pressure and persuasion is being used instead, a method which has a long history in Italy and has demonstrated its efficacy with respect to entire generations of intellectuals, although it is a method that works more successfully on persons who are already persuaded than on the newer elements which the party is seeking to attract.

PARTY SCHOOLS, ORGANIZATION OF CADRES,
CELL AND PRESS ACTIVITIES

Large-scale and continuous selection of new leaders is a must for a party that exercises such far-reaching influence upon society. Selections are made by the members only in the case of the cell and, sometimes, of the section leaders. Otherwise the choice comes from the top. From the cell and section leaders and from those who appear, from the personal records which each member must keep, most likely to perform well specific functions, the party selects the persons to be taken into the party apparatus. The party worker is given a paid job in the party itself or in one of its subsidiary organs.[2] Generally, salaries are not high, and persons of middle-class background who accept them are obviously inspired by motives other than economic gain.

At every level of the party structure, there are party schools. The cell schools are not really schools at all, but elementary propaganda courses dedicated to instilling in every member the rudimentary concepts of Marxism as now codified by Stalin, as well as the current party line. To synchronize the party's work at this level, materials are distributed monthly prescribing the manner in which problems of a general nature are to be met and answering in advance the opposition's objections. Correspondence courses are also organized, with questions for the students to answer and return to the school staffs.

A step higher are the section schools, which, like those of the federations, consist of courses taught by special instructors. For the party as a whole there are several national schools in which the higher ranks of the party are instructed. Three schools have been set up for this purpose: at Bologna there is a six-month curriculum of studies directed by Spinella; at Rome a three-month curriculum directed by de Giovanni; and at Milan six-month courses for women workers. In Rome, at the party's national headquarters, a seminar for advanced studies is held, dealing with such topics as "the periods of Italian history" and "Communist China." At a college for Roman party leaders hidden in the quiet of the Alban hills, thirty-five students attend lectures from eight until ten o'clock in the morning, while the rest of the day is devoted to reading, talking with professors, and preparing for discussion of the following day's subject. Even when the lecturer comes from the outside, the conclusions are always given by the resident staff.

[2]Members of the editorial and administrative staffs of the Communist press have had to give up ordinary forms of employment as newspapermen and become paid party functionaries.

The bureaucratic machine required by this large-scale operation is imposing. A personal record must be kept for each member of a cell. This record contains, in addition to essential vital statistics, data covering the member's profession, his status as a partisan, veteran, or political prisoner, the other party associations to which he belongs, the co-operative with which he is affiliated, the union in which he has a card, the cultural, athletic, or professional groups in which he takes part, the date of his enrollment in the party,[3] his status as an "activist" (positions held in the party or in Communist organizations), and his electoral and military classifications. These records are used to set up broader registries, which are always kept fully up to date. Each month the cells send to their section a list of changes in the register, and twice a year they send a "cell account," which is an over-all summary of the register. Similar data and charts on membership trends are kept by the sections, which send to their federation monthly, quarterly, and biannual reports of varying degrees of complexity. There is no doubt that the Communist party has a more complex and up-to-date personnel file system than an army.

The press is also a part of this army and is active at all levels. The Communist party puts out a daily newspaper, *Unità*, published in four regional editions at Milan, Turin, Genoa, and Rome, with a probable average circulation of half a million copies. This makes it the only political party daily that is self-supporting. In addition to *Unità*, there are para-Communist dailies such as *Milano-Sera, Progresso* of Bologna, *Corriere* of Florence, *Paese* and *Paese-Sera* of Rome.

The dailies are supplemented by popular weeklies such as *Vie nuove* and *Calendario del popolo,* and by a youth magazine called *Gioventù nuova.* The party theoretical monthly, corresponding to the French *Cahiers du communisme,* is *Rinascita,*

[3]The enrollment data bear an obvious relationship to the various phases of the party's history: (1) from its foundation to its suppression by the Fascist government on October 31, 1926; (2) from 1926 to the Spanish civil war; (3) from 1936 to the downfall of Mussolini; (4) from 1943 to the liberation. Since 1945 the classification is more detailed.

edited by Togliatti himself. Of the many unofficial Communist magazines which blossomed after the war, only *Società* has survived. The product of a number of publishing companies increases the flood: the Centro Diffusione Stampa, Rinascita's series of Marxist texts, Milano-Sera's collection of classical economic texts with Marxist prefaces, and the Edizioni Sociali. As a result, great quantities of low-priced books are at the public's disposal.

We come now to the military apparatus of the party. It is not improbable that the party today, as in 1924, has a secret machine, ready to spring into action in the event of another underground period, and even a military force. This is logical for a revolutionary party which advocates the use of force under given circumstances. But to try to describe this machine involves the obvious risk of using unreliable information. It will be enough to recall that in the parliamentary debate following the attempt on Togliatti's life, the Minister of the Interior, Mario Scelba, said in the Senate on August 4, 1948, that "local incidents demonstrated that it was not a question simply of spontaneous manifestations but of movements ordered in advance with a view to an open insurrection." Yet Communist military action is likely to take place only if certain national and international conditions, which did not exist in 1948, are present.

MASS ORGANIZATIONS: THE RELATIONSHIP OF COMMUNISM AND SOCIALISM

The Communist party acts not only through its own organization, but also through the mass organizations. The most important of these is the General Confederation of Labor. Its position is a singular one because, in addition to being a base for Communist activity, it is also an instrument of trade union action and, therefore, cannot be used by the party exclusively for political purposes. Also, while the Communists have been the majority group since the beginning and have had the initiative within the confederation, the latter was originally governed both at the center and locally by representatives of the three mass parties, the Communist, Socialist, and Christian-Democratic.

Early in 1944, in Naples, the first free workers' organizations sprang up again. Two distinct organizations were then formed: the Catholic Confederation of Italian Workers and the leftist General Confederation of Labor, composed mainly of Communists though not directed by them. With the arrival of Togliatti, this arrangement came to an end, and his views concerning labor "unity" prevailed. Togliatti made an agreement with the Catholic organization and took the Socialists under his own "unitary" banner. Thus, the General Confederation of Italian Labor was founded, the adjective "Italian" being added to the old pre-Fascist name to signify the re-establishment of the link between the masses and the nation. Its first secretaries were di Vittorio, Lizzadri, and Grandi, representing respectively the Communist, Socialist, and Christian-Democratic workers.

Born of a family of *braccianti* in Apulia, di Vittorio came to communism from prewar anarcho-syndicalism and rose through the various stages of the Communist hierarchy. Among other things he was, with Longo, a commissioner in the International Brigade in Spain and, returning to France because of ill health, there edited the party newspaper. He is a man of humane qualities, open to the suggestions of others, capable of compromise, yet sufficiently faithful to the party to control these inclinations when necessary. His stature as a syndicalist cannot be equaled by those placed beside him. Bruno Buozzi, the old Socialist leader, who had the experience and the toughness of an old Syndicalist and could, through his moderate position, attract the support of many old workers who knew his firmness and ability in negotiating, was murdered by the Nazis soon after the liberation of Rome. The Socialists replaced him with Lizzadri, a middle-class organizer with no real union or political experience and committed in advance to the Communist thesis. As for the Catholic representative, Achille Grandi, he was an able but sick man who soon was replaced by Rapelli, an intelligent but unstable person. After a short time Rapelli had to retire to a sanitarium. Giulio Pastore, his successor, had anything but the mobility and imagination of Rapelli; it would have been difficult, even if it had been possible, for him to have developed a union policy in competition with di Vittorio.

The Communists gained control of the unified Confederation of Labor in two ways. In the first place, they played the role of reformists and advanced the interests of labor within the government. They were not afraid of any competition on the left, for no other party had either revolutionary cadres or programs. In the second place, they used their machine, which was much more centralized and effective than that of the other groups. Since the Communists succeeded in placing their own men in the unpaid or poorly paid trade union jobs, the equal representation maintained among the three groups in the top confederation jobs was meaningless. In addition, the Communists operated according to a fixed policy set by the party's leaders; the Socialists approached each dispute on the merits of the case and relied on the common sense of their men. The Catholics had a stronger organization but few men. The most effective Christian-Democratic party workers have always been furnished by the clergy, and priests do not work in factories. So the Communists kept control of the confederation throughout the whole period of tripartite government; and even after the exit of the Communists from the de Gasperi cabinet in May 1947, the government parties remained a minority surrounded by a Communist majority, since the Communists had won the local trade union elections.

Although the strength of the Christian Democrats, then acting as the chief opposition force within the confederation, seemed improved for a time in 1948, there was never any real chance that they would conquer the majority of the organization by an alliance with the Social Democrats and Republicans. When the schism between Communist and non-Communist labor became a reality at the international level, first the Christian Democrats and later the Social Democrats set up their own independent federations.

Despite these defections the bulk of the organized workers remain within the fold of the General Confederation of Labor. Its losses have been significant only among teacher and white-collar unions. But for political reasons the Communists now proceed with greater caution in exposing their trade unions to defeat. All recent strikes have been short, of a general or demonstrative nature. Railroad workers have seldom been on strike.

An analogous evolution from a tripartite organism to a Communist one has occurred with the National League of Co-operatives whose president is Giulio Cerreti, a Communist deputy and former food commissioner. The same monotonous story repeats itself in the case of partisan organizations. The A.N.P.I. (Associazione Nazionale Partigiani d'Italia) was first set up with representation from all political groups, but today it follows the Communist party line.

To these mass organizations which have a national and permanent nature and therefore represent basic forces of the Communist party, should be added the temporary organizations established to attain specific contingent propaganda goals. In December 1947, when the campaign was launched for an electoral alliance with the Socialists under the auspices of a People's Democratic Front, the Communists created associations of all kinds to facilitate communications between the party and independent voters or mere sympathizers. In this way the Land Constituent Assembly, the League of Democratic Communes, the Committee for the South, the Labor Front, and the Cultural Alliance were formed. The latest of these leagues seems to be the International Partisans of Peace, whose Paris convention was directed by Pietro Nenni, leader of philo-Soviet Italian socialism.

To explain in detail the process by which the Italian Socialist party, the largest leftist party in the June 2, 1946, elections with 21 per cent of the vote as against 19 per cent for the Communists, was reduced to an appendage of the Communist party would be a long story. It would mean writing a detailed chronicle of Italian politics from 1921 to 1951. It would be necessary to go back to the birth of the Communist party, when the Socialist party shared the Communists' admiration for the Russian myth; to remember how few were the Socialist attempts to organize an underground resistance to fascism from 1926 to 1942; and to recall that these few attempts were almost all undertaken under the heretical banner, from the point of view of the Socialist tradition, of the Justice and Freedom movement.

For the purposes of this essay, the story will start with the underground reorganization of the Socialist party in 1942. By that time the old reformist leaders, Turati, Treves, and Morgari, had died in exile. A few Socialist parliamentarians of the days before fascism, men who had no national prestige nor experience in political struggle in underground conditions, survived. There were also some younger men who had joined socialism after the advent of fascism, but they were unknown. Finally, there were a few who had taken part in underground activity; but of these, Faravelli was in prison and Basso and Morandi lacked a conception of democracy at all different from that of the Communists.

At the head stood Pietro Nenni and Giuseppe Saragat. Nenni had joined the Socialist party in 1920, after a tumultuous political career which had included a Fascist interlude. When in 1934 the Communists suddenly changed their tactics from opposition to social fascism to support of the Popular Front, Nenni, who had suffered the artificial hostility organized against him among the Italian emigrants in France by the Communist party, became suddenly popular. For a temperament such as Nenni's, eager for the approval of the crowd, the change was decisive. If the aridity of bureaucratic relations with the Communists did not appeal to him, still he liked the new vaguely Jacobin climate of the Popular Front. Since that time Nenni has never deviated from the Communist line in anything he has done. He lost the secretaryship of the party in exile to Oddino Morgari at the time of the Stalin-Hitler pact because, although he expressed vague disapproval of it, he refused to follow the categorical condemnation pronounced by the Socialist party against the "betrayal." But soon afterward, given the Socialist-Communist ties which existed in Italy, Nenni returned to the party leadership, to which no other could aspire once the "unitary" policy was again adopted.

As for Saragat, he had never had a responsible position in the party prior to its suppression. He was a speaker of great ability, and, because of his culture, he was prominent among the noncultured Italian Socialists. He too longed for a great party, able to play a decisive role in Italian history.

The Communists had no great difficulties in forcing the Socialists to play their game. The Socialist party was to be pushed to the forefront and to be used as bait to gain control of the old workers who had been Socialists, of the intellectuals who were repelled by the too rigid discipline of the Communist party, and of the democrats who still believed in a new society. At the same time, the Communists aimed to keep it tied to themselves through infiltration by their own trusted men, through formal pacts of unity of action and joint party orders, and through all that complex action which it is easy for a party firmly controlled and organized for conquest to exercise upon a democratic party in which, on the other hand, policy and situations are openly discussed.

So it happened that heterogeneous forces came to the Socialist party for conflicting reasons. There were enlightened conservatives who felt the need, after the fascist reaction, to make sacrifices in favor of new forms of equality (it is said that Maria José, then Queen of Italy, voted for Saragat on June 2, 1946; as a legend this has its significance); young men who wanted non-Communist equality or who were tired of the rigidity and the empty political debates of the Resistance parties; and workers and intellectuals happy to extricate themselves from Communist tutelage without having to take a stand against it. But the greater this influx, the greater became the inclination to be independent of the Communists. The municipal elections of the spring of 1946 witnessed a great Socialist victory in some of the larger cities, where their vote proved 50 per cent larger than the Communist vote. These elections, showing that socialism still had the fascination of old, should have led the party to assert strongly its autonomy. But it was known that the Communists would look upon autonomous socialism as their worst enemy: "If the Socialist party," Togliatti had said in his Florence speech of October 1945, "should break with the working masses which follow our party, it will become little by little the center of reactionary forces."

The first encounter between Nenni and his fellow advocates of pro-Communist ideas and Saragat, firmly committed to autonomy, took place at the party congress held in Florence in April 1946. Nenni came out the loser though only by a slight margin: his motion received 338,000 votes against 300,000 for the motion of the center (which also spoke of a pact of unity of action) and 83,000 for the motion of the inflexible anti-Communist right.

This was enough to permit the organization of a solidly independent party even at the price of a grave internal crisis. But a compromise solution was reached whereby the presidency of the party remained with Nenni while a representative of the right, Ivan Matteo Lombardo, was appointed secretary. Under the circumstances, the Communists still had several cards to play.

There was the pact for unity of action, concluded for the first time on August 17, 1934, between the parties in exile and renewed in the period of semilegality on August 4, 1943, and on several occasions later. The pact was meaningful only insofar as the party leaders enforced it. The Socialist refusal to join in the second Bonomi cabinet, to which the Communists gave their support, had been a public indication that the two parties were still following separate policies. Another sign was the freedom with which the Socialists took their stand on many issues.

When the Socialists emerged from the elections of June 2, 1946, with a greater number of votes and of deputies than the Communists, the latter moved to attack. On September 17, 1946, in an interview with the Venice daily *Gazzettino*, Togliatti described as "frankly bad" the "present relations with the Socialist party." For some time something had been wrong: "The pact of unity of action has not worked for several months and this is the fault of the reformist antiunitarian groups who, in effect, control the Socialist party." The interview, instead of causing a rupture, led the two parties to a review of the pact and to a full agreement a month later. Such was the Communists' strength.

The Socialists who negotiated the pact were intent on obtaining, and obtained, a political formula much more liberal than the preceding ones with regard, for example, to attitudes toward the Soviet Union. But this was not what counted. What counted was that the country, and particularly party members, had the definite feeling that the link was now a real one. The new pact looked toward a "joint executive committee"; and where the extremists of both parties were already in control, as in Rome, "people's blocs" were launched which fused the two parties in a single political entity.

On November 1, Togliatti declared in the Leghorn *Gazzetta* that a joint struggle for power by the Communists and Socialists could be expected: "Every party, every bloc of parties (and the pact of unity of action creates a solid bloc of two brother parties) in a democracy has the right to fight and does fight for power.... The Socialists and the Communists together...will devote themselves...to a policy of unity." And he sounded the slogan of a "government under Socialist and Communist direction."

On the following day Pietro Secchia described the use Communist militants were to make of the pact:

Our cells, our sections ought to take the initiative, in agreement with our Socialist comrades, in convoking people's meetings in the factories, in the various quarters of the cities, in clubs, villages.... The problem is to create joint executive committees where they do not yet exist and to reinforce those which do exist by making them function permanently.

As a consequence of the new Communist offensive, Socialist voters moved in two directions: toward communism or toward the right. On November 13, in the new municipal elections held in many Italian cities, the Socialist vote declined while the Communist vote increased. Turin, Genoa, and Florence elected Communist mayors. The crisis was intensified, and early in 1947 Saragat brought about the first and most serious Socialist schism with the creation of a new Italian Socialist Workers' party.

For the 1948 elections the Nenni Socialists accepted a joint electoral list with the Communists in the so-called Popular Front. The Front lost the battle, but within the Front the Communists won. Through their greater control of the use of the preferential votes, they made sure that Socialist representatives in parliament would be few and "orthodox." After five years of this policy, the Socialist party has seen its membership drop substantially. But the party machine remains firmly in the hands of Pietro Nenni, who continues his policy of adhering to Russian and Communist directives.

Thus the Socialist party has become for the Communist party not only a base of preparation and recruitment, as are all other mass organizations, but something even more precious. It is a political auxiliary containing many who, because of their resistance to strict discipline or their independence of judgment, could not easily be directed by the Communist party itself. In Italy the phenomenon of the fellow traveler, elsewhere isolated or limited to the intellectual class, has organized bases upon which to develop. On the other hand, even in its present reduced condition the Italian Socialist party retains persons who could hardly be classified as true Communists, and the public sometimes has the fleeting impression that the party has managed to retain certain hidden sources of autonomous strength.

CONCLUSION

The extent of the Communist party's success is revealed in election results. On June 2, 1946, in the elections for the Constituent Assembly, the party received about 4,358,000 votes, approximately 19 per cent of the 23,000,000 valid votes cast. In the elections of April 18, 1948, the Popular Front got 8,137,000 votes or 31 per cent of the votes cast for the Chamber of Deputies. Of these, perhaps two-thirds were Communist votes. In the municipal elections of May and June 1951, the combined vote of the parties accepting Communist leadership increased to 36.9 per cent of the votes cast. But the most important beneficiaries were the Socialists and not the Communists. And though the Socialist party has identified itself with communism, its voters are not Communists.

The Communist party, in terms both of membership and votes, is strongest in central Italy. This is an area combining fairly prosperous and poor agriculture, not highly developed industrially, and with flourishing handicrafts. Here the proportion of Popular Front votes to total votes cast in the elections of 1948 reached 55 per cent in the provinces of Siena, Arezzo, and Grosseto in southern Tuscany; about 52.2 per cent in the provinces of Bologna, Ferrara, Ravenna, and Forlì, Italy's red belt; about 50 per cent in Florence; 49.5 per cent in Umbria; and 42 per cent in western Tuscany (Pisa, Leghorn, Lucca, Massa, and Carrara). In southern Lombardy, which is both industrial and agricultural, the Popular Front vote was near the dividing line between minority and majority: at Mantua and Cremona it was 46 per cent; it dropped below 40 per cent in the great industrial cities of Piedmont and Lombardy, with 37 per cent in the provinces of Milan and Pavia and 37 per cent in the cities of Milan and Turin; it dropped still lower in the hill or mountain areas of small industry and peasant-owned farms of Lombardy, Piedmont, and, particularly, Veneto, where the influence of the Catholics' organization was felt strongly though not uniformly. The Front received 25 per cent of the votes in southern Piedmont (Cuneo, Alessandria, and Asti) and northern Lombardy (Brescia and Bergamo); and about the same in the lake region.

In the south the Front vote oscillated between 20 and 25 per cent, with peaks registered in northern Apulia (Bari and Foggia, 30.5 per cent) and low points in the areas most backward politically and economically (Campobasso, 13 per cent). The poorest and most mountainous areas of Abruzzi (Aquila, Pescara, Teramo) show 27 per cent and the Basilicate, before which "Christ stopped," 25.2 per cent. The remote plains of southern Apulia show 21.6 per cent. In Sicily the highest percentages were reached in the western part of the island, the richest part economically (Palermo, Trapani, and Agrigento, 23 per cent) and the lowest in the east-central areas (Messina, Syracuse, Catania, and Enna, 20 per cent). About the same average was attained in Sardinia.

These Communist Front votes do not mean the same thing everywhere. A geographical analysis shows that Communist voters are more numerous where social struggle on the land is accom-

panied by a rather intensive urban development, with small industry and commerce. In the great industrial cities of the north,
amid the proletariat as among that middle class which votes Communist in Tuscany and Emilia, there still remains a sufficiently
important stratum of democratic Socialist voters. In the south,
with the exception of the intellectual and professional bourgeoisie, Communist votes come from the *braccianti,* the poor peasants,
and the industrial working class minority, where such a class
exists (as in Apulia). A majority of the members of the southern
middle classes, including particularly the lower middle classes,
vote for the right.

Interesting comparisons can be made between the elections of
1948 and those of 1919, the first elections to be held under a system of proportional representation and the first to witness the
play of the mass Socialist and Christian-Democratic parties on the
Italian political scene, in an atmosphere of messianic expectations. In the 1919 elections the Socialists received 32.2 per cent
of the votes as against the Communist Front's 31 per cent in 1948,
and the two percentages can be said to be the same when we take
into account the post-World War II enfranchisement of women —
by nature generally more conservative — and the greater turnout
in 1948, which undoubtedly operated to the benefit of the right-
wing parties. In 1919 the maximum strength of the left was in
Emilia, where it won 60 per cent of the votes; it won 46 per cent
in Lombardy and Umbria, 40 per cent in Piedmont, and 43.9
per cent in Tuscany.

Therefore, after twenty years of fascism, which came into power
to save Italy from the Communist danger, the Communist party
has succeeded in occupying nearly the same position held by the
Socialists in 1919. It has consolidated its electoral position and
obtained a far greater effective control over its voters. (The Socialist party in 1919 had less than 250,000 members.) If it has lost —
rather, it has never gained — the earlier Socialist position in the
great industrial cities where the movement originated, Milan and
Turin, it has made notable advances in the south, where it has
destroyed the old Liberal party.

Similar conclusions may be reached through a comparison of the social groups which were under the influence of the left in 1919 and in 1948. Success has been modest in both periods among the white-collar and rural propertied classes; more substantial success has been achieved among the workers of the large northern factories and among the poorer landless peasants. Important results have also been gained among the craftsmen and the members of the professions.[4]

The Italian Communist party did not succeed in winning a majority and installing itself in power after the fall of fascism when no democratic structure existed in the country and when all other parties were far less well trained than the Communist party for political life under the new conditions. This was its initial failure and from it comes its present stagnation and certain murmurs of discontent audible around its periphery.

On the other hand, in the years since 1945 the Communist party has succeeded in accomplishing what it had never been able to do in so complete a way even during the Fascist period and the struggle for liberation: it has managed to present itself as the only alternative to the present Christian-Democratic government. There have been and there continue to be attempts to create a third force, which could, in the event of a failure of Christian Democracy, assume control of the government. No matter how such attempts may be judged politically, the fact remains that they have not yet been able to develop a strength even remotely comparable to that of the Communist party.

The Communist party cannot mold Italy to its image. It can, nevertheless, make it impossible for a policy to obtain the support of some of the more active elements of the Italian population. As an opposition party in local administrations or in parliament, it sometimes assumes the role of a democratic opposition.

[4]Certain groups in particular (film directors and artists) seem especially susceptible to Communist recruitment. Thus the directors Visconti, de Santis, and Vergano are Communists; the actor Lamberto Picasso; and the painters Guttuso, Mafai, and Purificato. And amid the more articulate representatives of the academic world there are many members or sympathizers, such as Marchesi, Cantimori, de Martino, Luporini, Banfi, and della Volpe.

As a party controlling the unions it often works for specific and concrete ends, aligning itself with the industrialists in order to put joint pressure on the state. As a closed national party it opposes any expansion of the national horizon beyond its present limits, which are those of a state in crisis.

But while it temporarily fulfills these functions and to a certain extent impedes the formation of truly democratic parties, and even competes with the nationalists, the Communist party retains as its fundamental characteristic its role as one of the agents of the interests of the Soviet Union on the international front. It pursues its other activities *ad interim,* while waiting for the time when the war of movement in the international sphere can be resumed. Its most dangerous characteristic in a country like Italy, which has a tendency to stagnate, is precisely its contribution to the perpetuation of the country's lethargy and its success in blocking any forward step, especially any step in the direction of social progress and development, by holding the masses, whose active and friendly participation in such a development is indispensable, under lock and key.

Bibliographical Note

I COMMUNISM IN WESTERN EUROPE

A bibliography of French and Italian literature on communism, drawn chiefly from the years 1947 to 1950, can be found in Mario Einaudi, "Western European communism: a profile," *American Political Science Review*, March 1951.

On the Enlightenment and communism, see Voltaire, *Trattato sulla tolleranza,* with an introduction by Palmiro Togliatti, (Rome, 1949), and Roger Garaudy, *Les Sources françaises du socialisme scientifique* (Paris, 1948, pp. 284).

On early Italian communism and its illusions of freedom, see Piero Gobetti, *La rivoluzione liberale* (Turin, 1948, pp. 202), and *Antologia della "rivoluzione liberale,"* ed. by Nino Valeri (Turin, 1948, pp. xxix–523).

On the rebellion by dissatisfied Marxists against the bureaucratization of communism, see Aldo Cucchi, *Una delegazione italiana in Russia* (Florence, 1951, pp. 139); Valdo Magnani and Aldo Cucchi, *Dichiarazioni e documenti* (Bologna, 1951, pp. 45); Carlo Matteotti, *Capitalismo e comunismo* (Milan, 1951, pp. viii–221).

Official documents in connection with the 1950 and 1951 congresses of the Italian and French Communist parties are found in *Verso il VII congresso del partito comunista italiano: rapporto di Palmiro Togliatti, interventi di Longo, Secchia, Scoccimarro, d'Onofrio, Sereni* (Rome, 1950, pp. 156); *Documenti politici di organizzazioni democratiche di massa* (Rome, 1951, pp. 95); *VII congresso nazionale del partito comunista italiano: documenti politici del comitato centrale della direzione e della segreteria*

(Rome, 1951, pp. 478), and Maurice Thorez, *La Lutte pour l'indépendance nationale et pour la paix* (Paris, 1950, pp. 95).

The attitude of certain groups of French Christian progressives toward Marxism or communism is developed in Jean Boulier, *Un prêtre prend position* (Paris, 1949, pp. 79); Pierre Debray, *Un Catholique retour de l'U.R.S.S.* (Paris, 1950, pp. 140); André Mandouze, "Prendre la main tendue" in *Les chrétiens et la politique,* by Henri Guillemin, André Mandouze, Paul Ricoeur, Georges Hourdin, Daniel Villey, M. I. Montuclard (Paris, 1948, pp. 169); R. Vancourt, *Marxisme et pensée chrétienne* (Paris, 1947, pp. 301); Henri Bartoli, *Doctrine économique et sociale de Karl Marx* (Paris, 1950, pp. 418); Jean Lacroix, *Marxisme, existentialisme, personnalisme: présence de l'éternité dans le temps* (Paris, 1950, pp. 120). The monthly edited until his death by Emmanuel Mounier, *Esprit,* has repeatedly discussed the issue since 1945.

For a non-Communist point of view on the agrarian and political problems of the Italian South, Guido Dorso, *La rivoluzione meridionale* (Rome, 1945, pp. 328); Guido Dorso, *Dittatura, classe politica e classe dirigente* (Turin, 1949, pp. xiv–186); Manlio Rossi-Doria, *Riforma agraria e azione meridionalista* (Bologna, 1948, pp. 298). For the Communist viewpoint, Emilio Sereni, *La questione agraria nella rinascita nazionale italiana* (Rome, 1946, pp. 461); Ruggiero Grieco, *Introduzione alla riforma agraria* (Turin, 1949, pp. 333).

The following works deal with some of the religious, political, and constitutional problems that are discussed in the text in relation to communism: Gabriel Le Bras, "Géographie électorale et géographie religieuse," in *Etudes de sociologie electorale* (Paris, 1948, pp. 89); Arturo Carlo Jemolo, *Chiesa e stato in Italia negli ultimi cento anni* (Turin, 1948, pp. 752); André Ferrat, *La République à refaire* (Paris, 1945); Maurice Duverger, "L'organisation politique de la France," and François Goguel, "Les partis politiques en France," in *Encyclopédie politique de la France et du monde,* vol. I (2d ed., Paris, 1950, pp. 359); Jacques Fauvet, *Les Forces politiques en France* (Paris, 1951, pp. 346); François Goguel, "La démocratie en France," *Christianisme social,* December 1950, and January–February 1951; and Mario Einaudi, "The crisis of politics and government in France," *World Politics,* October 1951. See also Maurice Duverger, "Le dernier tournant," *Le Monde,* Jan. 11, 1951; "Une nouvelle gauche?," *ibid.,* March 12, 1951; "La troisième force sociale," *ibid.,* May 23, 1951, and "Dilemme socialiste," *ibid.,* July 4, 1951.

Important data on the economic problems of France will be found in Claude Chaballier, "Le société française est-elle menacée de sclerose?," *La revue socialiste,* May and June 1945; Jean Fourastié, *Le Grand Espoir du XXᵉ siècle* (Paris, 1949, pp. xi–223); Pierre George, *Géographie économique and sociale de la France* (Paris, 1949, pp. 247).

Basic information on the Marshall Plan is found in the progress reports of the Economic Cooperation Administration to Congress published at quarterly intervals (twelve have appeared for the period up to March 31, 1951) and of the Organization for European Economic Co-operation. The first was published at the end of 1948, the second in February 1950, and the third in June 1951, under the title: *Economic Progress and Problems of Western Europe.* Also see Howard S. Ellis, *The Economics of Freedom; the Progress and Future of Aid to Europe* (New York, 1950, pp. xviii–549).

II THE FRENCH COMMUNIST PARTY

Communist Sources

L'Humanité, the official daily of the French Communist party, occasionally publishes important articles on doctrinal orientation or problems of organization.

Cahiers du communisme, a monthly published by the Central Committee of the French Communist party, is the official review dealing with the doctrine and activities of the French Communist party and is the essential Communist source for any study of the party's ideology.

France nouvelle, official party weekly, reproduces in popular form the themes found in *Cahiers du communisme*. Its only useful content is the section entitled "Party problems," which publishes notes of "self-criticism" that enable one to follow concretely the French Communist party's difficulties in its federations and cells.

La Pensée, deals with philosophical and scientific questions; interesting because of its attempted synthesis of Marxism and French rationalism.

La Nouvelle Critique, a monthly, expresses the intransigence of the young Communist intellectuals who try to be "pure" Marxists.

On ideological and tactical orientation as well as on organizational problems, the works of Thorez are the most important. The party started the publication of his complete works in 1950. So far three volumes have appeared: *Oeuvres de Maurice Thorez,* vol. I: January 1930 to June 1931, pp. 230; vol. II: June 1931 to February 1932, pp. 238; vol. III: March 1932 to May 1932, pp. 252 (Paris, 1950 and 1951).

The reports presented by Thorez to the Communist party congresses between 1936 and 1945 are found in *Une Politique de grandeur française* (Paris, 1945, pp. 384). The report of June 1945 treats extensively the questions of organization and cadres. Other important speeches made by Thorez can be found in *Pour l'union: communistes et socialistes* (Paris, 1949, pp. 63) and *Pour l'union: communistes et catholiques* (Paris, 1949, pp. 47). The former pamphlet was written in collaboration with Duclos.

Thorez' autobiography, *Fils du peuple* (Paris, 1949, pp. 253), is useful for understanding the personality of the French Communist leader and at the same time the ways by which communism has been grafted on the French workers' tradition. This is a second edition to which passages glorifying Stalin have been added.

Other than these works, it is impossible to list the many speeches, studies, and pamphlets which echo the themes of Communist propaganda. However, with respect to organization, important statistics and information are found in *Deux années d'activité pour la renaissance économique et politique de la république française* (reports to the French Communist party congress at Strasbourg in 1947), pp. 400. The volume is for party members only.

On the history of the French Communist party, the main Communist sources are *Fils du peuple* and Florimond Bonte, *Le Chemin de l'honneur* (Paris, 1949), which tells the story of a group of Communist deputies between September 1939 and February 1943. There is still no complete Communist work on the French Communist party, and because of this, its history, especially between 1939 and 1943, is difficult to learn. The number of party members during this period has never been revealed. For an epic chronicle of the war and the Resistance, see Louis Aragon, *Les Communistes,* vol. I: February to September 1939, pp. 265; vol. II: September to November 1939, pp. 364; vol. III: November 1939 to March 1940, pp. 413; vol. IV: March to May 1940, pp. 335 (Paris, 1949 and 1950), and, also by Aragon, *L'Homme communiste* (Paris, 1946, pp. 246).

With respect to the intellectuals, see Laurent Casanova, *Le communisme, la pensée et l'art* (Paris, 1947, pp. 17); *Le Parti communiste, les intellectuels et la nation* (Paris, 1949, pp. 141); *Responsabilités de l'intellectuel communiste* (Paris, 1949, pp. 32).

Non-Communist Sources

Gérard Walter, *Histoire du parti communiste français* (Paris, 1948, pp. 391). This work traces the history of the French Communist party from its formation to 1939. A clear and objective book.

Angelo Tasca, one of the founders of the Italian Communist party, later expelled, has now become the chief historiographer of French communism. Writing under the pseudonym of A. Rossi he has so far published two volumes: *Physiologie du parti communiste français* (Paris, 1948, pp. xxxvi–465; abridged English translation: *A Communist Party in Action,* New Haven, 1949, pp. xxiv–301) and *Les Communistes français pendant la drôle de guerre* (Paris, 1951, pp. 365). The latter is particularly valuable because of the documents used to demonstrate the absence of the Communists from the Resistance until June 1941.

On the organization of the party, see the works of Walter and Rossi and an anonymous article in *Esprit,* May 1939, no. 80, "Le parti communiste," as well as the course taught by François Goguel, *La Vie politique de la société française contemporaine,* published in three multigraphed volumes (Paris, 1948–1949, vol. I, pp. 211; vol. II, pp. 338; vol. III, pp. 555). In addition, two articles by H. Chambre give essential information on the present state of Communist organization and influence: "Le parti communiste français depuis le libération," *Travaux de l'action populaire,* December 1948, no. 25, and "Le parti communiste français durant les 6 premiers mois de 1949," *ibid.,* September–October 1949, no. 33.

For the geographical and sociological studies of the Communist electorate, see the articles of François Goguel on electoral geography in *Esprit,* December 1945, February 1947, and September 1951.

For the tactics, themes, and influence of communism in France, see Raymond Aron, *Le Grand schisme* (Paris, 1948, pp. 346), which contains some penetrating sociological and philosophical observations.

Jules Monnerot, *Sociologie du communisme* (Paris, 1949, pp. 510). This is a psychological and psychoanalytical study of Communist mentality and methods. Although it deals with world communism, this book is of great value and any study of a Communist party must refer to some of its analyses. It likens communism to a "secular religion," to a "twentieth-century Islam." See also Henri Pollès, *Psychoanalyse du communisme* (Paris, 1949, pp. 569), and Lucien Martin, "Psychologie de la pensée communiste," *La Revue socialiste,* December 1949, no. 32.

With respect to the reasons for the influence of communism on youth and especially on young intellectuals, one must refer to the investigation made by *Esprit,* February and April 1946, nos. 119 and 121. The reasons that prompt French intellectuals to accept or reject communism are given by twenty-five writers in *Questions du communisme,* Confluences nos. 18–20.

The motivations of the Christians who are approaching communism are clearly stated in the contribution of André Mandouze, "Prendre la main tendue, in *Les Chrétiens et la politique* (Paris, 1948, pp. 169). The monthly organ of the Progressive Christians is *Position.*

The writers of Communist tendencies who came from the Resistance have recorded their views in *L'Heure du choix* by Claude Aveline, Jean Cassau, André Chamson, Georges Friedmann, Louis Martin-Chauffier, Vercors (Paris, 1947, pp. 170). They have since revised their positions, however: see in particular Jean Cassou and Vercors, "Il ne faut pas tromper le peuple," *Esprit,* December 1949, no. 162, and *La Voie libre* (Paris, 1951) by Aveline, Cassou, Martin-Chauffier, and Vercors.

On the Communist militant, the new type of man formed by Marxism, see Jean Lacroix, "L'homme marxiste," *La Vie intellectuelle,* August and September 1947. This study has been republished in Jean Lacroix, *Marxisme, existentialisme, personnalisme* (Paris, 1950, pp. 120).

III THE ITALIAN COMMUNIST PARTY

There is no complete study of the Italian Communist party. Adequate newspaper sources are not available owing to the dispersion of documents, for which the Fascists are responsible, and to the fact that after 1925 Communist publications went underground or appeared abroad.

Before the founding of the party in 1921, the following periodicals are of interest: the Turin edition of *Avanti!;* the weekly *Ordine nuovo,* published in Turin beginning May 1, 1919 (a single issue with the title *La Città futura* appeared before that date); and the weekly *Il Soviet* of Naples. After the foundation of the party: *Ordine nuovo,* now a daily (Turin, 1921–1922); *Il Comunista,* daily (Rome, 1922); *Il Lavoratore,* a Trieste daily.

The party magazine was *La Rassegna comunista* (1921–1922). The daily *Unità* appeared in Milan from March 1921 until its suppression in 1925 under the "exceptional" Fascist laws; it then carried on, quite irregularly, in the underground.

Before the founding of the Communist party, the position of the Russian revolutionaries was explained through the translation of such works as Bukharin, *Il programma dei comunisti* (Milan, 1920); Bela Kun, *Di rivoluzione in rivoluzione* (Milan, 1920). Once the party was founded and had developed its own publishing houses, a series of pamphlets was started under the title of "Biblioteca dell'internazionale comunista." The series included *L'ABC del comunismo* by Karl Radek and Preobrazhensky; *Tesi e risoluzioni* of the Third Congress of the Communist International; speeches on *La questione italiana al III congresso dell'internazionale comunista* and *I sindacati italiani al primo congresso dell' internazionale dei sindacati rossi,* and writings of Radek, Lenin, Zinoviev, Clara Zetkin, Lunacharsky *(Il cittadino Giacinto Menotti Serrati),* almost all dealing with polemics on the Italian syndical question. A separate "Biblioteca dell'internazionale dei sindacati rossi" was also published. Among the other publications of these earlier years, the following may be listed: *I documenti della scissione,* in which Ladislao Rudas collected documents dealing with the founding of the party; the speech of Kabakov at the Leghorn congress; biographies of Rosa Luxemburg and Karl Liebknecht; A. Bordiga, *La questione agraria;* the *Relazione del comitato centrale del partito comunista d'Italia al secondo congresso nazionale del marzo 1922 in Roma,* together with other material on this second party congress; a pacifist work by the philosopher Zino Zini, *Il congresso dei morti.*

The official magazine of the Communist party, *Stato operaio,* was published in France from March 1927 until 1938 and in the United States in 1941 and 1942. It remains the principal source for the history of the party in the years of the underground. The party also published first a weekly in France under various names *(Bandiera rossa, La Nostra Bandiera, Grido del popolo)* and then, from 1937 to 1939, a daily, *La Voce degli italiani.* The weekly, *L'Unità del popolo,* was published in New York in 1939. Between 1942 and 1945, there appeared the *Lettere di Spartaco* (from France); a more militant review, *La Nostra Lotta;* and various propaganda sheets such as *Il Combattente* and *Noi Donne.* The current party daily, *Unità,* began to appear intermittently in the south under allied occupation in December 1943; with the liberation of Rome in June 1944 it became a daily. It is now published in several regional editions in Milan, Turin, Genoa, and Rome. *Rinascita,* the party's official monthly review edited by Togliatti, began to appear in May 1944. The weekly *Vie nuove* has a large circulation, as does *Il Calendario del popolo, Il Lavoro* is the organ of the General Confederation of Labor, *Gioventù nuova* of the Young Communist Federation. *Letture per tutti* gives monthly reports on books put out by the party or by sympathetic publishing houses. Direct propaganda and information on the U.S.S.R. is found in *Rassegna della stampa sovietica* and in the *Biblioteca scientifica sovietica.*

Rinascita and the so-called "foreign language editions" coming from Moscow have published on a large scale the writings of Marx, Engels, Plekhanov, Lenin, Stalin, Zhdanov, Kuusinen, and the *History of the Communist Party (Bolshevik) approved by the central committee of the Communist Party (B) of the USSR.*

A brief study of communism is contained in the appendix of the *Enciclopedia italiana* for the years 1938–1949, I, 667–669. A good sketch of Communist politics from 1921 to 1945, from an official point of view, is found in the report of the party directorate to the fifth congress, Rome, December 29, 1945, published under the title *Per la libertà e l'indipendenza d'Italia* (Rome, 1945). Summary essays on the Communist party are found in *I partiti dell'Italia nuova,* ed. by Giovanni Gambarin (the essay on the Communist party was written by Giuseppe Turcato), (Venice, 1945), and in the *Storia critica dei partiti italiani* by Michele Dipiero (pseud. of A. Volpicelli), (Rome, 1946).

On the period from 1921 to 1926, see A. Malatesta, *I socialisti durante la guerra;* Gerolamo Lazzeri, *La scissione socialista* (Milan, 1921); Mario Guarnieri, *I consigli di fabbrica* (Turin, 1923); P. Gobetti, *La rivoluzione liberale* (Bologna, 1924; 2d ed., Turin, 1948, especially pp. 111–132). See also V. Gorresio, *L'esperienza di un dopoguerra* (Rome, 1943). The Lyon Theses were published in 1927 by *Stato operaio.*

On the underground period, the only two critical articles are "Il partito comunista dalle leggi eccezionali in poi" of Manfredo (pseud. of Riccardo Boatti) in *Quaderni di Giustizia e Libertà* Paris, March 1933; and "I movimenti proletari in Italia" of Federico Ricci (pseud. of Leo Valiani) in *Quaderni italiani,* Boston–New York, August 1942. See also Valiani, *Socialismo di oggi e domani* (Florence, 1946).

Several party leaders have written their memoirs: Mario Montagnana, *Ricordi di un operaio torinese* (2 vols., Rome, 1949); Germanetto, *Memorie di un barbiere* (Paris, 1929); Luigi Longo *Un popolo alla macchia* (Milan, 1947). Estella (pseud. of Teresa Noce) has written in the form of a novel a youthful autobiography, *Gioventù senza sole* (Paris, 1939). For each of the members of the directorate, the Propaganda Committee of the party in 1946 published pamphlet biographies under the title of *Dirigenti comunisti.*

The complete works of Antonio Gramsci are now in course of publication. Six volumes have appeared so far: *Lettere dal carcere* (Turin, 1947, pp. 260); *Il materialismo storico e la filosofia di Benedetto Croce* (Turin, 1948, pp. xxiii–299); *Gli intellettuali e l'organizzazione della cultura* (Turin, 1949, pp. xv–208); *Il risorgimento* (Turin, 1949, pp. xiv–235); *Note sul Machiavelli, sulla politica e sullo stato moderno* (Turin, 1949, pp. 371); and *Letteratura e vita nazionale* (Turin, 1950, pp. 400). A number of essays on Gramsci by Togliatti and other leaders of the party have been collected in *Gramsci* (Rome, 1945). The appearance of the first volume was followed by renewed discussion on the significance of Gramsci's thought.

The political writings and occasional speeches of Palmiro Togliatti have been gathered in book or pamphlet form: *Politica comunista* (Rome, 1945); *La politica d'unità nazionale dei comunisti* (Rome, 1945); *Avanti verso la democrazia* (Rome, 1945); *I compiti del partito nella situazione attuale* (Rome, 1945); *Discorso alle donne* (Rome, 1945); *Per la libertà d'Italia, per la creazione di un vero regine democratico* (Rome, 1945); *Rapporto al consiglio nazionale del partito* (Rome, 1945); *Rinnovare l'Italia* (Rome, 1946); *Per la salvezza del nostro paese* (Turin, 1946); *Minacce alla democrazia italiana* (Milan, 1948); *Linea d'una politica* (Milan, 1949); *Pace o guerra* (Milan, 1949). For works on Togliatti, see A. Murena, *Togliatti* (Rome, 1946); M. Ciatti, *Palmiro Togliatti,* with preface by A. Donini (Rome, 1946); and the article "Palmiro Togliatti" by Giuseppe Carocci in *Belfagor,* Jan. 31, 1949, pp. 62–75. On the "heresies" of Togliatti, see "Un'uscita di sicurezza" by Ignazio Silone in *Comunità,* September–October 1949. This article provoked a violent reply by Togliatti in *Unità* and new party condemnations of Silone. The Silone article is part of his essay published in *The God that Failed,* ed. by R. H. Crossman (New York, 1949).

Of works by other party leaders, those of Emilio Sereni might be mentioned: *Il mezzogiorno all'opposizione* (Turin, 1948); *Scienza, marxismo e cultura* (Milan, 1949).

On some particular problems of the younger generation now turned Communist, see L. Lombardo Radice, *Fascismo e anticomunismo* (Turin, 1945); and the essay by a former Fascist, Ruggero Zangrandi, *Il lungo viaggio* (Turin, 1948).

On party schools, see Mario Spinella, *Come studiare* (Rome, 1949), and Giorgio Granata, "La rivoluzione a scuola," *Il Mondo,* Rome, July 9, 1949.

Index

[The following abbreviation is used throughout: c.p. = Communist party.]

231